KAROL WOJTYLA

FAITH ACCORDING TO ST. JOHN OF THE CROSS

KAROL WOJTYLA

FAITH
ACCORDING TO
ST. JOHN OF THE CROSS

Translated by

JORDAN AUMANN, O.P.

IGNATIUS PRESS   SAN FRANCISCO

The original text
Doctrina de fide apud S. Joannem a Cruce
was a doctoral thesis presented at
the Pontifical University of St. Thomas Aquinas, Rome.

Cover by Victoria Hoke Lane

Translation and publication with the permission
of Libreria Editrice Vaticana, Vatican City
With ecclesiastical approval
© Ignatius Press, San Francisco 1981
Reprinted 1985, 1986
ISBN 0–89870–005–1 (PB)
ISBN 0–89870–010–8 (HB)
Library of Congress catalogue number 80–82265
Printed in the United States of America

Publication of this book was made possible by the generous donation of Mr. and Mrs. Walter Berg.

CONTENTS

PART TWO: SYNTHESIS

FOREWORD

As a young man, Karol Wojtyla was one of five members of a lay spirituality group, led by Jan Tyranowski, a working tailor. The group studied the writings of St. John of the Cross, a 16th-century Spanish mystic who co-founded the Carmelite Reform. St. John, a contemplative, a reformer, a poet, a gifted theologian and a friend of St. Teresa of Avila, wrote two treatises entitled *The Ascent of Mount Carmel* and *The Dark Night of the Soul*. In them he describes God's gentle hand in clearing the debris from the soul to make way for divine life. He insisted on purgation through suffering, self-discipline and fidelity to commitment.

As a young priest, Father Wojtyla, who had endured and witnessed much suffering under the Nazi terror, continued his studies at the Pontifical University of St. Thomas Aquinas in Rome. Under the direction of the renowned French Dominican theologian Père Reginald Garrigou-Lagrange, he wrote his doctoral thesis on "Faith According to St. John of the Cross". St. John's dominant interest as a theologian was not in the speculative and systematic, but in the spiritual and experiential dimensions of theology. In writing the thesis, Father Wojtyla shows a rare combination of the methodical procedure of a researcher and of a poetic spirit that was in harmony with the poems of St. John.

In March 1976, Cardinal Wojtyla preached the annual Lenten retreat to Pope Paul VI and his co-workers. The text of the twenty-two conferences given at the retreat were published under the title "Sign of Contradiction". These conferences show the great influence of the mystic St. John of the Cross in the moulding of Cardinal Wojtyla's soul. They provide insights into the mind and heart of our Holy Father. For the Christian, the Cross is a sign of contradiction which leads to the joys of resurrection.

Pope John Paul II has charmed and fascinated the world. Thousands and millions of peoples crowd to see and hear him. There has been a steady flow of literature, media reports, special articles and books, trying to capture and explain the charism, the magnetism, the human personality of the Holy Father.

Like each of us, Pope John Paul is a unique individual. He has had a variety of experiences seldom found in one human life. He has many talents, many accomplishments. He is equally at home with the people of the land, the coal-miners and quarry workers, the youngsters, as he is with the most renowned philosophers and theologians. He is a public figure, exhilarated by the crowds—in love with the people, especially the poor and the handicapped—yet he is a very private person intro-spective, reflective, prayerful to the point of being a mystic.

No single article and no single book can fully capture and explain his richly endowed personality. At the same time, the Pope's personality, his actions and his words, cannot be under-stood or appreciated without some knowledge of the influence of the mystic doctor, St. John of the Cross, upon the Holy Father. Like St. John, the Holy Father is not just a speculative and systematic theologian, his theology is spiritual and expe-riential. The Pope, like St. Thomas Aquinas, studied theology on his knees. He studied theology not merely to know and un-derstand and explain God, but to love God, to serve God, and to live the divine life.

The attraction to Pope John Paul is an attraction not just to the human charism and magnetism of the Pope. It is an attrac-tion to a profoundly spiritual human being, who lives Christ, radiates Christ, and resounds Christ. All of the speeches, hom-ilies, letters and the encyclical "Jesus Christ the Redeemer of Man" are a proclamation of Christ—the Way, the Truth, and the Light. The Pope is, in name and in fact, an "*Alter Christus*—Another Christ" as well as the Vicar of Christ.

To help us appreciate this basic spiritual element in our Holy Father, the gifted American Dominican theologian Jordan Au-

mann, who is the Director of the Institute of Spirituality of the
same St. Thomas Aquinas University in Rome, has translated
the Holy Father's doctoral thesis on "Faith According to St.
John of the Cross". The caliber of Father Aumann's translation
can only be described in superlatives.

Having known His Holiness for close to twenty years, and
having read many of the sincere efforts of capable writers to
explain and interpret the human personality of the Pope, I am
deeply grateful to Father Aumann for providing the English
reading public with such an indispensable insight into the Holy
Father's life, words, and works. He helps us to know not just
what the Holy Father says and does, but why his words and
actions have such an impact.

It is my fervent hope that the reading of this translation will
help many not only to know God better, but to live His divine
life—to that fullness of life promised by Christ.

JOHN CARDINAL KROL
Archbishop of Philadelphia

July 10, 1979

The first literary publications of Karol Wojtyla were on St. John of the Cross. First of all, he completed and defended his doctoral thesis in 1948: *Doctrina de fide apud S. Joannem a Cruce*; then, on his return to Poland he published an article on this same topic in *Collectanea Theologica* in Warsaw in 1950; lastly, in 1951 he published an article on humanism in St. John of the Cross in the Polish magazine, *Znak*.

Long before he arrived in Rome as a newly ordained priest in 1946, Karol Wojtyla had studied and discussed with a small group of friends the spiritual doctrine of St. John of the Cross. Therefore he was already well versed in the teaching of the Carmelite mystic, and it is only logical that he should have selected a theme from St. John of the Cross as the topic of his thesis for the doctorate in sacred theology.

On June 19, 1948, Karol Wojtyla successfully defended his thesis before a board of outstanding professors of the Pontifical University of St. Thomas Aquinas (known then as the Angelicum): Father Reginald Garrigou-Lagrange, moderator of the thesis, and the future Cardinals Paul Philippe and Luigi Ciappi.

The topic selected by the young doctoral candidate was a difficult one—the metaphysical and psychological nature of faith in the writings of St. John of the Cross. The Carmelite Doctor did not treat theology in a systematic and speculative manner; his approach was mystical, experiential and eminently practical. Therefore, it was necessary to make a deep and detailed analysis of the texts in which St. John of the Cross treated of faith, and especially in *The Ascent of Mount Carmel*, where the Mystical Doctor explained the purgation of the intellect by faith in the active night of the spirit. Karol Wojtyla, even in those early days of his priestly life, manifested a rare gift for languages (he wrote the thesis in Latin and quoted St. John of the Cross in the original Spanish) and also an acute metaphysical and theological insight.

This translation of Karol Wojtyla's doctoral thesis is as faithful as possible to the original manuscript but without, we would hope, being too slavishly literal. The translator has added a few explanatory footnotes, designated as (Tr.), and is responsible for the translation of the Spanish quotations from the works of St. John of the Cross.

A final word of special thanks is given to Sister Emilia of the Generalate of the Ursuline Sisters in Rome. She kindly read the first draft of the translation and offered many helpful suggestions for its improvement.

The translation itself is offered to Pope John Paul II in the name of his *alma mater*, the Pontifical University of St. Thomas Aquinas in Rome.

Jordan Aumann, O.P.

INTRODUCTION

Historical and biographical background

We shall treat of the historical and biographical data only in general; there are many books, both old and recent, that treat of this material, as can be seen in the Bibliography.[1] Only one point should be emphasized here, namely, the influence of the historical situation on the concept of faith that we intend to investigate in the writings of St. John of the Cross. It is well known that his works provided a strong and much-needed reaction against the exaggerated tendencies of his time, against heterodox movements and false doctrines in the field of mystical theology, where errors concerning principles have deplorable effects in practice. Traces of St. John's reaction are still vividly and palpably evident in his works.

Ecclesiastical authority had taken a stand against the dangerous deviations by means of a rigorous juridical process that was sometimes drastic. It evokes the name of Melchior Cano.[2] But the truth as lived and experienced was likewise a powerful means of resisting the pseudo-mystical movement, and in this respect the recent reform of Carmelite life was especially effective. As a result of this salutary counterattack, a fountain of pure mystical life and clear doctrine sprang forth. It not only

---

[1] Two works available in English translation are: Crisógono de Jesús, *The Life of St. John of the Cross* (London, 1958) and Léon Cristiani, *St. John of the Cross* (New York: Doubleday, 1962). (Tr.)

[2] Melchior Cano (1509–1560), a Spanish Dominican, was an outstanding professor at Alcalá and Salamanca, a theologian at the Council of Trent, and author of the work *De locis theologicis*. Many historians refer to him as an excessively severe inquisitor. (Tr.)

provided the weapon to overcome the *alumbrados*[3] but also a light that would illumine the true Church of Christ throughout the centuries.

However, it should be evident that we cannot make a detailed study of the historical situation, as if it were the only factor that prompted St. John of the Cross to write his works. As a matter of fact, his intention was to teach and only secondarily, by teaching, to combat error. He states as much in his prologue to *The Ascent of Mount Carmel*. Nevertheless, some reference to the historical background can be helpful, especially in view of the subject matter of the present study.

Against the false theories concerning union with God, the Mystical Doctor calmly maintained that *faith* is the proper means to that union—faith with all its consequences: in nakedness, austerity, and obedience of the intellect. Thus, Father Crisógono states:

> The way to react against those tendencies and doctrines was to glorify faith, which is opposed to vision; to make it the only means for attaining the loftiest grade of mystical union; to place it above any vision or revelation; to exclude from the mystical experience the immediate, face-to-face vision of God.[4]

The solution is clear. The deep-seated pseudo-mystical tendencies, rooted perhaps in the teaching of Averroes and in Arabian mysticism,[5] had recently been revived through a false

---

[3] The term *alumbrados* (equivalent to the term *illuminati*) refers to the Spanish pseudo-mystics who claimed to be under the direct guidance of the Holy Spirit and therefore not subject to any human authority. They claimed to be able to enjoy the immediate vision of God and to be thus rendered impeccable, with the result that no action, however base or evil, could be imputed to them as a sin. In their teaching and practice of prayer, they exaggerated the passivity of the soul in relation to God and thus fell into the error of quietism. (Tr.)

[4] Crisógono de Jesús Sacramentado, *San Juan de la Cruz: su obra científica y su obra literaria* (Madrid, 1929), vol. I, 327.

[5] Averroes was born at Córdoba, Spain, in 1128 and died in Morocco in 1198. Besides being an outstanding Aristotelian philosopher who had a great

interpretation of Flemish authors and the Rhineland mystics,[6] whose works were widely read in the Iberian peninsula. But the interior manifestation of the Spirit in the life of the Church corrects the errors of false mysticism by holding up the virtue of faith—that same faith whose saving power and ability to unite the soul with God had been extolled in Sacred Scripture. And the instrument by which the divine doctrine was to be propagated with new vigor in that period of disorientation was the humble solitary of Duruelo.[7]

The historical situation reveals another aspect that is more extensive and more significant for the life of the Church as a whole. We are in the second half of the sixteenth century, shortly after the crisis of the Reformation; that is, after the innovators had spread their erroneous doctrines and the Tridentine reform had been promulgated. Close as it was to that period of the Church's history, the teaching of St. John of the Cross has a value of even wider significance. Father Bruno touches on this point in the following passage:

> Brother John fights with the weapon of love, not with fire.[8] At the root of the error of Martin Luther was an uncontrolled desire for the sensible consolations of grace, which was a perversion of Tauler's mysticism. This led to the despair of ever becoming a "Friend of

---

influence on the English Carmelite John Baconthorpe (1290–1348), he was also involved with the Moslem mysticism that greatly contributed to the pseudo-mystical teachings of the *alumbrados*. (Tr.)

[6] The most influential writers among the Rhineland mystics were the German Dominicans, Meister Eckhart (1260–1327), John Tauler (1300–1350), and Henry Suso (1300–1366). John Ruysbroeck (1293–1381) is considered the leader of the Flemish school of spirituality. (Tr.)

[7] The first house of the Discalced Friars of the Teresian Reform was situated at Duruelo, a remote village in the western part of Castile. The house was opened officially in November, 1568, and the first occupants were St. John of the Cross and two companions from the monastery at Medina del Campo. (Tr.)

[8] A reference to the burning of heretics as practiced by the Inquisition. (Tr.)

God" and to the doctrine of salvation through a faith-trust that saves without works and is not vivified by charity. John of the Cross places in opposition to that corrupted Christianity the integral supernatural life and its supreme work of transformation and union with God through love. By word and example he insists that one should never linger at the sense level, which deceives, but should abandon oneself to pure faith, a living faith animated by charity and working through charity, a faith that is the only means proportionate to vital union with God. The illuminism of the *alumbrados*, condemned for the first time in 1568, could have no more vigorous adversary than the Doctor of Los Mártires,[9] that true Poor Man who immolated himself by being obedient even to the death of the cross.[10]

We can find similar statements in other works that emphasize the importance of the doctrine of St. John of the Cross in the history of the Church. Speaking of St. John's doctrine on faith as the means of union with God, they generally assert that it has not only great doctrinal value but historical value as well.[11] It is by reason of the doctrinal value of his writings that he was declared Doctor of the Church by Pope Pius XI in 1926.

Doctrine and sources

In composing his works the Mystical Doctor could rely on a varied theological preparation. First, the study of Scholastic theology provided the foundation, for he was a student at the University of Salamanca after the great Thomistic revival that began toward the end of the fifteenth century under the leadership of Francis de Vitoria. At that time he was known

[9] St. John of the Cross became prior at Los Mártires, Granada, in 1582. (Tr.)

[10] Bruno de Jésus-Marie, *Saint Jean de la Croix* (Paris: Plon, 1929) 94.

The last reference is to the extreme poverty practiced by St. John of the Cross, his heroic obedience, and his painful death at Ubeda in 1591. (Tr.)

[11] For example, Louis de la Trinité, *Le docteur mystique* (Paris, 1929).

as John of St. Matthias,[12] and he followed the courses of philosophy and theology from 1564 to 1568. Among his professors was Mancio de Corpus Christi, who lectured on the *Tertia Pars* of the *Summa theologiae* of St. Thomas Aquinas.

The study of Scholastic theology made a lasting impression on St. John of the Cross, as he testifies in his prologue to *The Spiritual Canticle*. Not only did he learn a sound theological method,[13] but even then he was laying the foundation for the mystical doctrine that he would later develop from sound theological principles. This supports the statement of Dom Chevallier[14] concerning the basic conformity between the teaching of St. John of the Cross and that of St. Thomas Aquinas.

In addition to the study of Scholastic theology, which surely did not end with his stay at Salamanca, although not done later in a formal and academic way, St. John prepared himself through the reading of mystical literature. We find evidence of this in his own writings, and some authors are cited by name; for example, Pseudo-Dionysius, St. Augustine, and St. Gregory the Great.[15] He was especially influenced by *The Imitation of Christ* and by the spiritual writers of Germany and the Low Countries, from whom he took many expressions and concepts. He did not change the meaning substantially, but he did adapt them to his own genius and experience. Father Crisógono gives the following examples: the doctrine on the mystical "touch" and the "simple and loving awareness", found also in

[12] St. John of the Cross was born at Fontiveros, near Avila, in 1542 and given the name of Juan de Yepes. On entering the Carmelite Order he took the name of John of St. Matthias, but when he made his profession as a member of the Teresian Reform at Duruelo in 1568, he changed his name to John of the Cross. (Tr.)

[13] Cf. Bruno de Jésus-Marie, op, cit., 42.

[14] Cf. Dom Philippe Chevallier, "La doctrine ascétique de Saint Jean de la Croix", *La Vie Spirituelle*, 16 (1927) 175–96. (Tr.)

[15] There are also explicit references to St. Thomas Aquinas, St. Bernard, Boëthius, and St. Teresa of Avila. (Tr.)

the works of Ruysbroeck; the "ground of the soul",[16] "naked and simple" faith, and the signs of transition from meditation to contemplation, likewise found in the writings of Tauler.[17] The works of Tauler were available in Spain either in the Latin translation made by Surius or in the Spanish version published at Coimbra in 1551. The works of Ruysbroeck were also accessible, having been translated into Latin by Surius in 1552.

Many other authors can be named who had an influence on St. John of the Cross, but perhaps to a less degree. Some were writers from past centuries, such as the Victorines, possibly St. Bernard,[18] Denis the Carthusian, Henry Herpes, John Gerson; others were contemporaries, such as Francisco de Osuna, Bernardino de Laredo, and St. Teresa of Avila, who was at once the spiritual mother and daughter of St. John of the Cross.

As regards all these citations, we should note an observation made by Father Bruno, for it is very helpful in enabling one to appreciate the doctrinal importance of St. John of the Cross, especially in the area that is the immediate subject of our investigation. Father Bruno refers to the relationship between St. John of the Cross and the Rhineland and Flemish mystics, for whom the Mystical Doctor had a great affinity.

> Ruysbroeck did not distinguish as clearly as did St. Thomas between the natural and the supernatural orders. The theology of St. John of the Cross is quite different in this respect and much more faithful to St. Thomas Aquinas. He did not accept, in the Augustinian theory of the image of the Trinity in the soul, the Platonic aspects that we find in Ruysbroeck. For him, in order for the soul to be united with God, nature must not only be purified by grace, but

[16] This expression was popularized by Meister Eckhart, the leader of the Rhineland mystics. (Tr.)

[17] Cf. Crisógono de Jesús Sacramentado, op. cit., 29 ff. and in particular 45 ff.

[18] We have already noted that St. John of the Cross mentions St. Bernard by name in *The Dark Night*, but this does not necessarily mean that he had studied the works of St. Bernard in depth. (Tr.)

it must be radically elevated, so that the work of union depends entirely on the essentially supernatural power of a living faith.[19]

The same author notes in another place that Ruysbroeck certainly admits that grace, the virtues, and the gifts reside in some part of the soul; St. John of the Cross, however, maintains that it is precisely these supernatural elements that lead to and produce union with God. This distinction between "union without intermediary" and the frequently repeated doctrine on the "means of union" immediately places St. John of the Cross in the theological tradition of St. Thomas Aquinas, which he had first absorbed at the University of Salamanca. This area of his teaching relates directly to our subject because faith is treated here precisely as a "means of union" between the soul and God.

In addition to these two sources, for the most part extrinsic, there are others that contributed to the elaboration of St. John's theological system. The first is the study of the Gospel and of Sacred Scripture in general, with which St. John of the Cross was so well acquainted. His writings testify to this.

The second is experience. We have already spoken of the experience of others as described in the mystical literature that St. John read. Now we refer to his own experience, whether drawn from his contact with other souls in spiritual direction or from his own interior life. And here, it seems, we touch a constitutive element of his works. They are not simply speculative treatises on mystical theology; they are a witness to mystical experience. We would say that speculative theology provided the principles, the spiritual authors gave the terminology and a vast area of comparative study, but the writings of St. John of the Cross are the fruit of experience. It was a vital experience of the supernatural reality that is communicated to the soul, a dynamic experience of participation in the intimate life of the

---

[19] Bruno de Jésus-Marie, op. cit., 281.

Blessed Trinity, and, finally, an experience of the unifying power of that which serves as a "means of union" with God.

Considering all this, we are faced with an important task. By means of testimony verified for the most part by St. John's personal experience, we learn what faith is as a means of union with God; what that reality means psychologically, on the one hand, and on the other, as a participation in the divine; how it exists and operates in the soul; and how the symbiosis is effected between the participated divine reality and the human intellect. Now we must investigate and discover the vital and experiential significance of one particular theological category. Such is the proper aim and incentive of our research.

Object of this study, difficulties, and method of procedure

We have before us the complete works of St. John of the Cross. The most important among them are the famous four: *The Ascent of Mount Carmel*, *The Dark Night*, *The Spiritual Canticle*, and *The Living Flame of Love*. These works provide the basic material for our investigation. The time of their composition is not known for certain,[20] but they contain an explicit teaching

[20] "The chronological order of these various works has remained rather obscure, and the reason, I believe, is that the first two works were never completed" (Gabriele di S. Maria Maddelena, *San Giovanni della Croce: Dottore dell' Amore divino*, Firenze, 1937, 16).

Jean Baruzi (*Saint Jean de la Croix et le problème de l'expérience mystique*, Paris, 1924) asserts frequently, and rightly so, that this is also the reason why we lack an *ex professo* treatment by St. John on contemplation and the "obscure understanding" of faith.

Efrén de la Madre de Dios, in his work *San Juan de la Cruz y el mistero de la Santísima Trinidad en la vida espiritual* (Zaragoza, 1947) gives the following chronological listing of the works of St. John of the Cross: *The Ascent of Mount Carmel*, 1579–1585, at Beas, Baeza, and Granada; *The Spiritual Canticle* (first redaction), 1584, at Granada; *The Dark Night*, 1583–1585, at Granada; *The Living Flame* (first redaction), about 1586, at Granada; *The Spiritual Canticle* (second

on the virtue of faith as the means of union of the soul (that is, the intellect) with God. After seeing the texts that treat of this question and collating them with what has been said previously about St. John's preparation for his work, we have selected the virtue of faith as the object of our research.

We have already seen that the doctrine we shall study is a testimony of experience. It is expressed in scholastico-mystical language, using words and concepts well known in Scholastic theology, but its primary value and significance is as a witness of personal experience. It is there, in fact, that we can discover the living and dynamic reality of the virtue of faith, its activity in the human intellect, its corollaries and the effects on the movement of the soul toward union with God. For that reason we take the experiential witness of St. John of the Cross as the material for our investigation. It will be our task to discover the concept of faith that can be gleaned from that witness and the theological precisions that are latent in it.

Our investigation will proceed from an analysis of the texts themselves in order to establish their precise meaning, that is, to identify the reality that lies beneath the various terms used to express it. That will comprise the first phase of our research. The method will be predominantly analytical, and therefore our study will concentrate on the very words of St. John of the Cross. Here we shall discover great lights, but also some difficulties. We are not referring to textual or critical problems, concerning which we shall say a few words at the end of this introduction, but to the difficulties intrinsic to the texts selected for our analysis.

---

redaction), about 1590–1591, at Segovia; *The Living Flame* (second redaction). 1591, at Peñuela. This chronology seems to be based on the one composed by Silverio de Santa Teresa, editor of the works of St. Teresa of Avila.

Translator's note: For a more recent chronology, see Kieran Kavanaugh and Otilio Rodríguez, *The Collected Works of St. John of the Cross* (New York: Doubleday, 1964) 32–33.

The works of St. John of the Cross have a special literary characteristic. They are not simply a series of speculative treatises; rather, they are, as we have already noted, the testimony of experience, and their aim is to trace and illumine the path that leads to mystical union. To achieve this, the Saint expressed himself in poetry and then later wrote commentaries on the poems. In fact Jean Baruzi described the composition of the works of St. John of the Cross as the concept of a treatise springing from a poetic inspiration.[21]

Whatever one may think of this theory, it is certainly evident from the texts themselves that the poetic element occupies a prominent place in the writings of St. John of the Cross. This is especially true of *The Spiritual Canticle*, which is a commentary on a lengthy lyric poem. On the other hand, the explanatory element predominates in *The Ascent of Mount Carmel* and in *The Dark Night*.[22] Even the prologue is a germinal exposition of the poem.

The commentaries themselves are not always composed with exact precision. I do not refer to the overall plan of each work, for that is characterized by a rigorous and incomparable logic, a logic that is evident throughout, from the fundamental principle to the ultimate conclusion. I refer rather to certain particulars regarding language—the words and phrases used by St. John of the Cross. They do not always have exactly the same meaning.

Each of the commentaries has a practical rather than a speculative aim. Consequently, although the expressions used are always more than adequate to achieve the practical purpose, they do not always suffice for the second. This gives rise to

[21] Jean Baruzi, op. cit., 19.

[22] The same poem of eight stanzas serves as the basis for the commentary in *The Ascent of Mount Carmel* and *The Dark Night*, whereas there are thirty-nine stanzas in the poem in the first redaction of *The Spiritual Canticle* and forty stanzas in the second redaction. (Tr.)

the first difficulty: it is necessary to examine each word in every new context in order to see whether it still has the same meaning. This applies especially to words and phrases that have a precise, technical meaning in philosophy and theology. This will be our task in the analytical part of our study, examining such words as *substance*, *essence*, *potency*, *means*, and many others that may have a different meaning in another context.

But here we should emphasize that the texts not only expound a theology based on experience, but to a great extent they do so in a descriptive manner. The description is often couched in Scholastic terminology, but the experience that is described will often give a different nuance or a new meaning to the technical terminology.

In view of the foregoing, a great part of our research will consist in an analytic investigation by which we shall try to verify the meaning intended by the author in the use of various terms. In this way we hope to arrive at an overall view of the teaching of St. John of the Cross.

But we should note that it is impossible to focus exclusively on the virtue of faith in his writings. This applies not only to faith as a distinct and separate virtue—since St. John always speaks of a living faith that operates through charity to unite the soul to God—but also to the virtue of faith as a separate problem. It is true that in his writings St. John of the Cross sometimes treats of the virtue of faith *ex professo*, but even then he does not study it as an isolated virtue in a purely speculative way.

Usually the virtue of faith is connected with other elements by which the life of union is increased in the soul until it attains its perfection. Therefore, we have to extract the concept of faith from St. John's whole theological system, noting at the same time the other elements that relate to faith as expounded in his writings. Only then, after we have separated all the other factors that intervene in the path to union, can we investigate the necessity, function, and particular importance of the virtue of faith; in other words, discern the intrinsic nature of the virtue of faith.

However, we repeat that one must not think that St. John of the Cross composed an exhaustive treatise on the virtue of faith; by no means. He treats of only one aspect of faith: its unifying power, which he elaborates with precision and utmost competence. There are other elements of particular importance in the theology of faith, but he leaves them aside. He takes them for granted or, if he does refer to them, it is only by an implicit reference.

Such is the subject matter of our investigation and such is the intent and purpose with which we shall study it. By now it ought to be clear how we ought to proceed. The analytical phase will be leisurely and progressive in order to determine the textual and doctrinal content and to define the limits of the material to be discussed. Conclusions will be drawn in the course of our study, and they will be noted even in the analytical phase but stated explicitly in the final synthesis.

May the Blessed Virgin, to whom I dedicate this work, graciously accept it as a token of filial homage.

Bibliographical and textual note

We intend to base our study on the critical edition of the works of St. John of the Cross published by Father Silverio: *Obras de San Juan de la Cruz, Doctor de la Iglesia*, Burgos, 1929–1931.[23] However, we should note that the controversy over the various redactions of the texts of St. John of the Cross, which started in the 1920's, is not yet settled. It has to do especially with the two versions of *The Spiritual Canticle*.

[23] E. Allison Peers translated this edition by Father Silverio into English (*The Complete Works of Saint John of the Cross, Doctor of the Church*, first published in London in 1935). (Tr.)

Father Gerardo de San Juan de la Cruz published the complete works of St. John of the Cross in 1912, and thereafter a question was raised concerning the authenticity of manuscript B of *The Spiritual Canticle*. Dom Philippe Chevallier denied the authenticity of this manuscript, asserting that only manuscript A is the work of St. John of the Cross.[24]

There are notable differences between the two versions: manuscript B is much longer; in manuscript A there are only 39 stanzas in the poem, but in manuscript B there are 40 stanzas. The internal arrangement of the stanzas of the poem has been changed in manuscript B and, as a result, the arrangement of the commentary as well (for example, stanza 22 in manuscript B is stanza 27 in manuscript A). There are also many changes in the text of the commentary on the poem. Dom Chevallier concluded that manuscript B is not the work of St. John of the Cross, but one of his disciples. Therefore, in his opinion, only manuscript A is authentic. This opinion was accepted by Jean Baruzi, who raised similar but less serious questions regarding the two versions of *The Living Flame of Love*.[25]

Modern Carmelite theologians, especially Father Silverio de Santa Teresa and Father Gabriel of St. Mary Magdalen, accept manuscript B as authentic. The interlinear and marginal notes are in the handwriting of St. John of the Cross, and some of the marginal notations in manuscript A refer to textual changes that later appear in manuscript B. Carmelite scholars continue to work on this problem in order to verify the authenticity of

[24] Dom Philippe Chevallier, "*Le Cantique spirituel interpolé*", *La Vie Spirituelle* (1926 to 1930).

Translator's note: Dom Chevallier first attacked the authenticity of manuscript B in the article, "*Le Cantique spirituel de Saint Jean de la Croix a-t-il été interpolé?*" (*Bulletin Hispanique*, 1922). He later published a series of articles in *La Vie Spirituelle*, noted above. He received support from Jean Baruzi (1924) and in 1948 Jean Krynen provided additional arguments against the authenticity of the manuscript.

[25] Jean Baruzi, *Saint Jean de la Croix* (Paris, 1924) 7–65.

the various manuscripts. We have listed some of the studies in
the Bibliography. Recently, Father Juan de Jesús María tried to
establish the opinion of his school more securely.[26]

Practically speaking, the following solution seems to be the
right one so far as this controversy relates to our investigation:
we shall use the critical edition of Father Silverio, which contains both redactions or versions of *The Spiritual Canticle*, the
work that pertains especially to our study. We shall consult
both redactions and indicate any variations that are pertinent to
our subject. In this way we shall be certain of having the substance of the text of St. John of the Cross as well as his
doctrine, which, so far as our investigation is concerned, is to
be found primarily in *The Spiritual Canticle*.

One final word concerning the Bibliography. The works
listed are those that give a total view of the teaching of St. John
of the Cross (and therefore make some reference to the virtue
of faith), or they concentrate on the specific problem of contemplation (for example, the controversy concerning acquired
and infused contemplation and the nature of each). The latter
works either treat of a particular aspect of the virtue of faith or
presuppose it altogether. We shall endeavor to bring the doctrine on faith into relief, even where St. John treats of contemplation, abstracting as far as possible his teaching on faith so
that the concept of the virtue of faith as such will be seen
clearly.

A work along these lines has already been published by
Father Labourdette,[27] although his study deals also with mystical knowledge and therefore treats of faith in its func-

---

[26] Cf. Juan de Jesús María, "*El valor crítico del texto escrito por la primera mano
en el códice de Sanlúcar de Barrameda*", in *Ephemerides Carmeliticae*, I (1947) 154–
62; "*Las anotaciones del códice de Sanlúcar son de San Juan de la Cruz?*" op. cit.,
313–66.

[27] Michel Labourdette, "*La foi théologale et la connaissance mystique d'après
Saint Jean de la Croix*", in *Revue Thomiste* 42 (1936) 593–629; 43:16–58; 191–
229.

tional aspect so far as it is operative in contemplation. Our work will concentrate rather on discerning the nature of the virtue of faith as described in the writings of St. John of the Cross. With God's help, we hope to succeed.

I wish to address the last word to the Very Reverend Reginald Garrigou-Lagrange, who consented to direct the writing of this thesis, giving suggestions and guidance out of his own vast experience and learning.

PART ONE

ANALYSIS

THE ASCENT OF MOUNT CARMEL

Means of union

Anyone who seeks in *The Ascent of Mount Carmel* whatever can be found there concerning faith will perhaps notice first of all how often St. John of the Cross repeats statements in which faith is referred to as the means of union with God. This manner of describing the proper function of faith, so evident in *The Ascent* and somewhat less frequent in *The Dark Night*, is not found at all in *The Spiritual Canticle* or in *The Living Flame*. In the first two works of his tetrology, as Father Bruno de Jésus-Marie remarks, St. John of the Cross praises the created supernaturality of the theological virtues, but in the other two works he glorifies the uncreated supernatural.[1] Faith is seen, therefore, as a means of the union of the soul with God. This is constantly stated in *The Ascent*, not always in the same words, but in different ways. In order to give a better idea of the various texts, some of them are listed here:

1) Very often it is simply stated that faith is the means of union with God (*la fe es medio para unir el alma con Dios*).

2) Not infrequently the same thing is asserted in equivalent terms, as when it is said that through faith the soul approaches or is directed to union with God (*acercarse a la unión;*[2] *enderezar en fe a la unión;*[3] *caminar por la fe;*[4] *ir* [or *subir*] *por la fe*).[5] The same thing is expressed in those words in which the task of leading (*guia*[6]) to union is assigned to the virtue of faith.

---

[1] Cf. Bruno de Jésus-Marie, *Saint Jean de la Croix* (Paris: Plon, 1929) 270.

[2] Cf. *The Ascent*, bk. II, chap. 4, no. 6.

[3] Cf. *The Ascent*, bk. II, chap. 26, no. 11.

[4] Cf. *The Ascent*, bk. II, chap. 1, no. 1.

[5] Cf. *The Ascent*, bk. II, chap. 1, no. 1; chap. 29, no. 5.

[6] Cf. *The Ascent*, bk. II, chap. 3, no. 6; chap. 4, no. 2; chap. 4, no. 3.

3) Sometimes the simple word "means" is qualified by an adjective, more literary and poetic than philosophical or exegetical, as when faith is described as the marvelous means (*el admirable medio*[7]) or similar instances.

4) Greater attention must be paid to those phrases, not infrequent, in which the word "means" has a precise significance in theological language and therefore needs a specific interpretation. The following are some examples: faith is "the *proximate means* for ascending to union with God";[8] "the *proper and suitable means* of union with God";[9] "the means *proximate and proportionate* to the intellect, whereby the soul can arrive at the divine union of love".[10] The term most frequently used is "proximate means", as is evident from the following texts: faith, "which of itself is the *proximate and proportionate means* whereby the soul is united with God";[11] "that it may advance by the *proximate means*, namely, by faith" (that is, advance towards union with God); [12] faith is the "*legitimate and proximate means* to union with God" (from the context of the chapter, "legitimate means" signifies the right means).[13] In *The Dark Night* there is only one expression of this type. It is used when St. John of the Cross says the soul must walk in faith as "the *proper and adequate means*" whereby it can be united with God.[14]

The foregoing terms are obviously from Scholastic philosophy, and for that reason, rather than state or presuppose anything *a priori*, we must verify their exact meaning in each case. This we shall do as far as possible, for we know how the Mystical Doctor uses Scholastic terms and how in his writings

---

[7] Cf. *The Ascent*, bk. II, chap. 2, no. 1.
[8] Cf. *The Ascent*, bk. II, explanatory title.
[9] Cf. *The Ascent*, bk. II, chap. 8, no. 1.
[10] Cf. *The Ascent*, bk. II, chap. 9, explanatory title.
[11] Cf. *The Ascent*, bk. II, chap. 9, no. 1.
[12] Cf. *The Ascent*, bk. II, chap. 24, no. 8.
[13] Cf. *The Ascent*, bk. II, chap. 30, no. 5.
[14] Cf. *The Dark Night*, bk. II, chap. 2, no. 5.

certain philosophical elements are intermingled with descriptive and poetical elements to show us in a very striking manner the effect of profound experience. We must therefore state at once that the adjectives we have cited above are not used simply for literary adornment; they serve to determine more accurately the function of faith as a means of uniting the intellect with God. Hence the meaning of those adjectives gleaned from the text can give us our first insight into the nature of faith. But the texts quoted do not give us the sufficient reason why faith is described here by one adjective and there by another. St. John of the Cross did not write his works with a view to the investigations of scholars or those engaged in higher studies; they are written for the purpose of directing contemplatives toward union with God, as is evident from the prologue to *The Ascent of Mount Carmel*.

If any of the texts quoted above can serve as a basis for our investigations, it is the one from chapter 8 of *The Ascent of Mount Carmel*. And there is good reason for this, because with this text we enter at once to the heart of the question. Actually, in chapters 8 and 9 of *The Ascent* St. John begins to explain the positive doctrine on faith whose influence extends throughout the entire teaching of St. John of the Cross. We also find in chapter 8 the concept of *means* illustrated by examples and later explained theologically:

> It is to be understood, then, that, according to the rule of philosophy, all means must be proportionate to the end; that is, they must have some connection and likeness to the end, such as is enough and sufficient for attaining the end that is sought.[15]

We have in this text something resembling a definition: a proportionate means should possess all the elements necessary for reaching the end, thus making it possible for one to attain the end. Therefore it is not a question of indiscriminate elements, but of

---

[15] *The Ascent*, bk. II, chap. 8, no. 2.

those determined strictly by the end itself, for they must render the means proportionate to the end and hence suitable and sufficient for attaining the end. Thus, in chapter 8 of *The Ascent* we note such phrases as "proper and suitable means . . . enough and sufficient for attaining the end that is sought".[16] Thus it is evident that the requirements of the end, objectively considered, qualify the means to the end and, indeed, determine the means to be used.

Since the elements required in the means have been described in terms of "connection and likeness to the end", we must investigate their nature in the passage that follows, where St. John explains the elements that should characterize the means of union with God. However, the examples given do not require all the elements previously mentioned. This is especially true of the first example, namely, that one wishing to go to a certain city must go by this way and no other; he must take the way that leads to the city. It is true that we find in the example the element of "connection" between the means (the road) and the end (the city), but how does it exemplify "likeness" between the means and the end?

The other example demonstrates much better all the requisites, and it is a classical one. "One has to combine and unite fire with wood; it is necessary that the heat, which is the means, first dispose the wood by enough degrees of heat so that it will have great likeness and proportion to the fire."[17] Thus, the transformation of wood into fire is effected by the heat that has the power to prepare for the igniting of the wood. But this will not happen until the heat reaches the required intensity so that the wood will burn. The example clearly illustrates the two requisite elements, connection or proportion and likeness.

What can we conclude concerning the "proportionate means" on the basis of these examples? When St. John of the Cross speaks of means, he seems to be referring to a specific real-

---

[16] Cf. *The Ascent*, bk. II, chap. 8, nos. 1 and 2.
[17] *The Ascent*, bk. II, chap. 8, no. 2.

ity, indeed, its very nature in relation to an end. He investigates its qualities and looks for a certain innate disposition by which the means is intrinsically proportioned to the end that is sought. We can conclude from this that a means is said to be a "proportionate means" when by its intrinsic disposition it is sufficient to attain an end. It requires something intrinsic to itself in order to attain the end, as in the examples, the direction of the road or the power of heat to ignite and burn wood.

Only the "proportionate means" has the distinction of being fully explained by St. John; the others do not. He uses the other adjectives in such a way that one can be substituted for another or serves to complete the meaning of another term. Thus, in the same passage in chapter 8 of *The Ascent* he uses the phrase "proper means" to describe the natural power of heat to transform wood into fire. However, there is a difference between "proper means" and "proportionate means". The former signifies that of all the things proposed as means to the end, this is the only one that suffices; the others do not. The latter term indicates clearly why a particular means is the only proper means of attaining the end. This distinction is evident from the passage cited, although both terms are used to describe the same thing. St. John does not bother to make any further distinctions, nor shall we.

We find something similar in book II, chapter 24 of *The Ascent* in the use of the expression "proximate means", which has the same qualities as the "proportionate means" discussed in chapter 8, namely the "connection and likeness" that make it an apt means for attaining the end. In book II, chapter 2 of *The Dark Night* we find the phrase "adequate means", but neither the terminology nor the context add anything new. It seems that the term belongs to the same category of means described above and hence expresses the same idea.

Lastly, we have the term "legitimate means", and perhaps this adds something new. The context in which it is used emphasizes the marked opposition between the means of union with God which rightly and lawfully deserves that title and those other means, such as "interior locutions", with which the legitimate means are compared and which, without any adequate title, would purport to perform the function of uniting the soul with God.[18] Their aptitude for performing such a function must be carefully investigated in the effects they produce—and this is done only with difficulty—so that the apt means can be separated from those that are not so. Once they are distinguished one from the other, it will become evident that those other means are insufficient and totally inferior to the legitimate and proper means which is faith. Hence the term "legitimate" can be used to express this idea.

We have seen that the various adjectives that describe the means have a Scholastic interpretation, but as used by St. John of the Cross they designate practically the same thing. Moreover, a separate analysis of each one would not produce very much that is new. In the text they are always used in conjunction with the word "faith"; examined in that context, their full meaning will be revealed.

The previous analysis of terms has been helpful in preventing us from attributing to them *a priori* anything more than is warranted. At the same time, it brings us closer to the heart of our question, for now we see that faith as a means of union with God should possess certain qualities that make it suitable for attaining that end. These qualities should be as proper to faith as are the direction to the road and the heat to the fire in the examples given above. With this we have identified the first distinctive element in faith as a means of union with God.

"Proportion of likeness"

We are still examining chapter 8 in book II of *The Ascent of Mount Carmel*. In the subsequent text St. John of the Cross proceeds to explain clearly the meaning of "proportionate means",

---

[18] Cf. *The Ascent*, bk. II, chap. 30, no. 5.

introduced by way of the two examples given. Now he makes the application: in order that the intellect can be united with God, it must use the means that unites it with God.[19] And this is precisely a question of faith.

> Wherefore, in order that the intellect may be united with God in this life, so far as is possible, it must necessarily use that means that unites it with him and has the greatest likeness to him.[20]

At this point the qualities necessary for the proportionate means are clearly manifested. It is a question of union with God, and this necessarily requires some kind of likeness, which no created thing possesses.

> Among all creatures, the highest and the lowest, there is none that is intimately united to God or has any likeness to his being.[21]

Applying the criterion already stated, we can rephrase the foregoing text in the context of causality: no creature can be united with God because no creature bears any likeness to his being. But immediately we may ask what is meant by "his being". St. John of the Cross explains in the text that follows:

> Although it is true, as theologians say, that all creatures have a certain relation to God and a trace of God (some more and others less, according to the greater or lesser perfection of their being), yet there is no essential likeness or connection between them and God. On the contrary, the distance between their being and his divine being is infinite.[22]

This text is very instructive because it shows how the word "likeness" should be interpreted. The Mystical Doctor agrees with all the theologians in stating that there is some kind of likeness between God and creatures precisely as beings, or by reason of their existence. By the very fact that they exist,

---

[19] Cf. *The Ascent*, bk. II, chap. 8, no. 2.

[20] Ibid.

[21] *The Ascent*, bk. II, chap. 8, no. 3. St. John of the Cross is referring to created things as such, in the natural order. (Tr.)

[22] Ibid.

created beings have a certain analogical likeness to God; indeed, the greater their perfection in being, the more they resemble God in this respect. What is denied is any "essential" likeness: between that which is God and that which is creature, however perfect, there is no likeness, but infinite difference. The text clearly indicates that there is a hierarchy of beings, and the words are very similar to those used in the statement of Lateran Council IV: "Between the Creator and the creature there cannot be found such a likeness that the difference is not even greater."[23]

The passage cited from St. John of the Cross clearly reduces the dissimilarity between God and creatures to the order of essence or nature. Consequently, no creature, even the most perfect, considered in its essence, can be compared to the divine essence. That which God is must be totally unlike that which any creature is. There is no likeness between divinity and any created nature.

On this point there is no ambiguity whatever in the mind of the Mystical Doctor. But we should emphasize that in that particular text St. John is speaking of the absolute distinction between the divine reality and created reality on the basis of the nature of each one. Under this aspect the text also makes a distinction between the natural and the supernatural. The precise reason for the infinite distance between God and creatures is not only the fact that creatures are infinitely different from God, but because they lack an "essential likeness" to God. The infinite distance referred to in the text is based on the distinction between the nature or essence of God and that of creatures.

The statement concerning the strict distinction between the natural and the supernatural serves as the major premise of a syllogism that is actually contained in the text. It pervades the

---

[23] Denz.-Schön. *Enchiridion symbolorum, definit. et declarat.* (Freiburg: Herder, 1963) no. 806.

entire mystical doctrine of St. John of the Cross and adorns his teaching with that incomparable logic that has been noted by many commentators.

But now let us find the minor premise in the text. To do this it will be necessary to recall how the whole question of "essential likeness" was raised. We have seen that it came from the concept of the "proportionate means", as something required by the very nature of that means. But since an "essential likeness" between divinity and any creature, however perfect, has been denied, the conclusion necessarily follows: because it lacks any essential likeness to divinity, no created thing can serve as a proportionate means for union with God.

But why does the creature lack this essential likeness? Because that which constitutes the creature in its very being is of the natural order. Consequently it is this nature and nothing else that is the precise reason and the proper cause of the dissimilarity that excludes any creature from serving as a proportionate means of union with God. There is nothing in the natural order that can provide a "proportion of likeness" between the Creator and creatures. That is why no created thing can serve as a means of union with God.

And now we must state further that no created thing can serve as a means of union with God with respect to the intellect. As St. John of the Cross says: "Created things cannot serve as a proportionate means by which the intellect can reach God."[24] The words "reach God" (dar en Dios) mean to bring the intellect into contact with divinity in an effective way until it attains to the intimate essence of God. The expression specifies the meaning of "likeness" in a new way, reducing it to the level of representation or similitude. No created thing as known in its very essence by the intellect can reveal the divine essence to the intellect.[25]

[24] The Ascent, bk. II, chap. 8, no. 3.
[25] Cf. Summa theologiae, I, q. 12, a. 2.

This is the meaning of the text just cited from book II, chapter 8, of *The Ascent*, where we saw that the distance and essential difference between God and creatures took on a special significance in reference to the cognoscitive power. But now the concept of "likeness" acquires a new dimension: it passes from the real order to the intentional order. All these observations—which we shall subsequently apply to the virtue of faith—give a wide perspective to the question we are treating, namely, the virtue of faith in the doctrine of St. John of the Cross.

The text of chapter 8 next states explicitly the opposition between faith and created things.

> Hence, speaking of celestial creatures, David says: "There is none like you among the gods, O Lord" (Ps 86:8), calling the angels and the souls of the blessed gods. And elsewhere: "O God, your way is holy; what great god is there like our God?" (Ps 77:14). It is as if he said: The way of approach to you, O God, is a holy way, that is, the purity of faith.[26]

Faith is thus elevated above the highest creatures. They are excluded as means of union with God, but the virtue of faith is acknowledged as the way to union. It is the *proportionate* means of union, and therefore it possesses an *essential likeness* to God. This means that the essence of faith and divinity somehow relate to one another and converge. But it should be noted at once that this happens in connection with the intellect, which is united to God with faith serving as the proportionate means. We can therefore conclude, and without any exaggeration, that the text in chapter 8 places before us the question of the virtue of faith. It likewise indicates, though only in a vague and general way, the entitative and intentional elements in the virtue of faith.

We mentioned previously that the text we are studying contains a syllogism that is the key to the entire "mystical logic" of

---

[26] *The Ascent*, bk. II, chap. 8, no. 3.

St. John of the Cross. It will be helpful to put it in proper syllogistic form:

No created thing, considered in its specific nature, possesses any essential likeness to God.

But such a likeness is required for anything to serve as a proportionate means of union with God.

Therefore, no created thing, considered in its specific nature, can serve as a proportionate means of union with God.

This first syllogism applies to the entire mystical doctrine of St. John of the Cross, permeating and informing it profoundly. A second syllogism pertains particularly to the virtue of faith, deducing from the former syllogism a fundamental statement concerning its nature:

The virtue of faith serves as a proportionate means for the union of the intellect with God.

But the proportionate means of union with God must possess an essential likeness to him.

Therefore, faith possesses that likeness to God (and hence it provides the "proportion of likeness").

The preceding analysis opens the way for our precise question. In fact, the term "essential likeness" leads us to the order of essences, for when an essential likeness is denied of created things, that negation applies to their essences; and when it is attributed to the virtue of faith, it refers to the essence of faith. Therefore the question concerning the nature of the virtue of faith is well put in St. John of the Cross: that by which faith is faith is something similar to the divinity. Faith consists in that particular likeness.

At the same time in the text cited this likeness connotes a relation to the intellect, because the virtue of faith possesses a likeness to the divine on the intellectual level and hence unites the intellect with God. In this respect also the text is of great importance for our study.

We can now postulate the following: faith makes God known to the intellect, and no created thing, however perfect, is capable of doing this. Because of its essential likeness to the divine, faith can unite the soul with God. To put it another way: faith possesses an essential likeness to God in virtue of its relation to the intellect. And thus we are brought to the intentional order.

Both of the points developed are contained in the same text we have been considering. As to the first, the distinction between the natural and the supernatural is established, and then the virtue of faith enters the domain of the supernatural. Consequently, it possesses the required "essential likeness and connection with God" which is lacking to all other creatures, however perfect. Here we touch the very essence of the virtue of faith, which enables it to serve as a means of union.

As regards the second point, since the "essential likeness" is attributed to the virtue of faith by reason of its relation to the intellect, faith is described as a virtue that enables the intellect to attain to God in his very essence. This is apparent from the text we have been discussing but will become even more evident in the following section.[27] Other created things cannot lead the intellect to the divine essence, nor can the intellect by its natural powers alone do so; but the virtue of faith is able to do so. Why? Because created things have nothing more than their own essences, but faith possesses in its very essence a likeness to the essence of God.

It is evident, therefore, that the virtue of faith can serve as a proportionate means for union with God, and this for two reasons: first, because of its essential likeness to God, since it belongs to the supernatural order; secondly, because this essential likeness relates directly to the intellect. These two aspects—the entitative and the intentional—make the virtue of faith a proportionate means for the union of the intellect with God. For this

---

[27] Cf. *The Ascent*, bk. II, chap. 8, nos. 4–5.

reason chapter 8 of book II of *The Ascent of Mount Carmel* is the key to our investigation.

NOTES

1. As regards the concept of the supernatural in the works of St. John of the Cross, Father M. Labourdette writes:

> The difference between the two orders is presented by him as a difference of levels. . . .[28] As regards the divine union, the "supernatural" was considered and defined from the point of view of its psychological, concrete presentation to the soul that receives it; moreover, it was described as a mode of activity totally different from the "natural" mode.

Father Labourdette then adds in a footnote:

> The term "supernatural" in the language of St. John of the Cross does not have a specific, determined meaning that always remains the same. Father Crisógono rightly states that its meaning must be sought each time according to the context. But Father Crisógono himself uses a defective method in starting from the theological concept supernatural *quoad substantiam* or *quoad modum* to determine, at least in some passages, the meaning of the term. It is true that the realities of which the Saint speaks can be reduced and understood by transposing them according to that distinction, but his vocabulary does not relate to it directly; his point of view here is always concrete.[29]

These words describe accurately what we find in the text of St. John of the Cross. Nowhere do we find a more detailed definition of the word "supernatural" than the one cited, which

---

[28] Father Labourdette is evidently referring to the passage in *The Ascent*, bk. II, chap. 4, no. 2: "The word supernatural means that which is above the natural; the natural, therefore, remains below."

[29] M. Labourdette, "*La foi théologale et la connaissance mystique d'après Saint Jean de la Croix*", in *Revue Thomiste*, 42 (1936–1937) 16–57; 191–229.

is a nominal definition. On the other hand, when it is a question of those elements that are essential and constitutive of the entire synthesis, they could not even be classified without this concept of the supernatural. This is true also of the text in question, which could not be understood without the distinction between the natural and the supernatural. This will be demonstrated when later we analyze the texts in which St. John of the Cross treats of natural union and supernatural union.

We can further state that St. John of the Cross distinguishes the two orders with great precision and on this distinction he constructs his entire doctrine, to the last detail. It is true that he uses a variety of expressions, but our study is not concerned with names, but with the reality. On the other hand, we should not approach the text with *a priori* concepts and distinctions and then force the text to fit those presuppositions. But when a reality is evident from analysis of the text, it seems to me that we can then apply a name to it. This is true of the present distinction between the natural and the supernatural; it will likewise apply to our subsequent investigation of the "active night of the spirit".

In regard to the supernatural, does the Mystical Doctor consider it "from the point of view of its psychological, concrete presentation to the soul that receives it"? Usually he does, but when speaking of the "union of likeness" (for example, in book II, chapter 5 of *The Ascent*), he states that God "communicates supernatural being" to the soul.[30] This reference supports our conviction that St. John of the Cross does not treat of the virtue of faith exclusively in its operative aspect—which he does particularly when treating of contemplation—but first he studies it from the entitative aspect. Indeed, the operative function of faith in contemplation depends on the entitative aspect and flows from it.

One last observation: the meaning of "supernatural" which Father Labourdette has extracted from the works of St. John of

---

[30] Cf. *The Ascent*, bk. II, chap. 5, no. 4.

the Cross can be explained in another way. It is true that there is very little in the works of the Mystical Doctor that is purely speculative and abstract. This material—which is studied theoretically in theology—is treated primarily from an existential point of view in the works of the Saint. Whenever speculative matters are discussed it is because they are related to experience or even proceed from experience, and this necessarily reflects on the manner of presenting the speculative elements and writing about them.[31] Consequently, it would be futile to seek in the works of St. John of the Cross an explicitly speculative theology, although from time to time he uses terms and concepts from speculative theology.

2. After considering the essential likeness of the virtue of faith with divinity, which is explicitly affirmed in book II, chapter 8 of *The Ascent*, the concept of faith proposed by J. Baruzi[32] and the designation of it by Dom Chevallier as a "mysticism of the universalization of the intellect"[33] must be rejected. Although some texts, considered individually,[34] actually state that the intellect, in tending to union with God, must transcend the limitations of "certain modes"—which transcendence is actually attributed to the virtue of faith—nevertheless the essential supernatural likeness of faith with divinity, especially as described in book II, chapter 8 of *The Ascent*, certainly precludes attributing this transcendency to any natural "universalization of the intellect". The correct interpretation must be based on the nature of faith as described in chapter 8, where it is clearly stated that faith transcends the order of creatures and the limitation of any modality because it is supernatural in essence, possessing an

[31] Cf. Venancio Carro, "*La naturaleza de la gracia y el realismo místico*", *La Ciencia Tomista* (1922) 362 ff.

[32] Cf. J. Baruzi, *Saint Jean de la Croix et le problème de l'expérience mystique* (Paris, 1914; 2nd edition, 1931) 612–21.

[33] Cf. Dom P. Chevallier, "*Saint Jean de la Croix en Sorbonne*", *La Vie Spirituelle*, 12 (1925) 188–212.

[34] See, for example, *The Ascent*, bk. II, chap. 16, no. 7.

essential likeness to divinity. That is why it can lead the intellect to union with the divinity. Hence, for St. John of the Cross, faith's transcendence over every limited modality is based on its essential likeness to divinity, on the fact that it is substantially supernatural.

Consequently, it is evident that the nucleus of the question concerning the virtue of faith in St. John of the Cross is contained in that short text in book II, chapter 8, of *The Ascent*. The essential likeness of faith to divinity and its concomitant ordination to the intellect constitute the measure by which faith is constantly evaluated in the works of St. John of the Cross. And now, to corroborate the teaching on the supernaturality of faith, we shall study chapter 5 of book II of *The Ascent*, where we find the *ex professo* treatment of union with God.

"What is meant by union of the soul with God"

St. John of the Cross treats of the union of the soul with God throughout all his works—what it is, the means to attain it, the various degrees of union and its definitive degree. All four treatises treat of this same subject, as is evident from the prologue to *The Ascent* to the last page of *The Living Flame of Love*.

Since the virtue of faith is subordinated to union, as the means to the end, it should be clear that it is important for us to have a precise understanding of what that union is. The means must be proportionate to the end that is sought; therefore, to study the end as such—in this case union with God—we shall obtain a much clearer understanding of the nature and function of faith.

In chapter 5 of book II of *The Ascent*, St. John of the Cross distinguishes two types of union of the soul with God. The first is a "natural" union, called substantial or essential union; the second is supernatural, and it is properly a union of likeness. The first union is effected by the substantial presence of God in the soul, even in that of a sinner: "God sustains and is present substantially in every soul, even that of the greatest sinner in the world."[35] This first type of union, resulting from the substantial presence of God in the soul, is a union on the natural level and is therefore related to creation and conservation: "God is always present to the soul, giving to the soul its natural being and conserving it by his assistance."[36] But it is not this union that St. John of the Cross is treating in his works; he discusses only the supernatural union. And in this text the Mystical Doctor explains briefly how the supernatural union is to be understood.

The element that distinguishes supernatural union from every kind of natural union is that it is a different kind of communication: "Wherefore, although it is true, as we have said, that God is always present to the soul, giving to the soul its natural being and conserving it by his assistance, yet he does not communicate supernatural being to it."[37] This second type of communication is effected only through grace and charity: "This is communicated only by love and grace, which not all souls possess."[38] Moreover, the supernatural communication admits of varying degrees by different souls, according to the intensity of grace and charity in each one.

Later we shall see the role proper to love in the union between the soul and God; for the time being, it suffices to note that in the present text the Mystical Doctor is simply emphasizing the importance of love for obtaining and increasing this union. Thus, the dynamic aspect of union becomes immediately evident: it consists in the communication of the supernatural being of God through grace and love, and it is precisely through love that the union is increased.

The Mystical Doctor designates the supernatural union through grace and charity as a new birth, as the generation of

---

[35] *The Ascent*, bk. II, chap. 5, no. 3.
[36] Ibid., no. 4.   [37] Ibid.   [38] Cf. ibid.

the children of God, referring to John 1:13 and 3:15. But it should immediately be noted that in this brief survey of union another word is heard—a word of greatest importance in the theology of grace and charity: *transformation*. It is applied to supernatural union because of love, as we shall see when we analyze chapter 4 in book I of *The Ascent*. Love increases the union, and it is likewise love that determines the degree of transformation. Moreover, the unifying and transforming power of love redounds to the will, and hence we have the quasi-axiom stated in book II, chapter 5 of *The Ascent* and in other places as well:

> Therefore God communicates himself most to that soul that has progressed farthest in love, which means that its will is more in conformity with the will of God. And the soul that has attained complete conformity and likeness of will is completely united and transformed in God supernaturally.[39]

Thus, through the intervention of love the union is reduced psychologically to the conformity between the human will and the divine. But the conformity of wills is discussed in terms of the object. Thus, St. John of the Cross states repeatedly: "The supernatural union exists when the two wills—that of the soul and that of God—are in complete conformity, so that there is nothing in the one that is repugnant to the other."[40] Consequently, the union is a supernatural communication that is augmented through love and by that same love manifests the psychological effect of a conformity of wills.

But love is also transforming power. What does transformation signify? St. John of the Cross immediately rejects the possibility of a pantheistic interpretation. It is not a question of a substantial or essential transformation but a "participation of

---

[39] *The Ascent*, bk. II, chap. 5, no. 4.   [40] Ibid., no. 3.

union".[41] St. John the poet explains his meaning by using the famous and well-known example of the ray of sunlight passing through a window. The cleaner the window, the more sunlight passes through it, communicating its own brightness, its luminous quality and proper characteristics. And if it finds the window completely clean and totally transparent, the sunlight will be communicated to the window to such a degree that the latter, perfectly translucent, will give the same light as the sun's ray and will itself seem to be a ray of light. Yet the window is not transformed essentially into a ray of light, but retains its own nature distinct from the light; it merely participates in the ray of light to a high degree. So St. John of the Cross states: "Although it seems to be identical with the ray, the window has a nature distinct from that of the ray itself, but we may say that the window is a ray or light by participation."[42]

That splendid example contains the whole theology of supernatural communication, grace and participated transformation. In a similar fashion the soul shares in the supernatural communication through grace and love, through which ultimately it is transformed by participation into the very light of divinity.

> The soul becomes illumined and transformed in God, and God communicates his supernatural being to it in such a way that it appears to be God himself, and possesses all that God himself has. And this union is effected when God grants the soul this supernatural favor, that all the things of God and the soul are one in participant transformation; and the soul seems to be God rather than a soul. It is indeed God by participation; although it is true that its being, although transformed, is as distinct in nature from the being of God as it was before.[43]

Complete transformation, therefore, never exceeds the limits of participation and, understanding this, the Mystical Doctor

[41] Cf. ibid., no. 5.   [42] Ibid., no. 6.   [43] Ibid., no. 7.

can say that "the soul is God by participation". All of this demonstrates how the truths treated in speculative theology can be expressed much more vividly after one has actually experienced them. Thus, union with God, which is the goal of the soul's striving, is presented as a supernatural communication with God, a sharing in divinity itself through grace and love. And because of the power of love, the union can reach the point of transformation—the transforming union in God. Love likewise explains the psychological aspect of union: the conformity of the human will with the divine, a convergence of wills on the same object ("there is nothing in the one that is repugnant to the other") and hence a conformity that constitutes a moral union according to the axiom: *idem velle, idem nolle*.

Such are the principal themes that comprise the entire doctrinal system of St. John of the Cross concerning union with God: *communication*, *participation* and *transformation*. Participation is the result of communication; it explains the intimate nature and limits of the latter; and at the same time, under the form and impulse of love it tends toward transformation within the limits of participation. In other words, it progresses to the participated transformation of love. The entire teaching of the Mystical Doctor on the union between the soul and God is found in germ in chapter 5 of book II of *The Ascent*; it evolves and grows throughout the rest of his writings.

For our purpose, namely, to study the nature of faith in the teaching of St. John of the Cross, chapter 5 has special significance. It is there, for example, that we find verification of our interpretation of the passage in chapter 8 concerning the distinction between the natural and the supernatural. The distinction corresponds exactly with the Mystical Doctor's teaching on the two types of union with God—natural and supernatural—given in chapter 5.

Every created thing is united to God by a natural union by

the very reason of its being, and, depending on the perfection of its being, it will be more or less a vestige of God. But this vestigial likeness to God, this natural perfection, is not capable of a supernatural union with God; it cannot pass beyond the limits of the divine essence and penetrate the intimate life of divinity. No perfections of the natural order suffice to attain union with God, for they all lack that "essential likeness" which would enable them to ascend to the order of the divine. But the virtue of faith does possess the essential likeness and is therefore able to lead to union with God. This means that faith enters the confines of the supernatural order and touches divinity itself; and hence it is capable of contributing in some way to the participated transformation of the soul that is gradually and successively effected through grace and love. The capacity to do this is rooted in the very nature of faith, from which evolves its unifying power. All this is manifested clearly, though not always explicitly, in the texts of St. John of the Cross that we have thus far analyzed.

Faith and the intellect

Before we can examine the precise nature of the virtue of faith, we must ask a previous question: is the intellect the subject of faith? [In other words, does the virtue of faith reside in the intellect? (Tr.)]

Nowhere in the writings of St. John of the Cross do we find an explicit statement of this kind, much less in Scholastic terminology. But perhaps we can find something similar expressed in metaphorical terms, as in chapter 16, book II of *The Ascent*, where faith is compared to a lighted candle in a dark place. In explaining the comparison St. John makes reference to the psychological subject of faith: "This place, which here signifies the intellect, the candlestick on which the candle of faith is set. . . ."[44] The comparison is clear; faith shines in the intellect like a candle in the candlestick. Therefore the intellect is the subject of the virtue of faith.

But the explanation does not suffice. In order to know how to explain the relationship between faith and the intellect, we must investigate the concept—however general—that the Mystical Doctor has concerning faith. He says that it is the means of the union of the intellect with God. But that statement is still insufficient. We must find something that will serve as a definition of faith. St. John of the Cross provides this when he explains the precise function of the means of union, which is the specific function of faith. At the same time he provides a division of the faculties, according to which he also divides the three theological virtues. All three of these virtues are instruments of union in respect to the faculties in which they reside. Therefore the Saint speaks of three superior or spiritual faculties in man,[45] because only the spiritual or superior part of the soul is capable of communication with God and union properly so called. St. John of the Cross describes it as "the part that relates to God and to spiritual things. . . , which is the rational and higher part."[46]

The theological virtues are assigned to the various faculties as follows: faith to the intellect, hope to the memory, and charity

[44] *The Ascent*, bk. II, chap. 16, no. 15.

[45] Concerning the threefold division of man's spiritual faculties, cf. Crisógono de Jesús Sacramentado, *San Juan de la Cruz: Su obra científica y su obra literaria* (Madrid, 1929) vol. I, 79–80; Marcelo de Niño Jesús, *El Tomismo de San Juan de la Cruz* (Burgos, 1930). The threefold division of the spiritual faculties of the soul seems to have been taken from John Baconthorpe, an English Carmelite. Carmelites were obliged to study the works of their own masters.

But there is still the question of how to interpret the threefold division as found in the works of St. John of the Cross. Authors do not agree on this point. Father Marcelo offers a Thomistic interpretation while Father Crisógono explains it in accordance with the teaching of John Baconthorpe. However, the problem is not which doctrine St. John of the Cross held or taught, but how he applied it.

[46] *The Ascent*, bk. II, chap. 4, no. 2.

to the will. Each of the virtues is capable of uniting to God the faculty in which it operates. The entire structure of *The Ascent* is based on this schema. Thus, we read in the title of chapter 6 of book II: "How the three theological virtues perfect the three faculties of the soul, and how said virtues produce emptiness and darkness within them." Then in the body of the chapter we read:

> The three theological virtues of faith, hope and charity—which relate to these three faculties as their proper supernatural objects, and by means of which the faculties of the soul are united with God— produce the same emptiness and darkness, each one in its own faculty: faith in the intellect, hope in the memory, and charity in the will. [47]

We have here something equivalent to a definition of faith and the other two theological virtues. Proceeding from their specified function as means of union with God, St. John then considers each theological virtue in its actual operation (*in actu exercito*) and describes what is proper to each virtue as a means of union. These quasi-definitions indicate that the theological virtues unite their respective faculties to God; they likewise describe briefly how the virtues perform this unifying function—by purging the faculties through "emptiness and darkness" and presenting themselves as supernatural objects of those faculties.

The phrase referring to the theological virtues as "supernatural objects" is a curious one. St. John states that "the three theological virtues of faith, hope and charity, which relate to these three faculties as their supernatural objects. . . ." [48] The statement presupposes the doctrine on the informing of a faculty by its object by means of its connatural act. Thus, in the operation of a natural appetite in which the will intervenes, the will is informed and actuated by the natural object of that

---

[47] *The Ascent*, bk. II, chap. 6, no. 1.   [48] Ibid.

appetite. (We shall examine this point later.) In like manner the spiritual faculties relate to their corresponding theological virtues as to supernatural objects. This means that through the operation of these virtues each spiritual faculty is informed or actuated in a supernatural manner in accordance with its nature and function. This will be clarified when we study chapter 4 of book II of *The Ascent*. For the moment it suffices to state that the quasi-definition of each of the theological virtues reveals at the same time the principal function of each one and the way in which the function is exercised. For St. John of the Cross this requires the expulsion of the natural form proper to the faculty and its penetration or information by a supernatural form. The theological virtues are thus the instruments that present a supernatural object to their corresponding faculties.

The foregoing also illustrates the relationship of the theological virtues to the spiritual faculties. It is not a relationship of one thing subjected or predicated to another, but a relationship of one thing inhering in another. Each theological virtue penetrates or informs, as it were, its corresponding spiritual faculty; it operates in it and through it, disposing it for union with God or participated transformation in the divine. Thus, the virtue of faith relates to the intellect as a virtue or power that operates within it. It permeates the intellect, expelling the natural forms and informing it with the supernatural, thus gradually detaching it from created things and uniting it with God.

Such is the intimate and dynamic interdependence of the intellect and the virtue of faith. Rather, we should say that such is the *fact* of the interdependence, for its mode, development and all that follows from the evolution of this vital cohesion constitute the object of a study of the psychological aspects of faith. In order to make such a study, we shall have to glean from the writings of St. John of the Cross a deeper knowledge of the nature of the "subject" of the virtue of faith, that is, the faculty in which it resides. For the moment it suffices to take note of and emphasize the fact of the interdependence.

In the course of our study, as the nature of faith is developed more and more in the text of St. John of the Cross, we shall be able to investigate more deeply the function of the intellect. Faith and the intellect are so closely related in the teaching of the Mystical Doctor that it is impossible to understand the nature of one without knowing the nature of the other. Therefore it is best to study them together. To summarize: faith is the means of supernatural union for the intellect and its participation in divinity.

NOTE

Before proceeding further in our analysis, it will be helpful to examine another text in chapter 5, book II of *The Ascent*, where St. John of the Cross states explicitly what is to be understood by union of the soul with God. He says:

> Here I treat only of the total and permanent union in the substance of the soul and its faculties as regards the obscure habitual union; but as regards actual union, we shall explain later, with God's help, that there can be no permanent union in the faculties in this life, but only a transitory union.[49]

Habitual union is already distinguished from actual union, and St. John asserts that in this life it is impossible to have actual union with God through the faculties of the soul in a permanent manner. It can be only a transitory union. This refers to the soul's faculties and not the substance of the soul.[50]

---

[49] *The Ascent*, bk. II, chap. 5, no. 2.

[50] At this point we should note that Father Labourdette (art. cit., *Revue Thomiste*, 1936–1937, 48 and 200) makes certain restrictions concerning the text in bk. II, chap. 16 of *The Ascent*. The term "substance" is not used in a Scholastic sense, as opposed to "potency" or faculty. Rather, St. John is using it simply to designate that part of the soul in which mystical knowledge is experienced. It is a typical example that shows how the meaning of the Scholastic terminology changes in the course of the works of St. John of the Cross. It passes from the strictly speculative meaning to a broader application to the mystical experience.

But what is meant by an actual and permanent union in the substance of the soul? Is it only the substance of the soul that is capable of actual union? According to the Mystical Doctor, it would seem not. The substance of the soul is incapable of acting, save through the medium of the faculties. But the substance of the soul together with the faculties is capable of permanent union in this life in a habitual and obscure manner. The faculties alone, on the other hand, are capable of actual union, though only in a transitory and not a permanent manner.

But is the actual union of the intellect an act of the virtue of faith? That is the object of our investigation. The virtue of faith is the proper means of union of the intellect with God, but we shall see later how and to what extent the *act* of faith can be called an *act* of union.

Another question arises: how is the habitual union of the intellect with God related to the virtue of faith? According to the text cited, it is necessary to maintain the distinction between "habitual union" and "actual union" (union *quoad habitum* and union *quoad actum*). We can see from that text that the Mystical Doctor uses those Scholastic terms in order to designate different perfections of the faculty. It is one thing to be united with God habitually (*quoad habitum*) and quite another to be united actually (*quoad actum*). This observation will be helpful for the subsequent investigation.

We can summarize all that we have treated in the previous sections by saying, in the first place, that the virtue of faith appears in *The Ascent* as the means of the union of the intellect with God. It is described as the proportionate, proper, proximate, accommodated, adequate and legitimate means. The various adjectives do not differ very much from one another; they

---

However, in the text that we have cited from chap. 5 it is evident that "substance" is strictly a Scholastic term.

[51] *The Ascent*, bk. II, chap. 8, no. 4.

all designate a means which by reason of its very nature and particular qualities is apt for attaining the end. And with respect to achieving union of the intellect with God, the means is faith.

The text in book II, chapter 8 of *The Ascent* is of particular importance for understanding the nature of the means to union, or rather, the fundamental exigencies of its nature. That text is the nucleus of the entire question concerning the virtue of faith. Its essential likeness with God, which is necessary for the proportionate means of union, places faith on the supernatural level, while the relation of this likeness to the intellect postulates its intentional or intellectual quality. The subsequent texts analyzed confirm what was stated in chapter 8. First, faith is the proportionate means of supernatural union, and through it the soul participates in the divinity which is communicated to the soul through grace. The union can be increased through love until it attains the highest degree of the transforming union. Secondly, we have seen how the Mystical Doctor understands the relation between faith and the intellect in the movement towards union or in the soul's progress towards God.

With this we have placed the state of the question, and the way is open for further investigation.

"Obscurity of faith wherein divinity is concealed"

We have seen the importance of the concept "essential likeness" for our study, and we noted in chapter 8 of book II of *The Ascent* the two meanings of the term, one referring to "being" and the other to the intellect. Both meanings apply to the notion of the proportionate means of union of the intellect with God; in fact, the second meaning applies because of the first. The Mystical Doctor states with certitude that created things, however perfect, cannot unite to the divinity the intellect that knows them and seeks God in them. Created things are not capable of uniting the intellect with God because they lack the essential likeness to the divinity; faith, on the contrary, does possess it.

The subsequent development of the doctrine of St. John of the Cross in chapters 8 and 9 of book II follows along the lines of the fundamental concept of "essential likeness". From it he derives the conclusion concerning the absolute incapacity and insufficiency of the intellect to attain union with God by its own natural powers. The Mystical Doctor excludes the possibility for two reasons.

> 1. For, if we speak of natural knowledge, since the intellect cannot know anything except what is contained in and is presented in the forms and images of things received through the bodily senses —which things, we have said, cannot serve as means—it cannot make use of its natural knowledge.[51]

This statement presupposes the entire theory on the nature of intellectual cognition which, in the state of the union of body and soul, depends on the senses. But what reaches the intellect through the senses is nothing more than natural things, indeed material things, that lack any essential relation or proportion of likeness to the divinity. Therefore the intellect, which in this life is ordained to the knowledge of such things, is excluded from the possibility of attaining to the divine essence.

> 2. If we speak of supernatural knowledge, so far as is possible in this life by its ordinary power, the intellect in its prison of the body has no disposition or capacity for receiving clear knowledge of God. Such knowledge does not belong to this state; and one must either die or not receive it.[52]

This is a simple statement of fact. A clear vision of the divine essence is excluded as long as the soul is united to the body. But let us proceed:

> Therefore no supernatural apprehension or knowledge in this mortal state can serve as a proximate means to the lofty union of

[52] Ibid.

love with God. Whatever the intellect can understand, the will experience, and the imagination portray is, as we have said, most unlike and disproportionate to God.[53]

This assertion, whose effects we shall see later, and especially in the "active night of the spirit", although it seems to be based on the same reason as previously given—namely, the natural operation of the intellect—actually goes much deeper. It touches the natural state of the intellect. The phrase, "whatever the intellect can understand", designates that state: of itself, the intellect is incapable of conceiving or receiving the likeness of the divinity, and hence, left to itself, it does not suffice for reaching the divinity. This denotes the basic incapacity of the intellect, described in chapter 3, book II of *The Ascent*.

Moreover, for the same reason "no supernatural apprehension or knowledge" that could be connaturally presented to the intellect in this life can serve as a proximate means of union with God. The reason is that these are things that the intellect "can understand". Hence their insufficiency for serving as a means of union; they are something connatural to the intellect. This means that the intellect, considered in its natural capacity, is incapable of attaining to union with God.

The last statement is of great importance for the question concerning faith, and we shall see later how this native insufficiency of the intellect is remedied by faith and in faith. But even now, in chapter 8, book II of *The Ascent*, St. John of the Cross speaks of the incapacity of the intellect for union with the divine:

In order to reach him, a soul must proceed rather by not understanding than by desiring to understand, by blinding itself and putting itself in darkness, rather than opening its eyes to approach the divine ray more closely.[54]

[53] Ibid., no. 5.   [54] Ibid., bk. II, chap. 8, no. 5.

The Mystical Doctor then adds some remarks about contemplation which, things being as they are, can never be anything more than a "secret wisdom of God; for it is secret even to the understanding that receives it. For that reason St. Dionysius calls it a ray of darkness."[55]

We can see that the concept of "essential likeness" permeates the entire doctrine that St. John of the Cross is expounding, and it dominates the transition from the entitative to the intentional order. We can also see that everything depends on this concept of "essential likeness", and conclusions of great importance for our study are rooted in it.

All of these considerations and precisions prepare the way for what St. John of the Cross will say in chapter 9. Even the descriptive title of the chapter is precise in determining how and in what sense the virtue of faith, according to the author, can serve as the means of union: "How faith is the proximate and proportionate means to the intellect so that the soul may reach the divine union of love." At the very outset he specifies the function of faith and indicates clearly the faculty in which it operates, namely, the intellect. Nor does he neglect to note the relationship of faith to the total union of the soul with God, a union that increases and is perfected by love.

The content of the entire chapter 9 depends especially on the concept of "likeness", which, as we have seen and shall see later, is the nucleus of the theology of union in St. John of the Cross. In the preceding chapter we saw that faith possesses an essential likeness to God, for which reason it is capable of uniting the intellect with God. Now the Mystical Doctor will determine what this likeness is and how it should be understood:

> Faith . . . alone is the proximate and proportionate means by which the soul is united with God; for such is the likeness between faith and God that there is no other difference except either to see God or to believe in him.[56]

[55] Ibid., no. 6. Cf. Pseudo-Dionysius, *De mystica theologia*, 3, 999. (Tr.)
[56] Ibid., bk. II, chap. 9, no. 1.

Here the "likeness" is placed immediately on the level of knowledge and is explained by the difference between faith and the beatific vision; that is, God as seen and God as believed. In the beatific vision the essence of God is clearly perceived by the intellect; the divine essence is present to the intellect as the known in the knower (*tamquam cognitum in cognoscente*). Through faith the divine essence is present to the intellect as the object known is in the knower (*tamquam objectum cognitum in cognoscente*), but with this difference between seeing and believing: the divine essence as perceived through faith lacks clarity. It is believed, not seen.

Such is the way in which the intentional or cognitive aspect of the "essential likeness" is presented, and it is in the light of this first text that subsequent passages will be understood. The Saint specifies obscurity as the distinctive note of faith, and he asserts that "beneath this darkness the intellect is united with God, and beneath it God is hidden."[57] To say that the intellect is united with God beneath the darkness is to say that it is in contact with the divine essence, and the union of the intellect with God consists precisely in this.

If one should now ask why the virtue of faith is the means of union for the intellect, the answer is that in and through faith the intellect attains to the divine essence and is joined to it, just as, when it functions naturally, it is united to any object of knowledge that is connatural to it. But there is always this difference: knowledge through faith is obscure, not clear. Hence, in faith God is a hidden God; he is hidden because through faith he is in the intellect as the object known in the knowing faculty.

The meaning of the text previously cited from chapter 9 depends entirely on the meaning given to "likeness". Since this term has been applied to the visual level and on that same level applied to the virtue of faith, it follows that the essential element in the union of the intellect with God is the relationship

[57] Ibid.

of the knower to the known, by virtue of which the knower is united to the known ("the intellect is united with God") and the known exists in the knower in the intentional order ("God is hidden"). There is, in other words, an "intentional" identification of the subject with the object,[58] that is, of the knower with the known. Nevertheless, the obscurity remains, the aspect of the not-seen (*de non visis*), and therefore the problem concerning faith arises again.

For the moment, however, the Mystical Doctor expatiates upon the statement made in chapter 9 to the effect that the intellect is united to God in darkness. That it may be fixed more clearly and deeply in the mind of the reader, he repeats it in various ways. To do this, he seeks examples in Sacred Scripture; for example, 1 Kings 8:12, where God promised that he would dwell in darkness in the newly constructed temple; Ps 17:10, which describes the vision of God rising above the cherubim and flying on the wind and setting darkness beneath his feet; and Job 38:1 and 40:1, where it is stated that God spoke to him from the darkness of the air. St. John then states:

> All these references to darkness signify the obscurity of the faith in which divinity is concealed when it communicates itself to the soul; an obscurity that will end when, as St. Paul says (1 Cor 13:10), that which is in part—namely, the darkness of faith—will be ended and that which is perfect comes, which is the divine light.[59]

Here again the same theme is developed: faith is compared to vision. In both the one and the other the divinity is attained, but with this difference: in faith the divinity is hidden in the darkness of the intellect of the wayfarer (man *in via*), while in the beatific vision it is manifested already by the divine light

---

[58] The *intentional order* or *intentional being* signifies the manner in which known reality is known and exists in the mind of the knower, as distinct from its existence in the real and concrete order of being. (Tr.)

[59] *The Ascent*, bk. II, chap. 9, no. 3.

(*lumen gloriae*).[60] Consequently, it is evident from these texts that in the transition from faith to vision, essentially the same relationship exists as is established by faith, the same union of the intellect with the divine object. But in the beatific vision the intellect is freed from the obscurity and darkness that are concomitant with faith. This is especially exemplified by the army of Gideon (Judges 7:16–20), whose soldiers had torches in their hands but could not see them because they were concealed in jars; but when the jars were broken, they began to see clearly. So also "faith, which is represented by those jars, contains divine light within itself; but when faith is ended and shattered by the ending and breaking of this mortal life, the glory and light of the divinity contained in faith will appear."[61]

St. John of the Cross explains the foregoing text by saying that one "must hold in his hands (that is, in the works of his will) the light, which is the union of love, though it be in the darkness of faith, so that, when the jar of this life, which alone obscures the light of faith, is broken, he may see God face to face in glory."[62]

The explanation connotes two things: first, the relationship between faith and the union through love in the present life and, second, the relationship between faith and the beatific vision, the face-to-face vision in glory. The light in the present life is the union of love hidden in the darkness of faith, but death dissipates the darkness of faith and the union is consummated in heaven in the light of the beatific vision. The light of the obscure union reaches its full brilliance in the luminous union of the beatific vision.

As can be seen, the virtue of faith is presented in chapter 9 as something at once bright and obscure. The brightness is the divinity itself, which is attained by faith, is united to the intellect through faith, is present there in an intentional manner,

---

[60] The *lumen gloriae* is a power infused into the intellects of the blessed in heaven so that they can see the divine essence in an immediate vision. (Tr.)

[61] *The Ascent*, bk. II, chap. 9, no. 3.   [62] Ibid., no. 4.

as we saw in our analysis of chapters 8 and 9. Or, to speak more exactly, the divinity is hidden precisely because through faith it is present only intentionally. And it is because the divinity is hidden that we deduce the other characteristic of faith, namely, its obscurity. This is something that requires lengthy and profound study. But what stands out as constitutive—if we may use a technical expression—seems to be the aspect of light. Thus, St. John states: "By this means alone, God manifests himself to the soul in divine light that surpasses all understanding. Therefore, the greater the faith of the soul, the more closely it is united with God."[63]

The meaning is clear: faith unites the intellect with God by means of the divine light whereby the intellect contacts God as God. But what does it mean to say that "God manifests himself to the soul"? It does not mean by way of vision, surely; rather, it means that the soul attains to the divinity and has contact with the divine essence. The manner of achieving this is not explained, for that always remains obscure; it is merely a statement of the fact.

We are led to this conclusion by a lengthy and careful analysis of chapter 8 and of the present chapter. The phrase "God manifests himself" signifies the reason why the soul attains to the divine being, indeed, the divine essence itself precisely as the divine. It is because of the "essential likeness", which is not found in any other creature, naturally considered, however perfect. Hence, chapters 8 and 9 lead to this interpretation of the phrase "God manifests himself to the soul", and the phrase itself verifies the "essential likeness" that is attributed to the virtue of faith.

God is manifested to the intellect, in the sense described, through the divine light and in the divine light which "surpasses all understanding", both quantitatively and qualitatively. In this statement St. John of the Cross responds to the question

---

[63] *The Ascent*, bk. II, chap. 9, no. 1.

raised in chapter 8. The reason why the virtue of faith surpasses every created nature and every intellect is the divine light that is present in faith. With this we arrive at a precise concept of the "essential likeness" attributed to faith. Indeed, essential likeness is predicated of faith in two ways: *entitatively*, so far as it surpasses every created natural perfection, and *intentionally*, so far as the light of faith enables the intellect to have contact with the divinity.

Consequently, the predominant element in the virtue of faith is "light", not in its mode of operation, but in its essence. This is evident from the text. The virtue of faith was designated at the outset as the proportionate means of union with God. If the concept of means applies to its very nature in the sense which we have seen in our analysis, namely, that it enables the intellect to attain to the divine essence as the object known—although obscurely—then the precise reason or basis for classifying it as a means of union is nothing other than the fact that in faith "God manifests himself to the soul in divine light that surpasses all understanding". Therefore the concept of "light" is essential to faith; it touches the very nature of faith. The virtue of faith is therefore "light"—indeed "divine light"—a light of the same order as the divinity and above all natural light.

Nevertheless, faith is also obscurity and darkness. St. John repeats this again and again. The divinity as known by the intellect through faith is not clearly manifested but is hidden in the intentional order of knowledge. For that reason the problem of faith in the teaching of St. John of the Cross requires an investigation from yet another aspect, namely, an investigation that concentrates on the psychology of faith. We have already seen that faith is the means of union; we have seen also why it is such a means; and now we shall investigate how it functions as a means of union. This last, as we have said, involves a study of the nature of faith from the psychological aspect and, with God's help, we shall now undertake this study.

"A certain and obscure habit"

The first thing to be noted is that the two characteristics, light and darkness, are so intimately related to the virtue of faith that either one can be predicated of faith with equal justification. Faith always appears to us as a light in the darkness, the true and inner light of divinity communicated through faith in the darkness that obscures it.

But before we proceed, we should take note of certain points contained in chapter 9 of book II of *The Ascent*. We must always be reverting to the fundamental concept of "likeness". We have seen how and in what sense this term applies to the virtue of faith, comparing the operation of faith with the beatific vision in glory. The Mystical Doctor further explains the darkness of faith by saying: "Since God is infinite, faith presents him to us as infinite; . . . and since God is darkness to our intellect, faith likewise blinds and dazzles our intellect."[64] This is the immediate explanation of why the concept of "likeness" to God is attributed to faith, as it is also to the beatific vision. And if considered carefully, the statement refers not only to the "why" but also to the "how", which leads us to our present investigation.

Faith is said to have and to cause a likeness to God for two reasons: first, because of its proportion to God; secondly, because of the state it produces in the intellect. The first reason is objective, since faith unites the intellect with God by proposing to it that which truly exists in God. The second reason is especially interesting, and it is typical of the concept of faith that is presented consistently in the works of St. John of the Cross. He says that faith bestows on the intellect a likeness to God because as God in himself, in his intimate nature, is darkness to the intellect, so faith obscures and darkens the intellect. This means that faith not only unites the intellect with God by proposing to

[64] *The Ascent*, bk. II, chap. 9, no. 1.

it the revealed truths which speak of God and what he is in himself, but it also presents the divinity to the intellect in a manner that is more "experiential". There is no other way of describing this aspect of the virtue of faith, for it not only enables the intellect to *know* God intimately and subjectively (which implies the presentation of an object to the intellect), but even more, to *experience* what God is. And this is no exaggeration.

This second reason why faith is called a "likeness" of the divinity with respect to the intellect should be carefully noted. For the moment it suffices to point out that while the proposition of revealed truths restricts the "likeness" of faith to God to the objective order, the second reason—namely, the actual experience of the relation of divinity to the intellect—indicates a "likeness" in the subjective sense. God is communicated to the intellect through faith and is received and experienced by a particular psychological state of this faculty. This psychological state or "psychological species" of the intellect as related to the virtue of faith—more exactly, the psychological species of the intellect which is identical with faith—brings us to the consideration of faith as a *habit*, which is discussed in chapter 3, book II of *The Ascent*.

We want to know whether the phrase "blinds and dazzles our intellect", which is a literary and poetic rather than technical manner of speaking, actually refers to the "psychological species" of the intellect which is faith. St. John of the Cross writes: "Faith, the theologians say, is a certain and obscure habit of the soul".[65] It is a habit, and this is perhaps the first and only time that the Mystical Doctor puts faith in this Scholastic category; and even then, the phrase "say the theologians" shows that he was referring to the common Scholastic teaching that faith is a habit.

It is true that in chapter 5, book II of *The Ascent* we found the

---

[65] *The Ascent*, bk. II, chap. 3, no. 1.

distinction "*quoad habitum*" and "*quoad actum*", and we can conclude that for him a habit constitutes a certain perfection of a faculty, inferior to the act as regards the mode of operation. Since in that text the habitual union of the soul and its faculties with God is distinguished from actual union, it is evident that actual union is more perfect; it constitutes a higher perfection for the faculty than does habitual union. The perfection of a faculty ordained to operation is measured by its manner of intervening in that particular operation; therefore the actuation of a faculty constitutes a certain definitive perfection in the order of operation and also, therefore, a definitive perfection in its manner of uniting with God. A habit, on the other hand, manifests a perfection on a lower level, farther removed from the definitive and ultimate perfection, more latent, but of the same specific perfection.

It is certain that such is the meaning of "habit" as related to "act" in the works of St. John of the Cross. The name and the definition come from Scholastic philosophy, where the term "habit" signifies a certain perfection of a faculty ordained to operation. However, we do not find in his works the definition of habit as "a quality difficult to remove". And it is within these limits that we should analyze the present question.

To say, therefore, that faith is a habit signifies that it is a certain perfection of the intellect, ordained to a particular mode of operation and, indeed, to the ultimate in that order, which is the act itself. This is what is meant by "the theologians say", to whose speculations the Mystical Doctor refers. This is what he teaches in agreement with them, although his doctrine comes from other sources and is expressed differently.

Faith, then, is a certain and obscure habit. St. John of the Cross introduces this concept immediately and then explains why it is an obscure habit. The basic reason, or rather, the form of expressing it, is extremely simple: "because it enables us to believe truths revealed by God himself".[66] This simple for-

---

[66] Ibid.

mula, readily understood by those for whom he was writing—
the contemplatives of Carmel and elsewhere, not all of whom
knew theology—contains a profound teaching: the divinely revealed truths "transcend every natural light and exceed all
human understanding beyond all proportion."[67]

We are once again in the familiar atmosphere of "essential
likeness" and "proportion of likeness". Now it is clear that the
"proportion of likeness" applies to the virtue of faith in its objective aspect, because the divinely revealed truths that the intellect believes through faith surpass all understanding, beyond
any proportion. They truly present the divine essence to the intellect and therefore pertain to the same divine order and are a
participation in God's essential perfection. For that reason there
is no proportion between them and any human intellect, however perfect, because they belong to an order that transcends it
completely.

St. John then proceeds to a consideration of the subject that
receives the revealed truths and, in them, the divine essence expressed in revelation. The transition from the objective to the
subjective aspect of faith is not made immediately and explicitly, but it appears gradually in the text:

> Hence, the excessive light that is given in faith is thick darkness for
> the soul because the greater overwhelms and eclipses the lesser. The
> light of the sun overwhelms all other lights, so that they do not
> seem to be lights at all when it shines and overwhelms our power of
> vision. It blinds the eyes and deprives them of sight because its light
> is excessive and beyond all proportion to the faculty of vision. In
> like manner the light of faith, by reason of its excessive intensity,
> oppresses and overwhelms the light of the intellect, which, of its
> own power extends only to natural knowledge, although it has a
> capacity for the supernatural, whenever our Lord wishes to actuate
> it supernaturally.[68]

The first statement in the foregoing passage refers to the objective aspect of the virtue of faith, but gradually the subjective

[67] Cf. ibid.
[68] *The Ascent*, bk. II, chap. 3, no. 1.

aspect of faith as an obscure habit comes to the fore. We can probably suppose that throughout the entire text reference is constantly made to the revealed truths which, like the excessive light of the sun to the eye, are too dazzling for the intellect. For that reason they blind the intellect, as the bright sun blinds the eyes. But while the eyes close in the brilliant light of the sun, the intellect opens to the light of divine truths, not by its own power, which is disproportionate and insufficient, but by the light of faith, the supernatural light that our Lord has placed in the intellect.

The intellect has a certain passive or "obediential" potency[69] in relation to the supernatural, but it is only through the reception of a supernatural power that the natural cognitive faculty is supernaturally activated. In other words, once the intellect is disposed supernaturally by a divine infusion, it is capable of receiving the light of divine truths. Then, when the objective element (the revealed truths) has been provided and the subjective element (light) has been infused, faith is engendered. It comprises both the revealed divinity that is received through the divine light of faith and the divine light that receives the divinity of the revealed truths in the intellect.

Such is the origin or birth of faith in the intellect, wherein the objective and subjective elements are joined and blended, and both are expressed in the phrase that describes the light as "excessive and beyond all proportion". The blending or fusion of the objective and subjective elements is expressed as a victorious invasion of the human cognitive faculty: it "oppresses and overwhelms" the natural light of the intellect. Thus, the light of faith (both objective and subjective) overwhelms the natural light of the intellect, so that the latter does not shed its own light, does not intervene as a light when the light of faith, an excessive and supernatural light, begins to shine.

Such are the words and the meaning of the light of faith in the intellect as found in the text of St. John of the Cross. In

[69] The *Editio princeps* (Alcalá, 1618) of *The Ascent* uses the Scholastic term "obediential potency" in the text cited above.

these terms he describes for the first time the symbiosis of the supernatural with the natural in view of the union that is ultimately to be achieved. And this is not outside the scope of our investigation. It suffices to recall the proportion—or rather, the disproportion—described in book II, chapter 8 of *The Ascent*. It is, in fact, a summary of the entire doctrine of the Mystical Doctor on faith, which is portrayed as a light that establishes a proportion between the intellect and divinely revealed truths, truths containing the divinity. It is, therefore, an infused light that presupposes nothing more in the intellect than the obediential potency that coincides with the natural light of the intellect. It causes, as it were, a tension, but the divine light prevails; then the intellect possesses the virtue of faith and is capable of attaining divinity through the virtue of faith.

We should note how St. John describes the struggle and the ultimate victory of faith. It is implied in the text that the natural light of the intellect strives by its own power to arrive at the revealed truths but fails to do so. It can extend no farther than natural knowledge. Then the "excessive light" comes to the aid of the intellect's insufficiency and overwhelms it by reason of its excess and its supernatural proportion to divinely revealed truths. This manner of describing the intervention of the divine light in the natural light of the intellect deserves careful attention, and perhaps we shall have to return to it later.

The foregoing description also explains to some extent the mystery of light and darkness that we already noted in our analysis of chapter 9. The virtue of faith is at once light—an infused, excessive light whereby the intellect attains to divinity by a light that is not proper to itself—and it is darkness. Why is this so? Precisely because the divine truths cannot be attained by the natural light of the intellect; in fact, the light proper to the intellect is positively excluded from the knowledge of such truths. The intellect is restricted to the lower level of knowledge and activity that lie within the scope of its natural power. Consequently, the virtue of faith provides a knowledge of divine things to which the intellect attains by a borrowed light;

its own light does not reach that far, and hence the natural power of the intellect falls short of such knowledge.

Nevertheless, it is a curious fact that in the very act of knowing, faith is still a darkness. This is explained psychologically by the fact that the intellect attains the object of knowledge but at the same time is prevented from knowing it. At first glance, therefore, faith seems to be an obstacle to the intellect's natural craving for knowledge and, indeed, as regards its highest act of knowledge.

The virtue of faith is thus presented as uniting and fusing with the human cognitive faculty. We could call it the psychological aspect of faith. But to discover what lies beneath this first impression, it is necessary to study some particulars in greater detail. And the first thing to consider is the subject—the intellect—which is described in the text as overwhelmed and oppressed by "excessive light".

We stated previously how and in what sense the subject of the virtue of faith is understood in the works of St. John of the Cross. We described its nature, which is not defined immediately but only gradually in the teaching of the Mystical Doctor, as the need arises to explain it. We likewise stated that the explanation was necessary because of the intimate connection between the two, namely, of faith and the intellect. Indeed, faith is explicitly named as the means of the union of the intellect with God. Therefore, in discussing the union of the soul with God, the Mystical Doctor treats of both faith and the intellect because in his opinion it is not possible to investigate the one without the other.

We also emphasized his teaching in chapter 8 concerning the absolute insufficiency and incapacity of the intellect for attaining union with the divinity by its own power. The human cognitive faculty is dependent on the internal and external senses in its natural operations, and through them it can acquire knowledge of material things from which it abstracts their essence. The contact of the intellect with an object proportionate to itself is described by St. John of the Cross in chapter 8, where he states that the function of the intellect is "to form concepts and strip them . . . of sense species and phantasms."[70] We could say that his expression, "strip them", is a general way of stating the Scholastic teaching on the power of abstraction proper to the agent intellect. He explains this in greater detail when he treats of the function of the passive intellect:

> The soul can neither do anything nor receive any knowledge except through the sense faculties and the spiritual faculties. By means of the sense faculties, as we have said, the soul can make discursive meditation and search out and gain knowledge of things; by means of the spiritual faculties it can enjoy the knowledge it has already received through the faculties previously mentioned, without the faculties themselves functioning.[71]

In this passage the entire work of preparing for knowledge of an object is attributed to the senses; the function of the agent intellect is not mentioned explicitly. Nevertheless, we already know its function from the passage in chapter 8. Here, however, the Mystical Doctor is stressing another point of his doctrine—the transition from meditation to contemplation—and hence he refers to another dimension of the theory of knowledge and considers it from another aspect. He is treating of the "fruition" of the spiritual faculties, and especially of the intellect, in contemplation; the satisfaction and quiet of the cognitive faculty, once it has attained knowledge of its object.

Something similar can be found in book III, chapter 13, where "form, figure and image" are given as the material of human cognition. St. John calls them "the rind and accident of the substance and spirit that lie beneath the rind and accident. This substance and spirit," he adds, "do not unite with the faculties of the soul in true understanding and love until the

[70] *The Ascent*, bk. II, chap. 8, no. 5.
[71] Ibid., bk. II, chap. 14, no. 6.

operation of the faculties ceases."[72] Then the goal of the operation is attained, which is "that the substance understood and loved through these forms is received in the soul."[73] This seems to be nothing other than the essence of the thing known by the intellect—if we raise the question of the faculty involved—present to the intellect according to the nature of the knowing subject and united with it in the intentional order. Hence the phrase, "substance understood".

But now arises the problem of interpreting what the Mystical Doctor says about the nature of human knowledge. This problem is not outside the scope of our study; rather, as we have already noted, it has an important bearing on the role of the intellect in union with God. The various opinions are given below in the footnote.[74]

---

[72] Ibid., bk. III, chap. 13, no. 4.   [73] Ibid.

[74] The question is treated by the commentators who discuss the philosophical aspects of the teaching of St. John of the Cross. Fr. Marcelo de Niño Jesús explains the text in a Thomistic sense (cf. op. cit., 134–54), but Fr. Crisógono de Jesús Sacramentado (cf. op. cit., 27) maintains that St. John of the Cross follows the Aristotelian doctrine as interpreted by the English Carmelite John Baconthorpe. The difference lies in the very process of knowledge and not in the preparatory acts. Thus, Fr. Crisógono states that "for St. John of the Cross the intimate essence of the object is formally and *per se* intelligible". Therefore the act of understanding does not consist in forming an intelligible species in which the passive intellect rests by possessing the intentional form of the object in its own mode, but only in the application of the light of the intellect to this "stripped substance"; that is, to the object itself so far as it is intelligible. Fr. Crisógono emphasizes the axiom quoted in chap. 3, no. 2: "*Ab objecto et potentia paritur notitia*" (Knowledge is born from the object presented and from the faculty). Therefore, the object to be known and the light of the intellect suffice for knowledge; there is no need for the intelligible species. Accordingly the verb "to strip" does not refer to abstraction, that is, the operation of the agent intellect whereby the object perceived by the senses and existing in a sense image is made intelligible. Rather, it refers to the penetration of the object by the intellect to discover its innate intelligibility, which is always present in a state of potency and reduce it to act. The acts that prepare for knowledge, such as perception by the senses and the production of the sense image, serve to stimulate the penetration of the object by the intellect. According to Fr. Crisógono,

Whatever one may rightly conclude concerning this particular question, for our purpose, which is to investigate the nature of the virtue of faith in the works of St. John of the Cross, it suffices to emphasize the dynamic quality that he perceives in the intellect, by virtue of which it is joined to faith in order to attain union with divinity.

In many places the Mystical Doctor mentions explicitly the natural limitations of the intellect and the necessity of a natural proportion for its operation. This proportion is provided by subsistent material things to whose essences the intellect naturally tends in order to unite them to itself according to its proper intentional modality. When such knowledge is acquired naturally, the intellect rests and enjoys fruition. This is the rest and fruition of the "possible intellect". It is the teaching of St. John of the Cross that this process is surely facilitated by the "stripping" by the intellect—this time the "agent intellect", which utilizes the impressions received by the external senses and retained by the internal senses.

---

this is the theory of knowledge that is proper and special to St. John of the Cross.

Do the texts justify such an interpretation? In the first place it seems to us that the texts do not have such speculative precision that this theory of knowledge can be found there, delineated in all its details. Moreover, in some of the texts cited (e.g., bk. II, chap. 6) it would seem that many points refer to the theory of abstraction by the agent intellect, which separates all the accidents from the image perceived by the senses—everything sensible—to reach the ultimate "substance understood". Now the question is how one should understand the "substance understood": as an intelligible species or *verbum mentale* that is the terminus of intellectual cognition or in the sense proposed by Fr. Crisógono. He is a great authority on the works of St. John of the Cross, and he has investigated in particular the philosophical aspects, something that we do not intend to do here. We simply state his interpretation and note the contrary opinion of Father Marcelo and many others who see in the texts the process of abstraction by an agent intellect. Finally, St. John of the Cross does not explicitly teach any theory of human knowledge in his writings. He merely applies in a general and practical way what he had learned in Scholastic philosophy and theology. This will also be the norm for our investigation.

All of the foregoing elements are Scholastic doctrine and are of special help in determining the distinction between meditation and contemplation.[75] In meditation the soul's activity is more evident; in contemplation it is more a matter of "rest and fruition". The same doctrine is repeated in *The Spiritual Canticle* and is closely related to our study and investigation.

Thus, St. John of the Cross usually speaks of the intellect as a faculty, possessing its own nature, acting in accordance with its nature and, within its proper limits, manifesting its own peculiar dynamism. In book II, chapter 3 of *The Ascent* the intellect receives the supernatural infused light, the excessive light that is faith, a supernatural virtue infused into the natural faculty and capable of uniting the intellect with God. Then, in chapter 6 he states that "the spiritual faculties are emptied and purified of everything that is not God, and they remain in the darkness of these three virtues" or, as he stated earlier, "setting each faculty in darkness concerning everything that does not pertain to these three virtues".[76] It would appear that the life and destiny of the intellect are intimately related to unifying faith from now on and will be profoundly dependent on all that faith provides.

But what does faith provide? We have already seen that it supplies an excessive light through which divinity is attained in revealed truths. And since this takes place in the intellect, it will necessarily produce certain effects in that faculty. And what are these effects?

In the first place, we have already seen that the intellect of itself is incapable of reaching divinity in the truths revealed. St. John has stated that the light of the intellect extends only to "natural knowledge". He says this clearly, and then he explains it on the basis of the premises concerning the nature of human knowledge as we have already seen in the pertinent passages from *The Ascent*. Thus, natural knowledge depends on the

[75] Cf. *The Ascent*, bk. II, chap. 14.
[76] *The Ascent*, bk. II, chap. 6, no. 6.

senses. It is elaborated from the images and phantasms of external objects and terminates in intellectual apprehension. But it is evident from the whole process of cognition that knowledge cannot be had without an immediate sense experience; that is, without the phantasms or species of the internal senses. Therefore, the Mystical Doctor continues, not just any kind of sense experience suffices for providing knowledge, that is, for uniting the intellect with the object known, but that which enables the interior sense to produce its species or image. But what kind of species is this?

St. John of the Cross replies with an example. It does not suffice that the ear receive the sensation of sound if the interior sense cannot form a phantasm of what has been received from outside. In other words, the sound must be referred by association to something in the sensible world from which the interior sense can form the phantasm, at least vaguely. Lacking these elements of association, it would be impossible to form a species in the internal sense. That which was heard would remain only a sound, unable to be assimilated by the internal senses or constructed into a sense phantasm and therefore unable to be perceived by the agent intellect. As St. John of the Cross states in the example of the man born blind, "since he has never seen colors or anything like them by which he may judge them, he would be left with only their names. These he could know through hearing, but not their forms or figures."[77] Another classical example is that of the blind man who tries in vain to imagine a certain color that he knows only through hearing (*ex auditu*). This is exactly the case with the virtue of faith.

> So it is with faith in relation to the soul. It tells us of things we have never seen or understood, in themselves or in anything that resembles them, because there is nothing that resembles them. And thus we do not know them by the light of natural knowledge because

[77] *The Ascent*, bk. II, chap. 3, no. 2.

that which has been revealed to us has no proportion to any sense faculty. We know it by hearing, believing what we are taught, blinding our natural light and bringing it to submission. For, as St. Paul says, *Fides ex auditu* (Rom 10:17). It is as if he were to say: Faith is not a type of knowledge that enters by any of the senses; it is only the assent of the soul to what enters through hearing.[78]

All things considered, we see at once that the revealed truths present some reality to the cognitive power considered in its totality, and then this power turns to the revelation in its usual manner, making use of the senses. But there is no proportion between the sense faculties and that which is revealed, and therefore the agent intellect finds no material from which to abstract the intentional species. Its activity is frustrated because there is no likeness between the revealed truth and anything in the natural order.

Once again the fundamental concept of "likeness" appears, and not just any likeness, but a strictly "essential" likeness, because that is what the intellect seeks. The sense faculties cannot find anything they can associate with the revealed truth; it remains for them only a word or the name of something unknown. Meanwhile, the intellect, which can accomplish nothing because of the insufficiency of the senses, is seized, as it were, and raised above itself, drawn to the divine essence by the power of the light that is infused into it. In this sense the intellect is "overwhelmed and oppressed", for it is attracted and joined to things that lie beyond its competence. Of itself, the intellect cannot investigate the revealed truth; it cannot perform its normal task of abstracting ("stripping") the essence and finally enjoy the rest and fruition proper to the possible intellect. For this reason, according to St. John of the Cross, it approaches the revealed truths as if void of knowledge, without any of the forms or species that are connatural to it. Nevertheless, by virtue of the "excessive light" of faith, it approaches and is united to the divine reality.

[78] Ibid., bk. II, chap. 3, no. 3.

Such is the meaning of St. John's statement that faith is not science. The word science is not taken here in the Scholastic sense of certain and evident knowledge acquired by demonstration. What is emphasized here is the nature of the intentional species received by the intellect. In the works of St. John of the Cross faith is always compared to and distinguished from the beatific vision, wherein the intellect attains to the very essence of divinity and enjoys its presence in a clear manner. In faith, on the other hand, the divine is impressed on the intellect as something hidden and obscure in the intentional order. Therefore the concept of science in the foregoing statement does not refer to the process by which one acquires knowledge nor to the evidence the intellect discovers in the process, but only to the form or species received by the intellect. Hence the statement "faith is not science" does not mean for St. John of the Cross the lack of demonstrative evidence, but the lack of a species of the divine in the intellect.

This teaching of the Mystical Doctor applies in a very special way to the disposition of someone who ardently seeks union with God. Such a person is not afflicted so much by any deficiency in the cognitive process as by the absence of the Beloved, as expressed in the first line of the poem in *The Spiritual Canticle*: "Where have you hidden?" In chapter 3, at least, St. John of the Cross uses the word "science" to refer especially to the acquisition of an intentional form or species of the object known, and this involves the operation of the agent intellect and the ultimate quiet and fruition of the possible intellect. In this context we can speak, with St. John of the Cross, of the "substance understood".

From all that we have said it should be evident that the brief passage in chapter 3 is very meaningful and fruitful for our investigation. Consequently, we should analyze it carefully in order to discover all that is contained in it. It summarizes everything that St. John of the Cross teaches concerning the psychology of faith, and it cannot be appreciated unless all the details are clearly stated. This text is such that it touches the overall doctrine—taking doctrine in a strict sense—and the theological system of St. John of the Cross, especially when it applies to the path to union. It is well structured, concise and full of implications. Nothing is lacking in his theological system, although all the elements are not always found in any particular text.

What is of great importance for our study in the text from chapter 3 is the manner in which the "excessive light" of faith is conjoined to the natural intellect. First of all, we should note the natural orientation of the agent intellect, as indicated by the Mystical Doctor, to attain to the essence of anything presented to it by the senses; that is, to grasp their intelligibility and to unite this intelligibility to itself by an identification in the intentional order, wherein the intellect comes to rest.

Now this tendency of the intellect must also be operative in regard to the revealed truths, but immediately there is a difficulty, indeed an impossibility. That which is given in revelation cannot be expressed by a species proper to the senses, and for that reason the operation of the intellect is precluded. The intellect cannot penetrate the revelation, cannot acquire a species from that which is revealed nor make the essence stand out clearly. Therefore the intellect cannot come to rest and fruition. At basis it is a question of the "essential likeness", which is denied of every created thing in relation to divinity, however excellent its nature. The activity proper to the human intellect is restricted to the level of created things, and by nature it is excluded from anything higher.

The following statement should be well noted because it was of special importance to St. John of the Cross: the intellect naturally seeks the essence of things. The statement is also crucial to the concept of faith presented by the Mystical Doctor, because the natural tendency of the intellect to know the essence of things applies also to the infinite reality contained in revealed truths. But in this case it necessarily terminates in "darkness". We already know the role played by this "darkness" in the

Mystical Doctor's concept of faith, for we discussed it in our analysis of chapter 9. Now we shall explain some of the characteristics of this darkness in greater detail.

The natural tendency of the intellect to the essence of things presented to it is not proposed here as an isolated and solitary fact. Through faith it enters into the inner dynamism of that "excessive light" in which, according to chapter 9, "God manifests himself to the soul". This infused light takes control of the intellect, and St. John of the Cross tells us of its power in forceful terms: It "overwhelms and oppresses that of the intellect"[79], meaning, of course, the natural light of the intellect that, in the given situation, wavers helplessly before the unknown. The "excessive light" seems to extinguish the natural light of the intellect, just as "the light of the sun overwhelms all other lights, so that they do not seem to be lights at all."[80] The natural light of the intellect is of no avail for grasping the reality presented to it; it must be replaced by the infused light of faith.

This does not mean that the intellect is perfectly illuminated; not at all. On the contrary, the Mystical Doctor states that the intellect is blinded by the infused light. What the "excessive light" does is to make the intellect adhere to the supernatural reality made known to it through revelation. It unites the intellect to the supernatural reality or divine essence to which it naturally tends. However, the natural tendency, if left to its own resources, would terminate in only a word or a name, as does the blind person in regard to a knowledge of color. The intellect adheres to the divine essence, but without possessing the species or form of it as the intellect is wont to do. And this is very curious, for according to the premises established by St. John of the Cross, the intervention of the "excessive light" satisfies the natural tendency of the intellect to the essence of things and at the same time obstructs it. This is what the

---

[79] *The Ascent*, bk. II, chap. 3, no. 1.   [80] Ibid.

Mystical Doctor means when he says that faith "enables us to believe".[81]

This should clarify what the Mystical Doctor means by the tension that exists in the virtue of faith. For him, the virtue of faith involves an organic, intimate and dynamic conjunction or cohesion of the intellect with "excessive light". And what are the consequences of such a symbiosis?

In the first place it produces the oppressive darkness. St. John speaks of "this excessive light that is given in faith" as "thick darkness". Should this be ascribed to the fact that the intellect receives the revealed truths in the form of human concepts, that is, that they are known to the human mind through human language, *ex auditu*? No, because this phenomenon cannot be explained by the manner in which revealed truths are received. It is due rather to the natural tendency of the intellect to know the essence of things presented to it—to abstract the essence, to analyze it, to penetrate it, as it were, and finally assimilate it to itself in an intelligible species. But in the case of the virtue of faith, this natural tendency is exercised, not by the intellect's natural power, but under the impulse of the excessive divine light in which the intellect shares and through which it attains to the essence. But precisely because of this effect of the divine light, darkness envelops the intellect. The intellect does not attain to the divine species or form, in spite of its actual tendency; it remains empty and in darkness. It is not "science"; it is adhesion to the divine essence, contact with divinity by the intellect, but without arriving at its normal goal, which is to rest in and enjoy the "substance understood".

On the other hand, the obscurity and darkness enable us the better to understand the "excessive light" of faith. That light, although preserving all its connatural power in relation to that which is revealed, does not illumine the intellect intrinsically; rather, it elevates it beyond its natural capacity and beyond its

---

[81] *The Ascent*, bk. II, chap. 3, no. 1.

natural incapacity for attaining the essence of that which is revealed. It elevates rather than illumines; it elevates the intellect
to a higher receptivity while leaving it in its natural condition.
When shared by the intellect through the virtue of faith, the
power of that infused light seems somewhat limited, according
to the teaching of St. John of the Cross. It is limited by the very
nature of the intellect that receives it. For the intellect, which
attains to the divine by the excessive light of faith, does not do
so by its own power, although it does so according to its own
mode of operation. The intellect is not changed intrinsically
through the light of faith; it knows in the divine light and by
the power of that light, but it does not know as interiorly
changed or transformed by that light. This is the basic reason
for the darkness that it experiences.

All the foregoing elements are indissolubly linked together.
On the one hand, the darkness resulting from faith shows that
it effects some kind of real union with the divine essence. On
the other hand, the same darkness that accompanies contact
with the divine essence of revealed truth indicates the nature
and degree of intervention by the divine light in faith. It never
reaches the point of intrinsic transformation of the intellect into
divine light or a participation whereby the intellect is capable of
receiving the divine species and can know it in the manner of
the infused light. The intellect, as we have stated, retains its
natural mode of operation. The intellect knows by virtue of
that divine light and under its influence, but not precisely *in*
that light. If such were the case, it would be the beatific vision,
not faith. And that sums up the reason why faith is an obscure
habit, as explained by St. John of the Cross in book II, chapter
3 of *The Ascent*.

Such also seems to be the basis of the tension that exists in
the virtue of faith as St. John of the Cross describes it. The
symbiosis of the divine and the human that is effected by faith
does not resolve the essential difference and disproportion that
exist between the divine and the human. The difference can be

noted not only by an objective consideration and comparison, as we have seen in chapter 8 of *The Ascent*; it is also evident in the symbiosis itself, in the intrinsic structure of the virtue of faith, which possesses an essential likeness to divinity and at the same time something psychological, an intellectual habit.

There are still some observations to be made in concluding the analysis of this basic text in book II, chapter 3 of *The Ascent*. However, before proceeding in our study, there are several points that we should explain in greater detail.

NOTES

1. In the article to which we have referred,[82] Father Labourdette concentrates especially on the transition from the words of revealed truth to their content or essence. Thus, he states:

> Just as a blind person attains through words to the realities (colors) which he can in no way attain in themselves (since there is no direct proportion between the words and the realities for one who has no other way of knowing the realities), so in faith, through the medium of human words "which enter through the ear", we are presented with superior realities that the natural light of our intellect could no more attain than could the ear of a blind person know colors. . . . But—and here the example fails—while the blind man has no other way of knowing colors and even then knows them only as words, the believer receives from God the "certain and obscure habit" that enables him to attain to the supernatural realities from which pure reason was barred.[83]

Father Labourdette is speaking of the virtue of faith in relation to contemplation, while we are studying the nature of faith as expounded by St. John of the Cross, although we shall take

[82] Cf. M. Labourdette, art. cit., *Revue Thomiste*, 1936–1937.
[83] Cf. ibid., 21–22.

note of its role in mystical contemplation, as we shall see later. Father Labourdette states that by means of the habit of faith the intellect can truly attain to the supernatural object or content through the words of revelation, words which in themselves have no direct proportion to that object or content. Since the purpose of our study is to analyze the nature of faith, it is incumbent on us to ask how this happens. The answer to this question will lead us to an understanding of the nature of faith.

Our investigation proceeds, as we have already noted, from certain premises already noted in the text of St. John of the Cross. The first concerns the type of relationship that prevails between faith and the intellect—or better, between the intellect and the light that is infused by faith. It is an intimate and vital type of relationship whereby the intellect is joined to God through faith; indeed, the intellect becomes divine by participation[84] and thus attains its supernatural perfection.

The second premise stems from the description of the natural operation of the intellect which, as St. John of the Cross explains, naturally tends to abstract and to unite to itself in an intentional mode the essence of that which is the object of its knowledge.

Proceeding from these two premises, we discover in book II, chapter 3 the same tendency of the intellect in relation to the divine essence that is presented to the intellect through the revealed truths. This tendency, which is ineffectual if left to its own resources, is realized through the intervention of the infused light which is the constitutive element of faith. But now we must investigate how the transition from the words of revelation to the essence or content of revelation, effected by the virtue of faith and studied in its objective aspect by Father Labourdette, is manifested within the subject that is illumined by the divine light of faith. It is here, in the subjective aspect, that the habit of faith emerges.

[84] Cf. *The Ascent*, bk. II, chap. 6.

2. Perhaps one will ask in what sense we are to understand the divine and excessive light that is part of the very structure of the virtue of faith. A careful reading of the text will reveal that St. John of the Cross sees it as something comparable and yet opposed to the natural light of the intellect, which "extends only to natural knowledge".[85] It seems, therefore, that the natural light of the intellect signifies nothing more than the operative capacity or cognitive power of the intellect; not the act of intellection, but the power or capacity from which the operation proceeds. Hence, when compared to and opposed to the natural cognitive power of the intellect, the "excessive light" signifies a certain superior capacity for cognition, that is, a power of supernatural cognition. When we add the following statement of the Mystical Doctor, it is evident that we are dealing here with an intervention of divine knowledge: "By this means alone [by faith] God manifests himself to the soul in divine light that surpasses all understanding [which is equivalent to saying excessive light]."[86]

We can conclude from this that there is operative in faith an element of divine knowledge that illumines the intellect. That is what is meant by the phrase, "this excessive light that is given in faith". Divine knowledge somehow permeates the knowledge of the intellect—or better still, the incapacity of the intellect to know the reality revealed. Hence it is evident that by means of this light, the intellect can attain to the reality beneath the revealed truths.

But how does this happen? Let us see what can be culled from the texts of St. John of the Cross and, first of all, as regards the divine light that intervenes in the virtue of faith. We are already familiar with the important principle of "participation" stated in book II, chapter 5 of *The Ascent*. It permeates the entire mystical doctrine of St. John of the Cross. We find it in

---

[85] Cf. *The Ascent*, bk. II, chap. 3, no. 1.
[86] *The Ascent*, bk. II, chap. 9, no. 1.

The Dark Night,[87] *The Spiritual Canticle*,[88] *The Living Flame*,[89] and wherever he treats of the highest degrees of union. He always states that in the transformation the soul becomes divine or that the soul becomes God by participation.

This clearly presents the ontological aspect of the question. Indeed, the notion of participation runs through the whole of the unitive way and all the degrees of union, establishing with great precision the limits between that which is created and natural and that which is supernatural and divine. Moreover, the means of union—the virtue of faith—is described as pertaining to the same order and the same level as divinity itself, as we saw in book II, chapter 8 of *The Ascent*. Faith possesses an essential likeness to the divine and can therefore bridge the infinite gap between God and other created things. This further substantiates the Mystical Doctor's teaching on participation as found in chapter 5.

Consequently, the intervention of the "excessive light" whereby faith is infused into the intellect—or, to state it another way, that union or quasi-blending of the divine light with the human intellect so that it can attain the divine essence through faith—cannot be understood as anything less than the participation of the intellect in divine knowledge. To put it another way, it is a communication to the intellect of the divine light that is present in faith by participation. St. John of the Cross uses the term "communicate" in chapter 5, no. 4.

And now, what are the limits of the communication of divine light received in the intellect through faith? We have already answered this question to some extent. The infused divine light makes it possible for the intellect to be united with the essence of revealed truths, and thus it elevates the intellect. The text of the Mystical Doctor clearly states the native insufficiency of the intellect in this respect, but the divine light raises

---

[87] *The Dark Night*, bk. II, chap. 20, no. 5.

[88] *Spiritual Canticle*, chap. 22, no. 3.

[89] *Living Flame*, chap. 3, no. 78.

it beyond its natural capacity and enables it to adhere to the divine reality. This is what is meant by the expression "it enables us to believe truths revealed by God himself."[90]

But, as we have already seen, the operation of faith is accompanied by obscurity or darkness. The intellect that is drawn to the divine reality does not receive an intelligible species of the divine; the divine essence is present to the intellect in darkness and obscurity. The darkness substitutes, as it were, for the intentional species of the divine essence. All of this proves that the intellect attains to divinity through faith and that it does so in accordance with its natural disposition, because the participated divine light does not replace this in the operation of faith. Faith does not transform the intellect intrinsically; it simply elevates the intellect and unites it with the essence of revealed truths. Throughout a person's earthly life the virtue of faith will continue to work interiorly, preparing it gradually, through the grades of contemplation and the purgation of the dark nights, for the beatific vision in glory. The entire mystical evolution takes place within the limits of the obscurity of faith.

This should suffice to explain the degree of participation in the knowledge of divine things, communicated through faith, and what are the limits of the virtue of faith itself. Faith is the proper means for the union of the intellect with God, but it is only indirectly a means of transformation, presupposing the intervention of charity. But we shall see this more clearly later on.

3. Now that the foregoing analysis has clarified the relation of faith to vision, we should see how this matter is treated in the works of St. John of the Cross, especially in book II, chapter 9 of *The Ascent*. It would seem that faith and vision are essentially the same, if we take the word "essentially" to refer to participation in the infused divine light and its principal effect, namely, the elevation of the human intellect to the divine object of that

---

[90] *The Ascent*, bk. II, chap. 3, no. 1.

divine light. But if faith is considered in itself, as a virtue that operates in the natural mode of the intellect, with the obscurity that accompanies any contact with the divine in a human mode, then the distinction between faith and vision is evident. But why faith is a virtue for man *in via* and in what sense it is such a virtue, this will be explained in the considerations that follow.

4. We have already emphasized how the principle of "essential likeness", first noted in the teaching of St. John of the Cross in book II, chapter 8 of *The Ascent*, is observed with great exactness in the symbiosis of the divine with the human, which originates and develops in the virtue of faith. Then we saw how that principle specifies the ontological aspect of faith, since "essential likeness" to the divine places in relief the infinite distance between supernatural reality and natural created reality. At the same time it confirms that faith transcends the order of every created thing, however perfect in its nature, because it possesses a "proportion of likeness" to the divinity that is lacking to all other created things.

Moreover, this particular text brings the concept of the "proportional likeness" of faith to divinity into the ambit of the knowing intellect, that is, to the order of knowledge. This becomes especially evident later on, in book II, chapter 9, where the precise basis of likeness between divinity and faith is described as essentially the same as in the beatific vision, but with this distinction: there is a clear perception of the divine essence in glory, but the knowledge proper to faith is obscure (described also as *intentionaliter abscondita*).

And now, our analysis of the text in book II, chapter 3, prompts us to state once more the application of the principle of "essential likeness", but this time in relation to the intrinsic structure of faith itself. Properly speaking, the "proportion of likeness" between the intellect and divinity as known through revelation consists in the element of "excessive light", that is, in a certain participation in divine knowledge. This is the reason for attributing an "essential likeness" to faith. The proportion of likeness caused by a participation in the divine light then produces the primary effect of faith: union of the intellect with God. In this sense the principle of "likeness" intervenes in the virtue of faith in an ascending direction, so to speak; but there is also a descending or negative movement by reason of the concomitant obscurity. It is precisely here that the intellect's human mode of operation is evident as it approaches and attains to God by means of the divine light in which it participates through faith.

Now, if the intellect operates in a human mode, it does not attain to divinity as such nor acquire a clear species of divinity. Rather, it knows the divine as hidden in the intentional order, which is to say that the infinite transcendence of divinity is manifested only obscurely to the intellect that adheres to it through faith. This follows logically from the principle of "essential likeness".

5. The intervention of the participated divine light—which makes possible the contact with the divine object—and the resulting obscurity in the intellect—which attains to the divine without any substantial change in its human mode of operation (as is clear from book II, chapter 3)—show that for St. John of the Cross faith represents for the human intellect an intrinsic proportion to God. But the proportion is one not only of likeness but also one of incapacity and insufficiency. These two elements enter into the very essence of faith; they are intimately related and always occur concomitantly, as we shall see later. The proportion of likeness is essential to faith because it is on that score that faith qualifies as the proportionate means of union with God. The other element—namely, the obscurity— pertains to faith secondarily and by way of redundance; yet it is also essential to faith insofar as faith is only a limited communication of the divine light and hence a limited participation in the divine.

Moreover, this twofold aspect of faith explains the combination of light and darkness that we have already noted. The simultaneous presence of these opposites is a clear indication of the intimate and intrinsic proportion between the intellect and divinity. It is hardly necessary to add that we are speaking of a *supernatural* proportion, for that is presupposed, granted the principle of "essential likeness". There can be no other kind of proportion in relation to divinity.

6. The intimate proportion between the intellect and the divine is also manifested in the order of operation, that is, in the effective striving for union with God. In this context it is described as an "obscure habit". We already know in what sense St. John of the Cross uses the word "habit": the perfection of a faculty in the order of operation, a perfection inferior to act because it is ordained to operation. We now ask whether all that we have said in analyzing the text of book II, chapter 3 of *The Ascent* refers properly to the act or to the habit of faith.

Our answer is that all that we have said applies simply to faith. St. John of the Cross does not put the question this way; first treating of the habit of faith and then of its act. All the elements we have treated from chapter 3 and elsewhere pertain simply to the structure of faith, both as a "certain and obscure" habit and as the act of faith. In the first case these elements are constitutive of that "obscure habit of union" of which the Mystical Doctor speaks in chapter 5, no. 2; in the second case the same elements are manifested more clearly in the order of operation. Whether they likewise play a part in the act of "transitory union with respect to the act", of which the Mystical Doctor speaks in the same passage, is something we must investigate.

7. Finally, we should add that insofar as it enables the intellect to attain to divinity from the revealed truths by means of the participated divine light, faith elevates the intellect and satisfies its intimate and innate tendency to grasp in its connatural manner the essence of things presented to it by the senses. In this

respect we cannot say that faith causes any privation in the intellect; on the contrary, it elevates it and bestows a great favor on it.

But the intellect retains its human mode of operation in attaining the divine and this is the reason for its obscurity. It is under this aspect we can speak of a privation. By its power of cognition the intellect tends to grasp the nature of things in the intentional order and to find rest and fruition in that apprehension. But this is lacking in the operation of the virtue of faith, and for that reason the intellect suffers a privation. Yet, to be faithful to the teaching of St. John of the Cross, it must be noted that the privation does not consist in the lack of intellectual evidence, which the intellect has in any cognitive process, but in the lack of a species or intentional form.

Here faith is compared to and contrasted with immediate vision. As compared to vision, faith operates on the intentional or cognitive level, for through faith the divinity is present to the intellect on the intentional level; as contrasted with vision, the knowledge through faith has a negative characteristic: God is in the intellect as hidden, he is present in the intellect in obscurity. God is present to the intellect through faith, but the intellect never fully comprehends or possesses him through faith.

And now a word should be said about faith as a "certain habit". St. John of the Cross simply affirms the certitude of faith, but he does not give any explanation as he does for faith as an "obscure" habit. The certitude of faith would seem to derive from the communication of the divine light and indeed to be a quality intrinsic to the intellect's participation in that light. What is implied here is St. John's statement that "the light of faith, by reason of its excessive intensity, oppresses and overwhelms the light of the intellect."[91] It is obvious that there would be no victory over the intellect if the certitude of faith were lacking. However, since the concept of obscurity is more

[91] *The Ascent*, bk. II, chap. 3, no. 1.

closely related to the Mystical Doctor's treatment of faith, the concept of certitude, which connotes evidence, does not receive as much attention.

Returning to the text, faith as an obscure and certain habit terminates psychologically as "the assent of the soul to what enters through hearing".[92] Assent, however, is opposed to knowledge acquired by demonstration. Therefore we can say that the assent of the intellect comprises all that we have discovered in our analysis of the text: obscurity and certitude at the same time. From a doctrinal point of view, this teaching has always been commonly held; what is properly and specifically the teaching of St. John of the Cross is found in those texts that we investigated previously.

We turn now to consider a passage that appears later in chapter 3:

> Faith . . . not only produces no knowledge and science, but, as we have said, it blinds the soul and deprives it of all other knowledge and science which cannot judge [faith] well. Other kinds of knowledge can be acquired by the light of the intellect, but the knowledge that is of faith is acquired without the light of the intellect. Faith negates the natural light, and if that light is not darkened, faith is lost. . . . It is evident, then, that faith is dark night for the soul, and it is in this way that it gives light; and the more darkness it causes, the greater light it gives.[93]

This text serves as a corollary to the preceding analysis and also as a preparation for the investigation that follows. The "knowledge that is of faith", referred to in the text, can be understood according to the results of our preceding analysis, in which case it would signify the lack of any species acquired through faith. But the context seems to indicate that it should be interpreted as "the general, confused and obscure knowledge given by faith", which is contemplation. This knowledge is not

---

[92] Ibid., no. 3.   [93] Ibid., no. 4.

acquired by any natural light; there is no human knowledge that corresponds to it; rather, it is a negation of such knowledge. And this concept of negation touches the essential psychological element of faith and also connotes the abnegations of the active night of the spirit.

When St. John of the Cross states that other sciences and knowledge cannot judge faith well, this indicates the essential inaccessibility of faith to any natural power of the intellect. And faith is inaccessible because of its mysterious and obscure transcendence. Ordered as it is to the divine essence, faith can lead the intellect to the divine only through the infused divine light, and this, in turn, requires that the intellect relinquish all naturally acquired knowledge. In its essential adhesion to the divine, which is at once certain and obscure, faith has the intrinsic power of transcending all human knowledge.

To conclude, faith is a dark night for the soul and precisely as such it illumines the soul. The more it darkens the soul, the more it illumines it. We already know that these paradoxical qualities are both verified of faith and are always predicated of faith. They express the whole intrinsic nature of the virtue of faith, its inner tension, and its proportionate likeness to the divine, accompanied by a psychological disproportion. Faith is a dark night, and this statement leads us to our next consideration.

"Faith is a dark night"

The word "night" is one of the most frequently used terms in the works of St. John of the Cross. It gives his mystical theology a "nocturnal" quality which, in contrast to the "solar" aspect of St. Augustine's theology, can most certainly be traced back to the pseudo-Dionysius. However, the word "night" is not always used in the same sense by the Mystical Doctor, and hence it must be interpreted in different ways, according to the context.

The word is used in the very first pages of *The Ascent*, where the Mystical Doctor, conscious of the importance of this symbol, gives us an explanation. "What we here call night", he says, "is a deprivation of the pleasure of the appetite in all things."[94] Here the word "night" has a general meaning; it signifies the privation of the pleasure of any appetite or desire. But later St. John of the Cross distinguishes the various types of appetible goods and further specifies various nights according to the particular privations.

The reason for using the term "night" is that, just as night designates the privation of the light by means of which objects are visible to us, so metaphorically it signifies the privation of the psychological light whereby naturally desirable objects are presented to the appetite and thus stimulate a desire for them. Thus, St. John states that "the mortification of desire may be called a night of the soul, for when it is deprived of the pleasure of the appetite in all things, the soul remains, as it were, empty and in darkness."[95]

We also find here the notion of "mortification", which is explained in detail in the famous method proposed in book I, chapter 13 of *The Ascent*. However, night does not have exactly the same meaning as mortification. It refers only to the emptiness of the faculty which, deprived of its connatural object and, as it were, of its own proper light, remains in darkness. Such is the concept of night, a concept that is fundamental in the doctrine of St. John of the Cross. It is, as we have seen, a psychological concept that describes the condition of a faculty deprived of its proper object.

St. John of the Cross does not fail to observe that the desired objects are presented to the faculties in the natural way — through the senses — in the state of the union of body and soul. Then he asks whether the soul can eliminate completely the perception of things naturally presented to it by the senses. His

---

[94] *The Ascent*, bk. I, chap. 3, no. 1.
[95] Ibid.

response is that the concept of "dark night" is ultimately reducible to the acts of willing and desiring, and therefore to the will. It is not a question of contact with the object presented by the senses; rather, what is opposed to the dark night is the adherence of the will to the object or good with a view to satisfying the appetite or desire. He states this clearly: "It is not the things of this world that occupy the soul or cause it harm, for they do not enter it; rather, it is the will and desire for them, for these dwell within it."[96]

The foregoing statement defines the scope of the dark night. It does not apply to things in themselves, but to things known in the intentional order and then accepted by the appetite—or more strictly, the will—to satisfy one's desire. The dark night is opposed to this intentional modality of created things and therefore requires that the will be emptied of them and turned away from them.

The foregoing analysis brings us to a consideration of the philosophical basis of the doctrine of union as explained in book I, chapter 4 of *The Ascent*. But before coming to this, we should note that for St. John of the Cross all created things are pure darkness in relation to God. We have here another trace of the "dark night" or, better, the "nocturnal doctrine" does not contradict the concept of night explained above, but reinforces it. St. John of the Cross states and repeats in several ways throughout chapter 4 of book I that in comparison with God, the creature has nothing of goodness or beauty or even of being; rather, the contrary is true—it is evil, ugly and almost nothing.

What is the source of such statements? They are used in the text when he speaks of union with God. We are already familiar with this manner of speaking from our study of book II, chapter 8 of *The Ascent*: there is no essential likeness between created things and God; therefore they cannot serve as means of

---

[96] Ibid., bk. I, chap. 3, no. 4.

union with God.[97] Objectively speaking, the reason is that they lack a proportional likeness to God, but here in chapter 4 of book I the reason is a subjective one: the soul clothed with these things (or more properly, clothed with desires for such things or with voluntary attachment to such things) is not capable of union with God. "All the affections it has for creatures", says St. John of the Cross, "are pure darkness in the eyes of God, and as long as the soul is clothed with these affections, it is incapable of being enlightened and possessed by the pure and simple light of God."[98]

But we may further ask why this is so. St. John of the Cross replies: "The reason is that two contraries (as philosophy teaches us) cannot coexist in one subject."[99] From this principle he concludes that it must be either affection for creatures or union with God, but it cannot be both.[100]

The last response gives us the basic reason why affection for creatures and union with God are mutually exclusive, and the same reason applies to the constitutive element of union, which is love. For love has the power of making the lover and the beloved similar or equal; therefore, when it is a question of the union of likeness referred to in book II, chapter 5, no. 3, love alone is the unifying force. Now when love for created things prevails, the innate power of love makes the soul subject to creatures because love not only makes equals, but it subjects the lover to the beloved. When this happens, the soul is bound fast and imprisoned by its likeness and subjection to the object loved. It cannot escape, and it cannot be transformed by the divine union. It is, as St. John says, "incapable of pure union with God and transformation in God",[101] until the will puts aside its love, affection—or better, its attachment to creatures—

---

[97] Cf. Fr. Marcelo de Niño Jesús, op. cit., 27, 164–71.

[98] *The Ascent*, bk. I, chap. 4, no. 1.

[99] *The Ascent*, bk. I, chap. 4, no. 2.

[100] Cf. Fr. Marcelo de Niño Jesús, op. cit., 27, 89–98.

[101] *The Ascent*, bk. I, chap. 3, no. 3.

and thereby opens the soul to that other love. Such a detachment or deprivation of the desire for created things known through the senses is experienced as a "dark night".

The text in book I, chapter 4 teaches us two things with great insistence:

1) *the definitive power and essential characteristic of love—and therefore of the will—in union, as conceived by St. John of the Cross.* The power and essential characteristic of love flow from its very nature insofar as it causes likeness and subjects the lover to the beloved. Hence if it is a question of union of likeness, love must necessarily be the unifying factor. Moreover, since love operates through the will, it draws the whole person to the object loved. This explains what the Mystical Doctor repeats time and time again: union consists in the total conformation of the human will with the divine will, even transforming it to the point that no other thing contrary to the divine will is found in it. Rather, in all things and through all things the divine will alone is fulfilled in the operations of the human will.[102]

2) *the nature and function of the "dark night".* This follows necessarily from what we have just said. If we exclude from the appetitive power—the will—the possibility of two contrary forms possessed simultaneously by love, there is no other way in which the soul can progressively participate in the divine form through love, from which follows the union of likeness, than by the negation of the appetite's attachment to things perceived through the senses. And such a privation constitutes the "night" referred to in book I, chapter 3 of *The Ascent*.

We should note that throughout the entire tetrology of St. John of the Cross the succession of will—love—night is characteristic of his doctrine on union with God. However, the concept of "night" is not restricted to the description given in book I, chapter 3 of *The Ascent*, but it is later expanded to include the intervention of the virtue of faith. Up to now the

---

[102] Cf. *The Ascent*, bk. I, chap. 11; bk. II, chap. 5.

concept of "night" was explained as a mortification or privation of the appetite in regard to its connatural object, but now
we must examine the dark night as a way of union of the soul
with God or as a necessary condition for the entire path to
union.

This aspect of the night first appears in book I, chapter 2 of
The Ascent, where the Mystical Doctor says that "this journey
made by the soul to union with God is called night". There are
three reasons for this. The first is by reason of the *terminus a quo*
or point of origin. We already know what this origin is—it is
the soul, which is naturally incapable of anything but what is
presented to it through the senses. It is "like a smooth, blank
board on which nothing is painted, and, unless it knows things
through its senses, nothing is communicated to it naturally."[103]
Now there takes place in this *terminus a quo*, which is the soul, a
negation, or rather an abnegation of all the things to which the
soul is naturally drawn by the senses and by which it is informed and filled. This is the first night, which, as we already
know, consists in the "negation and privation [that] are, as it
were, night to all the senses of man."[104]

The second reason why the way to union is called night—or
the second part of the dark night—is by reason of the means to
union with God, which means extends throughout the entire
journey to union. And the means to union is the virtue of faith,
which, the Mystical Doctor states, "is also as dark as night to
the intellect".[105]

The third reason for the dark night is the *terminus ad quem* or
the goal of the journey, which is God alone, "who is likewise a
dark night to the soul in this life."[106]

There is a special relationship between the second and third
reasons (or parts of the dark night). In the first place, the second
night or phase of the night, which is described as the means by

---

[103] *The Ascent*, bk. I, chap. 3, no. 3.

[104] Ibid., bk. I, chap. 2, no. 1.

[105] Ibid., bk. I, chap. 2, no. 1; cf. also no. 5.   [106] Ibid.

which the soul travels to union, is not the exclusive means to that union, for the soul "abides alone in faith, not to the exclusion of charity, but of other knowledge acquired by the intellect".[107] It is so in a particular way with relation to the intellect, for which it is both a means of union and a dark night. We have here another aspect of union, of which the proper and necessary means, as we saw in the previous analysis, is love. Faith is something else; it is a particular means, and it gives a distinctive note to the entire journey toward union. As is evident from the title of chapter 9, book II of *The Ascent*, its distinctiveness lies in its relation to the intellect and consists in the fact that it presents God (the *terminus ad quem*) in total obscurity.

We should also note the difference between the first part of the night, which is "abnegation" or withdrawal from created things, and the second part, which is the approach to God, and as such is closely related to the third part of the night. Thus, St. John of the Cross states: "God, who by means of the second night, which is faith, continually communicates himself to the soul in such a secret and intimate manner that he is another night to the soul".[108]

What does this mean? It has the same meaning as we already saw in the passage from book II, chapter 9, but expressed in different words: in communicating himself to the soul through faith, God remains hidden. There is union with God through faith and the adhesion of the intellect to divinity, but all takes place in darkness. Faith is therefore a proper means of union wherein divinity is communicated to the soul; but at the same time it is a dark night because the communication of the soul with God is effected through faith, which is obscure. This twofold characteristic of faith extends throughout the entire path to union, pervades it and gives it the element of darkness.

Evidently this reason for the dark night differs from the first one, which pertains to the privation of the appetite or desire

---

[107] Ibid., bk. I, chap. 2, no. 3.   [108] Ibid., bk. I, chap. 2, no. 4.

with respect to its connatural sensible goods. The second reason refers to the unifying communication of God, although in darkness, and therefore it refers to union in some way. Nevertheless, the obscure mode of communication with God causes an intensification of the night in the soul that deprives itself of created things on account of God. Hence, faith is described as the darkest part of the night or as midnight, wherein the soul, now totally cut off from all created things, receives the communication of divinity, but in total obscurity.

What are the results of this analysis? Do we have any new elements to add to our synthesis of faith? Yes we do, and the first one is that we have a clearer notion of the word "night" that is used so often in the works of St. John of the Cross. Secondly, the foregoing analysis shows us how faith intervenes in the dark night. Moreover, since the whole question of union with God—of which faith has been frequently identified as the means—is closely related to the notion of "night", we are able to understand the virtue of faith more exactly within this context.

It is clear that for St. John of the Cross the union of likeness caused by love involves some conceptual apprehension whereby the object loved is presented to the will. And once we recall the nature of this faculty and its proper act, which is love, it is also clear how and in what sense the will is assimilated to the object and transformed. The transformation is nothing other than the total adhesion of the will to the object loved, since love draws the will completely to the object loved and makes it inhere to that object to the exclusion of everything else.

Such is the force of love, whose proper function is to effect union and, indeed, union in the psychological sense. For that reason the Mystical Doctor dedicates practically all of book I of *The Ascent* to a consideration of love of created things, which the soul experiences through its natural appetites and desires. If the soul seeks such things, it is drawn to created things, becomes like them and nullifies its innate superiority over created goods of the sensate order. And the soul's superiority consists precisely in this, that it is capable of being illumined by the divine light and informed by the divine reality through sanctifying grace and can ultimately attain to the transforming union by its growth in supernatural love.

In other words, the soul is capable of making the transition from created things to the divine reality, but this transition requires a twofold night: the night of privation of created things that constantly stimulate the desire through sense knowledge to draw these things to itself; and the night of union with God, who is communicated to the soul through faith, without clarity or natural satisfaction to the cognitive faculty, but rather in total darkness. Two things are evident from this analysis:

1) *the relationship between faith and love in the path to union.* Faith is called the means of union with God; it is frequently so called in the works of St. John of the Cross and for that reason we have used it as the starting point in our study. But love is also the means of union with God. Hence, both faith and love are means, but in different senses. Love produces the union of likeness by its native power and by reason of its psychological quality. Consequently, it can lead the soul to the height of union and likeness which is called the transforming union, as we have already seen.

Faith, on the other hand, as can be seen in book I, chapter 2, and book II, chapters 8 and 9 of *The Ascent*, produces union by presenting divinity to the intellect and uniting this faculty with God. But, as we saw in book II, chapter 3, the unifying power and the psychological aspects of faith are weak and insufficient as regards the fullness of union because the intellect is not transformed in divinity through faith as the will is through love. In faith the divine species or form is perceived only obscurely and in darkness, and not clearly, as are the forms of created things received through the senses. This, as we have seen, is what constitutes the night of faith: the intellect is informed by divinity, but its splendor is always inaccessible to the intellect.

The "night" of faith extends throughout the entire journey to union, and for that reason St. John of the Cross says that the entire road that the soul must travel is as a dark night to the intellect.[109] Divinity is presented to the intellect through faith and dwells there without being seen clearly by the intellect: such is the psychological character of faith as a habit. One can also keep in mind at this point what has already been said concerning revelation, by which divine truths are proposed to the intellect for its assent. This also pertains to the virtue of faith.

However, the intrinsic limitation of the unifying power of faith does not detract from the perfection of faith in the union itself; in fact, the divine reality communicated to the soul could be described in some sense as identical with faith, but clothed in the obscurity that is typical of faith. This would suggest that in the very essence of faith as a means of union there is a certain participated likeness of God in the intentional order. And in spite of the obscurity of the intentional form, it serves the soul and the will as the basis of transformation through love. Indeed, the note of obscurity provides a special quality to union in this life, for God, "by means of the second night, which is faith, continually communicates himself to the soul in such a secret and intimate manner that he is another night to the soul."[110] Thus, through love the soul is transformed into God by participation, but through faith the divinity to which it is united—although always in darkness and not clearly—becomes the principle of knowledge, assimilation and union.

2) Through faith the soul makes the transition to union with God, but *the entire way to union is obscure and dark as night*. The soul is united to God through faith, and this fundamental union is the basis of all progress on the path to union and of the increasing supernatural transformation of the soul to the highest degree possible in this life. And now the Mystical Doctor

---

[109] *The Ascent*, bk. I, chap. 2, no. 1.
[110] Ibid., no. 4.

wishes to introduce us to this path to union, carefully pointing out its various stages.

The path to union consists of four stages that are commonly called "nights". Two of them are active, and these are described in *The Ascent*; and two of them are passive and are explained in *The Dark Night*. Such is the projected plan of the Mystical Doctor. But our purpose is to study the doctrine on faith in the active nights, and especially as it pertains to the active night of the spirit.

The active night of the senses, which normally precedes the active night of the spirit, pertains to the lower faculties and is more external;[111] therefore it is not the night of faith, properly speaking. It is true, of course, that faith is operative throughout the entire path to union, and the abnegation of the external senses has its roots in faith, but since the abnegation is effected through the purging of the sense faculties, the process is not called the night of faith. Rather, it pertains, as the Mystical Doctor says, to the "yearnings of sensate love",[112] which do not pertain to the exercise of faith in a strict sense.

But in the later stages, when it is a question of the higher, spiritual faculties of the rational and interior part of the soul, the virtue of faith intervenes explicitly. Then the night at this stage is rightly called the active night of faith, which signifies the active purification or night that is effected through the virtue of faith. For this reason it is described as a most dark and difficult night, comparable to midnight, where no light of any kind remains. The light of created things, which shines in the soul through its desire, has been extinguished in the preceding night; the divine light is in the soul through the virtue of faith, but it does not shine. The reason is that although the divine reality alone remains in the soul when created things have been rejected, it is not seen clearly by the intellect through faith.

Therefore the soul remains alone with God, but God is present to it only through faith, and its possession of God is in

111 *The Ascent*, bk. II, chap. 2.   112 Ibid., bk. II, chap. 1, no. 2.

proportion to its faith. This means that the soul truly possesses God alone without any admixture of creatures, but psychologically the soul experiences nothingness or *"nada"*. There is no satisfaction or fruition in the intellect and no natural operation of the cognitive faculties, even though the soul adheres to divinity through faith. The adhesion, as we have seen in book II, chapter 3 of *The Ascent*, is an "assent", or it is like the species of color to a blind man, who knows them only by hearing. Thus the virtue of faith is a passage through the *nada* or a psychological nothingness.

The foregoing doctrine is found in book II, chapters 1 and 2 of *The Ascent*, where St. John of the Cross begins his discussion of the second part of the "nocturnal journey" which is by faith. Faith is presented as the night that is proper to the superior, spiritual faculties of the soul. Then an equation or correspondence is immediately set up between faith and God:

> Naturally speaking, God is as dark a night to the soul as is faith, but when these three parts of the night are ending [still the same schema as in book I, chapter 2], which are naturally night to the soul, God then begins to illumine the soul supernaturally with the ray of his divine light, which is the beginning of the perfect union that follows.[113]

There is also an antithesis here between the natural and the supernatural. God is nothing less than total night for the soul—or rather for the natural capacity of the intellect. Because of the lack of essential likeness between the divine essence and the nature of any creature, God remains completely inaccessible. Nevertheless, he can illumine the intellect with his divine light, which serves as the principle of perfect union with God. But the divine light is operative in the virtue of faith, as we have seen in book II, chapter 3, although it so greatly transcends the natural light of the intellect that it causes only darkness. Hence faith terminates in the darkness of the intellect that is caused by the excess of divine light.

[113] *The Ascent*, bk. II, chap. 2, no. 1.

Such is the virtue of faith, with its essential disproportion. And "naturally speaking", God is for the soul as dark a night as is faith. Faith is night for the intellect considered in its natural capacity; God, who is communicated through faith, is also night to the intellect. The light of faith is completely super-natural, and therefore the intellect obtains nothing from that light that is proportionate to the intellect or corresponds with its natural powers. There is a line of absolute separation be-tween the excessive light of faith and the natural light of the intellect, and this distinction between the natural and the super-natural, between the created and the divine, has a bearing on the very nature of faith and its operation.

We should add, finally, that the Mystical Doctor's teaching on faith is supported by the statement of St. Paul: "Faith is confident assurance concerning what we hope for, and convic-tion about things we do not see" (Heb 11:1). On that Pauline principle St. John of the Cross constructs his doctrine on faith and on hope and charity as well. He sees the three theological virtues as three means by which the spiritual faculties of the soul—intellect, memory and will—are "placed in perfection", that is, are united with God. At the same time, however, each of the corresponding faculties experiences darkness and empti-ness in regard to its natural objects or, as St. John of the Cross puts it, the three theological virtues "produce the same empti-ness and darkness, each one in its own faculty."[114]

How this happens in regard to the virtue of faith we have already explained to some extent, and we shall discuss it in greater detail later on. For the moment we note that the Mystical Doctor states in this same passage: "Faith . . . tells us what cannot be understood by the intellect."[115] Then, in ex-plaining the text of St. Paul, he says:

We understand this to mean that faith is the substance of things hoped for; and although the intellect gives a firm and certain assent

[114] Ibid., bk. II, chap. 6, no. 1.   [115] Ibid., no. 2.

to them, they are not things that are manifested to the intellect. If they were manifested to it, there would be no faith. So faith, although it gives certitude to the intellect, does not bring clarity, but obscurity.[116]

To summarize, the whole doctrine of the Mystical Doctor on faith, its very "substance", is based on those "things hoped for", all of which are received through faith as the object of the intellect and exist in the intellect, but without "evidence". Or perhaps the text of St. Paul would be better interpreted to mean without intellectual evidence that provides the intellect with the conclusion of scientific knowledge.

The Mystical Doctor's "conviction about things we do not see" is the same here as in book II, chapter 3, for he says: "They are not things that are manifested to the intellect. In other words, the things that are hoped for are present to the intellect through faith, but they are not there as something seen. The knowledge of them received through faith is by that same faith veiled and obscured. If it were otherwise, it would not be faith. Consequently these two things pertain essentially to the virtue of faith: the possession of the divine truths by the intellect and the obscurity of those truths in relation to the intellect.

Faith in the active night of the spirit

We have already mentioned that the night proper to faith is the active night of the spirit, which is explained at length in book II of *The Ascent*. We also stated that an analysis of book II would reveal the precise operation of the virtue of faith and how it leads to union. When the question was raised in chapter 8 of book II as to whether faith, as a proportionate means of union with God, possessed any likeness to the divine essence, we were

[116] Ibid.

given a static view of the virtue of faith. This could be considered as an entitative analysis of faith; that is, the nature of faith and its ontological quality and excellence. This was examined first, and rightly so, although not entirely in the same order as treated by St. John of the Cross.

However, the ontological basis leads us immediately to the dynamic aspect of faith in order to discover whether and how the virtue of faith causes union with God. The dynamic totality of the virtue of faith will explain union with God and the path that leads to union. And all the elements that contribute to union will be discovered, not through an abstract and theoretical consideration, but as actuated in the unifying process itself. They will be known through their operation. In this way also we can investigate the nature of faith more deeply, and this should not be considered a digression because the mode of operation follows from the mode of being or the nature of things.

In order to understand the active night of faith, it is necessary to note at the outset that, in passing from the general treatment of faith as a means of union to more particular matters—cf. *The Ascent*, book II, chapter 10—St. John of the Cross makes a division of the types of knowledge that the intellect can receive. But in the text we find various terms, such as "apprehensions", "concepts" and "knowledge" that mean substantially the same thing. He makes the division by means of elimination. Thus, there are two ways in which the intellect can receive knowledge, the one *natural* and the other *supernatural*. By the natural way is meant all the knowledge for which the human intellect suffices by its very nature, receiving it directly through the senses or by its own power, though even here, according to the theory of knowledge proposed by the Mystical Doctor, the knowledge would depend indirectly or remotely on the senses. Supernatural knowledge signifies that which exceeds the natural power of the intellect. It is knowledge that the intellect could never attain by its own efforts—as explained in book II, chapter 3 of *The Ascent*—because the knowledge was not gained through sense experience of the things themselves or their representations. The natural power and capacity of the intellect do not extend to such things and for that reason, says the Saint, they would be known in a supernatural manner.

There is a further division of the knowledge received supernaturally. The supernatural knowledge that is received through the external or internal senses is called *corporeal* supernatural knowledge; that which is received directly into the intellect without the intervention of the senses is called *spiritual* supernatural knowledge. The latter is again subdivided into *distinct, particular* knowledge and that which is *confused, general* and *dark*. Finally, the distinct, particular knowledge is of four kinds: *visions, revelations, locutions* and *spiritual feelings*; the general and dark knowledge, however, is of one kind only, which is "*contemplation* that is given in faith".[117]

It is evident from the various types of supernatural knowledge and even more so from the explanation given by the Mystical Doctor that his classification is based on the cause from which supernatural knowledge proceeds and not, as the names would indicate, on the content of the knowledge in question. Moreover, this manner of procedure indicates clearly the experimental and inductive character of the works of the Mystical Doctor. After explaining all the types of supernatural knowledge, he proceeds to reject this knowledge in accordance with the nature and function of faith already explained. The entire section of *The Ascent*, from chapter 10 to chapter 31 of book II, explains how and why certain elements or aspects of this knowledge are in accord with the attainment of union through faith, and how and why other elements or aspects must be eliminated.

[117] *The Ascent*, bk. II, chap. 10, no. 4.

In this particular section of *The Ascent* there are two questions that pertain to our study and which we must treat in order. The first question deals with the role of the virtue of faith in the active night of the spirit, wherein all the apprehensions and knowledge that cannot serve to unite the intellect with God must be rejected by the power of the virtue of faith. The second question concerns "the obscure and general type of knowledge . . . which is contemplation that is given in faith", as noted above. This is the knowledge that the intellect can attain in this life under the impetus of its natural tendency, within the limits of the virtue of faith, and aided by other supernatural powers. However, we should note immediately that the second question is of interest to us in this study only so far as it may shed some light on the nature and operation of the virtue of faith.

One should always keep in mind the reasons given in the teaching of St. John of the Cross for the absolute necessity of the dark night for union of the soul with God. The basic reason is given first in chapter 8 of book II of *The Ascent*, where he compares the Deity with created nature. His conclusion is that the Deity is not comparable to any creature; rather, there is an infinite distance between the divine reality or divine essence and all created things, considered in their very natures.

The second reason for the dark night—not in chronological order but in logical sequence—is found in book I, chapter 3 and especially in chapter 4, where St. John states that union with God is effected by some kind of informing or, as he says in chapter 5, by a participation in divinity. He then states a second principle: in such an informing of the soul by divinity, any relationship of coexistence is impossible. Why? He answers: because the bond of union is love.

At this point St. John of the Cross seems to find a third reason for the necessity of the dark night, one that is proper to love so far as love is a transforming power. By its nature love makes things equal and hence makes the lover similar to the beloved. The lover possesses the beloved in an intentional form which captivates the will and then the innate power of love causes the lover to adhere to the beloved. This means that the lover is united to the beloved and transformed into the beloved by participation. It is in this sense that love is exclusive, because by its very nature it tends to transform the lover into the beloved.

From these three reasons or premises the necessity for the dark night follows as a logical and inexorable conclusion. This night is a privation of the desire for anything that is not God; therefore its relation to love is immediately evident because it prevents one from loving any created or natural form. If it followed its innate tendency, love would establish a relationship with created things and thereby exclude the assimilation of the soul to God. By the same token, it would obstruct the soul's intimate union with God, given the inchoate tendency of love toward participated transformation. In this sense the dark night also pertains to love.

But faith also intervenes, and as a result we could say that the dark night is duplicated. Of itself, the virtue of faith contacts divinity, but it does so precisely by means of the dark night, which signifies that the intellect attains to the divine essence through faith, but at the same time it lacks the intentional form of divinity and is left in its natural condition. Faith unites the soul to divinity but does not transform the soul intrinsically, as is the case with the beatific vision. Thus, because of the mixture of light and darkness, faith is properly described as a dark night or non-vision and is at the same time the cause of the dark night that characterizes the entire passage to union. For although faith does not enable the intellect to possess the form of the divine in a manner that gives it satisfaction and fruition, nevertheless, as we tried to explain previously, it does bestow on the intellect a certain "measure" or proportion of divinity, in the sense that it does not confuse divinity with any created thing nor replace God by anything it can attain by its natural powers. How this is effected in practice, one can learn from experiencing the active night of the spirit. But before proceeding further, we must examine the passage found in book II, chapter 4 of *The Ascent*:

> Faith is a dark night to the soul, and . . . the soul likewise must be dark, or in darkness as regards its own light, so that it can let itself be guided [*se deje guiar*] by faith to this high goal of union.[118]

The word *"guiar"* means to direct or lead; hence the virtue of faith is the director or guide of the soul to union, but it guides the soul in darkness, not only as regards the lower sense faculties, but the higher faculties as well. The soul "must also be blinded and darkened according to the part that relates to God and to spiritual things, which is the rational and higher part".[119]

Why is this so? St. John explains immediately: "Because, in order that the soul may attain supernatural transformation, it is clear that it must be darkened and rise above everything contained in its nature, which is sensual and rational."[120] The Mystical Doctor always returns to the basic question of supernatural transformation, and he insists that in view of this goal, not only in the sense faculties but also in the superior or rational faculties, one must rise above everything that is purely natural, for as such it is opposed to supernatural union and transformation. So St. John gives the etymological definition of the word supernatural as "that which soars above the natural; the natural self, therefore, remains beneath it."

The absolutely supernatural character of the transforming union determines the nature of the way and the means to union. The soul must reject everything that falls within its natural capacity, whatever its source, from above or below.[121] It must empty itself of everything that can be received by a

---

[118] *The Ascent*, bk. II, chap. 4, no. 1.
[119] Ibid., no. 2.   [120] Ibid.
[121] Cf. *The Ascent*, bk. II, chap. 10, where St. John of the Cross treats of various kinds of apprehensions.

natural faculty or can be expressed by any psychological species. Then God can accomplish in the soul what he wills.

It is the virtue of faith that provides this disposition of soul, as the Mystical Doctor explains:

> [The soul] must be like a blind man, leaning upon dark faith, taking it for its guide and light, and leaning upon none of the things that he understands, experiences, feels and imagines. Because all this is darkness that will lead the soul astray. Faith transcends all that one can understand, experience, feel and imagine. And if the soul is not blinded to this, and does not remain in total darkness, it will not attain to that which is greater, namely, what faith teaches.[122]

Note that faith is said to be not only above all that the intellect naturally acquires or can acquire, but it also teaches. The first aspect denotes its intrinsic relation to the divine; the second denotes its objective relation to revealed truths whereby the divine is attained. The Mystical Doctor then continues his explanation with scarcely any change of style. Quoting the biblical statement, "Anyone who comes to God must believe that he exists" (Heb 11:6), he translates it as follows: "He that would strive for union with God must believe in God's existence."[123] This means that the soul must not adhere to anything felt, imagined or understood, even if it be the highest thing that can be felt and experienced concerning God in this life. (This will be of great importance later in describing the heights of mystical experience.) Nothing—"*nada*"—because whatever can be felt, imagined or understood naturally is infinitely removed from God and from the pure possession of God. All this calls for faith; this is what it means to "enter into the abyss of faith", mentioned in book III, chapter 7 of *The Ascent*.

In fact, in all these statements concerning abnegation, the concept of faith is always a key factor. The whole concept of the dark night is based on the structure and intrinsic logic of faith. That is why we stated that the virtue of faith duplicates

---

[122] *The Ascent*, bk. II, chap. 4, no. 2.   [123] Ibid., no. 4.

the dark night. At the same time it serves to explain the dark night, for if love requires a dark night lest the will be attracted to some natural object and be captivated by it, the virtue of faith adds still another reason for the dark night: God is not like or comparable to any created thing. Therefore every created thing must be rejected if one seeks divine union. Faith forbids that any creature be substituted for God.

The virtue of faith also explains the dark night because, by its very nature, by its intrinsic connection with the divinity in the intellect, and by its essential proportion to the divinity, in spite of the obscurity—or rather, because of it—it cannot be confused with any created or natural reality. Faith observes its own proper mode and limitations as regards union, but these suffice to communicate the divine to the soul. The Mystical Doctor describes it as follows:

> Wherefore, on this road, to enter the road is to leave the road or, to express it better, it is to pass on to the goal and to leave one's own way, and to enter upon that which has no way, which is God. For the soul that reaches this state no longer has any ways or methods, still less is it attached to them nor can it be attached to them. I mean ways of understanding, of experiencing or of feeling. Nevertheless it has within itself all ways, in the way that one possesses nothing, and yet possesses all things. For, having the courage to pass beyond its natural limitations, both interiorly and exteriorly, it enters the domain of the supernatural, which has no way, yet in substance has all ways.[124]

All of the foregoing is connoted in the phrase "the abyss of faith". Moreover, the Mystical Doctor's manner of speaking in the cited passage undoubtedly led J. Baruzi to his interpretation of the Saint's doctrine on faith, described by Dom Chevallier as a "universalization of the intellect".[125] It is true that the text can be interpreted in that way if one considers isolated passages, but

---

[124] *The Ascent*, bk. II, chap. 4, no. 5.
[125] Cf. J. Baruzi, op. cit., 19; P. Chevallier, op. cit.

there is another point that Baruzi does not seem to have developed sufficiently: the modality of faith derives from the fact that it transcends the limits of the natural capacity of the intellect and enters into the domain of the supernatural, which is something essentially divine. And it is precisely by transcending the natural limitations that faith is able to lead us to God.[126]

But there is no such power within the natural scope of the human intellect. Indeed, the Mystical Doctor constantly affirms that the more closely the soul approaches God, the more profound is the night it experiences. And this, as we have already seen, is due to the reaction of the intellect to the excessive light. Therefore, there is no intrinsic intellectual elaboration of anything divine, but a truly supernatural communication through the intervention of grace. The intellect does transcend itself, so to speak, but not by its own power. It is effected by the strictly supernatural "proportion" to the divine that faith provides, and then, by the dynamic growth of faith, the intellect achieves an ever greater awareness and experience of the divine.

From this we can see the importance of the dark night for understanding the virtue of faith in the works of St. John of the Cross. Moreover, the careful study of chapter 4, book II of *The Ascent* leads us to a detailed analysis of the active night of the spirit, which has already been designated as proper to the virtue of faith. It is here that we must investigate all the "apprehensions", "perceptions" and "understandings" that provide material for particular and distinct knowledge. They must be studied, not speculatively and critically—though we do not entirely prescind from this—but with a view to the experiential, practical and normative function of faith. In a word, they are to be judged and examined in the light of the experience of faith as essentially proportionate to the divine and as a means of union with God.

---

[126] J. Baruzi, op. cit. 471: "Our effort to transcend all types of being is considered as making us enter into God. Faith is an abyss."

Once having made the division of various types of "apprehensions", the Mystical Doctor treats of those things that can reach the intellect by supernatural means, not excluding those that pertain to the external and internal senses. This he does in chapter 10 of book II of *The Ascent*. All these things are supernatural by reason of the mode or manner in which they come to the intellect; they are not received through any natural cognitive operation but outside of it. Perhaps we can better understand all these distinct and particular "apprehensions" or "perceptions" as "species". All of them, to be sure, whether purely spiritual or received by the intellect through the senses, bespeak something distinct and particular for St. John of the Cross. They are all well defined and clear in the intentional order of knowledge, as opposed to "the obscure and general type of knowledge ... which is contemplation that is given in faith."[127] The obscure is opposed to the clear, and the general to the particular, and both of these attributes are predicated of the virtue of faith.

In chapter 10, book II of *The Ascent* the Mystical Doctor begins the lengthy practico-mystical treatment of faith, which is an application of the theoretico-mystical doctrine previously explained. We could say, indeed, that having stated the doctrinal principles, the Mystical Doctor now begins to discuss "mystical cases". It should be noted that these "cases" are taken either from his own experience or that of others, and, in the latter instance, from incidents known to him personally or taken from books. There are many books that treat of these matters and to some extent even give priority to such matters.

The Mystical Doctor's method of procedure is to describe the particular type of apprehension, investigate its nature, and then make a judgment as to how one should react to it so that it will not be an obstacle to divine union. Thus, in chapter 11 of book II, he raises the question of "those apprehensions that

---

[127] *The Ascent*, bk. II, chap. 10, no. 4.

come to the intellect by way of that which is presented supernaturally to the external senses". He first examines what they
are; he then asks whether they can come from God, and he
replies in the affirmative but advises great caution. Lastly, he
investigates their worth in relation to union with God, and here
he judges them with irrefutable logic and great severity, as is
his wont.

His general principle is that such things must not be sought
or desired. Why? For many reasons, all of which bear on the
manner in which the soul should relate to God. All these apprehensions are essentially corporeal, they pertain to a bodily
faculty, and therefore they are far removed from the spiritual.
Hence, when they are compared to faith, their slight value becomes apparent, and they must be rejected because of faith.
And here the Mystical Doctor states his fundamental reason:

> Faith is gradually diminished because things that are experienced by
> the senses derogate from faith; because faith, as we have said, tran-
> scends every sense.[128]

Thus, all apprehensions received through the senses fall far
short of faith, which bespeaks an intimate proportion between
the intellect and divinity. St. John of the Cross does not deny
that such things may come from God nor does he say that they
must be rejected because they are all illusions; not at all. He
simply evaluates them in relation to union with God, which has
already been well defined. Seen in this context, they reveal their
natural and even corporeal dimension; and even if they are
caused by God, they are received in a manner that is connatural
to man and not to God. As a result, the soul tends to be
promptly drawn to them, but this attraction derogates from
union with God, according to the principle that it is not the
thing itself that is a hindrance to union with God, but its
natural aspects so far as they occupy the will through the soul's

---

[128] *The Ascent*, bk. II, chap. 11, no. 7.

attraction to them. Then these supernatural apprehensions, with their natural modality that makes them naturally perceptible and desirable, are compared with faith, which is the proper means of union and, as a participation in the divine, establishes a proportion between the intellect and the divine. It is evident from the comparison that the corporeal apprehensions must be rejected and not desired or sought. Such is the answer to the question proposed and the reasons for the answer.

We should also note the manner in which the Mystical Doctor gives the answer. He advises the soul not to seek or be attached to such things because if they truly come from God, then God surely intends to produce some spiritual effect in the soul through them. However—and this is very important—the effect will be produced independently of the soul's "effort or capacity", because "this is something that is produced and works in the soul passively. Therefore whether the effect is produced or not does not depend on the soul's wanting or not wanting."[129]

Such is the way in which the laws of the divine activity in the soul are deduced from experience, and experience itself provides the principle of non-active intervention. Why is this so? The reason should be as clear as day, now that we have seen the strong statements in chapters 4 and 7 of book II. There we learned that whenever any faculty intervenes actively in that which is from God and therefore supernatural, it does so according to its own mode of operation, which is human and necessarily natural. This is the first practical principle, and the second derives from it: if the soul concentrates on the sensible aspect of supernatural apprehensions, "it does not receive so fully the spirit that they cause, which is impressed and preserved more surely by negating all things of sense, which are very different from pure spirit."[130]

[129] Ibid., bk. II, chap. 11, no. 6.   [130] Ibid., no. 7.

This "spirit" which God intends—presupposing that the apprehension comes from God—would be something that increases the degree of grace and charity in the soul, and consequently of union also. The sensible aspect contributes somewhat to this, but not directly; all it does is provide an adaptation to the human mode of operation. But at the same time the individual possesses faith in his intellect and faith, as we have seen, possesses an intrinsic proportion to the divine and is the proper means of union with God. As such, it requires the individual to reject everything on the sense order because that has no likeness to God. So it is that in this quasi-separation or elimination of everything communicated to the senses, faith fulfills its proper function and performs the operation that is peculiar to its nature.

We have here an example of how to solve a "mystical case" by the practical doctrine of the active night of the spirit. The case was very easy to resolve because the principles were immediately evident; however, the manner of working out the solution should be kept in mind. More difficult cases will be presented, but they are not discussed at this point since the second type of apprehensions also pertains to the sense order, but to the internal sense.

In chapter 12 of book II St. John of the Cross gives his teaching on the imagination and fantasy[131] and at the same time prepares for the succeeding chapters by explaining how the internal sense faculties function in discursive meditation. Chapters 13 to 15 contain the famous analysis of the transition from meditation to contemplation, which we shall examine later. Then, in chapter 16, the Mystical Doctor states that he will discuss "the imaginary apprehensions that are supernaturally

[131] As used by St. John of the Cross, imagination refers to the reception and recall of sense images by that faculty, and fantasy refers to the formation of new images out of the impressions already received. The latter is sometimes called the creative imagination. (Tr.)

represented in the phantasm." Here he repeats what he had said previously, namely, that "supernatural communications . . . likewise belong to the senses, since they come in the shape of forms, images and figures."[132] Consequently, he gives the same practical advice as he had given before: faith must, as it were, separate itself from and eliminate and negate everything of the sense order, which is present because of the natural weakness of the intellect. It must not seek the sensible in any way so that it can more clearly perceive the spiritual alone. "It is [the spirit] that leads the soul to union in faith, which is the proper means."[133]

St. John of the Cross treats of "the apprehensions of the intellect that come in a purely spiritual way" in chapter 23. They are so described because they are communicated directly to the spiritual part of the soul without passing through the external or internal senses. They are also known as "intellectual visions", as the Mystical Doctor explains: "To the spiritual eyes of the soul—namely, the intellect—all that is intelligible causes spiritual vision; since, as we have said, to understand a thing is to see it."[134]

The intellectual visions or apprehensions are manifested to the intellect after the manner of the species derived from the five external senses. Thus, what is presented to the intellect as something seen (that is, experienced by the intellect like something received through the sense of vision) is called a *vision*; that which is received after the manner of hearing is called a *locution*; the perception of something previously unknown is called a *revelation*; and lastly, anything received after the manner of the remaining external senses is called a *spiritual feeling*. Note, however, that these apprehensions are received "after the manner of" and not by means of the external senses because they are communicated directly to the intellect in a supernatural man-

---

[132] *The Ascent*, bk. II, chap. 16, no. 1.
[133] Ibid., no. 12.
[134] Ibid., bk. II, chap. 23, no. 2.

ner. It is a purely subjective impression that the apprehensions are received as if they had come through the external senses.

St. John of the Cross then states the practical norm regarding intellectual apprehensions: "From these, also . . . , it is necessary that we free the intellect, leading and directing it beyond them into the spiritual night of faith, to the divine and substantial union of God." This is the response we would expect from St. John of the Cross, in spite of the fact that he remarks almost immediately that "these apprehensions are nobler and more profitable and much more secure than the corporeal imaginary ones, since they are interior and purely spiritual and are less susceptible to the devil's intervention because they are communicated to the soul more purely and subtly, without any act of its own or of the imagination." [135]

Yet, St. John of the Cross is consistent in his teaching: all these things must be rejected in favor of the virtue of faith, which operates in the dark night and, by reason of its intimate proportion to divinity, surpasses any experience in which the natural faculties, however much purified, can find fruition and satisfaction. Faith, as we have seen, is the means of true and proper union with God, who by his essence incomparably transcends every created nature; for that reason faith surpasses even the most lofty mystical experience.

We cannot at this point go into further detail in analyzing the text, for that would take us beyond our stated purpose. We shall merely make a few observations, the first of which has to do with visions.

As stated in chapter 24, visions can have as their object either corporeal or incorporeal substances. The Mystical Doctor then makes a statement that will be of great value later on in judging the nature of mystical experience. He asserts that the incorporeal substances cannot be seen clearly by the intellect in this life but that they can be experienced to some extent in the

---

[135] Ibid., bk. II, chap. 23, no. 4.

substance of the soul. "They can be felt in the substance of the soul, with the gentlest touches and unions, all of which pertain to spiritual feelings."[136] It would seem that the word "substance" is not used here in the Scholastic sense but in an adapted sense, as applied to mystical experience.

As regards our subject of investigation, we find in this same chapter 24 a clear statement:

> These visions, since as they are of creatures, with which God has no essential likeness or proportion, cannot serve the intellect as a proximate means to union with God. Therefore the soul must be completely negative regarding them . . . in order that it may proceed by the proximate means, which is faith.[137]

Moreover, the Mystical Doctor affirms that although such visions may arouse the soul to the love of God, it is stimulated much more by faith, and faith itself will be much more deeply infused and rooted in the soul by the rejection of even the most lofty representations of created things. St. John of the Cross then makes some further observations that we shall cite and explain later, because they contain some explicit teaching on the increase of faith, together with hope and charity.

The Mystical Doctor begins to treat of revelations in chapter 25, and he distinguishes two kinds: "intellectual knowledge or understanding" and "manifestation of secrets and hidden mysteries of God". The former is of great value because it is "knowledge of God himself and delight in God himself. . . . For this kind of knowledge relates directly to God, and the soul has a sublime experience of some attribute of God."[138] The statement savors of *The Living Flame of Love*. As a matter of fact, these divine manifestations are "pure contemplation"; they are an effect of union with God and, indeed, "they are themselves that union, and to receive them is equivalent to a certain

---

[136] *The Ascent*, bk. II, chap. 24, no. 4.
[137] Ibid., no. 8.
[138] Ibid., bk. II, chap. 26, no. 3.

contact of the soul with the divinity. Hence it is God himself who is perceived and tasted there."[139] However, we shall omit what pertains to the composition and structure of the mystical experience as such.

As it progresses along the path to union, the soul is always accompanied by faith, and that is our primary concern: to know how faith intervenes in the aforementioned phenomena —faith, which is only a means in relation to the elements that, in the words of the Mystical Doctor, "are themselves union" or are "a part of the union".[140] And in regard to the supernatural knowledge that St. John is discussing here, the soul is instructed to act differently under the impetus of faith. It need not act negatively and reject the first type of apprehensions ("intellectual knowledge or understanding"), but should merely be humble and resigned and not cling to them as one's own. Such is the "just mean" that the virtue of faith should apply to the actual experience of union with God.

The Mystical Doctor then proceeds to discuss revelations in which, since they are strictly supernatural in cause, the soul knows with certitude unknown facts or happenings concerning created things, for example, the secrets of hearts. This type of knowledge is normally given by divine decree only to holy persons who are already in the state of union. Such gifts are known in theology as graces *gratis datae*. So far as the virtue of faith is concerned, St. John of the Cross makes the following judgment: "Knowledge such as this . . . can be of very little help for the progress of the soul on its journey to God if the soul is attached to it."[141] Then almost immediately he adds: "The soul should take great care always to reject this kind of

[139] Ibid., bk. II, chap. 26, no. 5.
[140] Cf. Ibid., no. 10.
[141] Ibid., bk. II, chap. 26, no. 18. The emphasis here is on supernatural intellectual knowledge that brings certitude to the knower about hidden or unknown events or facts. It is closely related to the spirit of prophecy and infused discernment of spirits. Cf. loc. cit., no. 11. (Tr.)

knowledge and endeavor to journey to God by the way of un-knowing." And the "way of unknowing" is the modality proper to faith.

According to the explanation given by the Mystical Doctor, the graces *gratis datae* (others are described in chapter 26, no. 12) may be indicative of the soul's union with God, but they are not necessarily so. Therefore they relate to union only extrinsically, and to desire them would be to step outside the path to union. The terminus of the path is the union itself, and the proper means for union of the intellect with God is faith. The conclusion follows logically when one carefully considers the following facts. Supernatural revelations concerning unknown facts or created things are granted by divine good will as graces *gratis datae*; usually, but not necessarily, they presuppose union of the soul with God; therefore it is evident that the soul should not desire or seek them. Such is the "just mean" or prudent judgment of the virtue of faith in regard to such revelations.

The role and function of faith is shown to be quite different in chapter 27, where St. John of the Cross discusses another type of revelation which he calls the "disclosure of secrets and hidden mysteries". This type of revelation pertains to the articles of our faith or to further revelations touching the course of events in general or in particular. Sometimes the deeper meaning of the truths of faith is revealed, "a manifestation or declaration of what has been revealed already".[142] But in this matter the Mystical Doctor is especially suspicious of possible diabolical intervention, particularly if something new and different is revealed. (St. John of the Cross was well acquainted with the excesses of the *alumbrados*.) For that reason he insists repeatedly on the necessity of submitting such things to the teaching and judgment of the Church.

The role of the Church in matters that touch the faith is not restricted to the objective proclamation of revealed truth; it also

[142] Ibid., bk. II, chap. 27, no. 2.

touches the intrinsic nature of the virtue of faith, as we shall see in a later analysis of the teaching of St. John of the Cross. For the present it suffices to note that this type of supernatural communication relates to the virtue of faith and for that reason it necessitates recourse to the authority of the Church, since revealed truths must be believed in the sense defined by the Church and proposed by the Church for belief and not because of any private revelation or interpretation. The basic reason for this teaching is that "it is very good for the soul not to desire to understand clearly many things pertaining to faith, so that it may preserve the merit of faith, pure and entire."[143] Note that sometimes the Mystical Doctor speaks of the merit of faith, but always with special reference to the attainment of union with God.

The third type of purely spiritual "apprehensions" is classified as locutions or "interior words", which St. John discusses in chapters 28 to 31. He divides locutions into various kinds: successive words, formal words and substantial words. He explains clearly the nature of each one, showing how they differ from one another and how they function in the intellect. The successive words or locutions always occur when the individual is recollected and is reflecting on some supernatural truth under the direction and guidance of the Holy Spirit, who assists in the formation of new concepts derived from the truth that is contemplated. The soul "successively forms in itself the other truths connected with the one on which it is thinking."[144] But even though these concepts are formed under the guidance of the Holy Spirit, there is always great danger of error, either because of intervention by the devil (and as a teacher of great experience, St. John of the Cross offers some signs by which one can distinguish locutions of diabolical origin from those supernaturally confected) or because of the limited capacity of

---

[143] Ibid., bk. II, chap. 27, no. 5.
[144] Ibid., bk. II, chap. 29, no. 1.

the intellect, which is often incapable of receiving and following the successive locutions without error, or because the locution is so subtle that the intellect lacks the natural facility to
formulate it properly.

But even if all the dangers are avoided and one can presuppose the guidance of the Holy Spirit in a given case, the value
of successive locutions is minimal when compared to faith. The
Mystical Doctor says as much in the following passage, the
force and meaning of which we shall apply to other matters as
well:

> Although it is true that in this illumination of truths [the Holy
> Spirit] communicates a certain light to the soul, the light of faith,
> which does not give clear understanding, is as different from this in
> quality as is purest gold from the basest metal, and in quantity as is
> the sea from a drop of water. For in the former, wisdom is commu-
> nicated concerning one or two or three truths, etc., but in the other,
> all the wisdom of God in general is communicated, namely, the Son
> of God, who communicates himself to the soul in faith.[145]

The text does not immediately compare successive locutions
with the virtue of faith, but with the obscure and general
knowledge—contemplation—which is given in faith. Therefore the full significance of the text will appear only when that
type of knowledge is investigated in greater detail. For the
present, however, the advice of the Mystical Doctor concerning
locutions is clear: they are not to be sought and the soul should
pay no heed to them, when the "abyss of faith" beckons to the
soul. The communication received from God through faith is
impeded by things that are particular, clear and of little value.
The solution is obvious from a comparison of the objective
value of the two types of knowledge to which the intellect is
united in the one and the other.

St. John of the Cross states his teaching on "formal locutions" in chapter 30, contrasting them with faith, which he de-

[145] *The Ascent*, bk. II, chap. 29, no. 6.

scribes as "the legitimate and proximate means to union with God".[146] As regards the third type, the "substantial words" or locutions (chapter 31), they cause in the soul what the words indicate—for example, when the Lord says, "Love me," the soul immediately experiences and truly receives love for God. The judgment of the Mystical Doctor concerning these substantial locutions is the same as he made concerning supernatural knowledge or apprehensions of God in chapter 26: they call for great humility and resignation. The substantial words are neither to be sought nor rejected, for when God wills to give them, they are very fruitful and contribute greatly to union.

The last type of the spiritual communications listed in book II, chapter 10, does not pertain directly and immediately to the intellect, but to the will. In chapter 32 St. John describes these communications as "spiritual feelings", supernaturally infused into the will, from which redound to the possible intellect "apprehensions and knowledge and understanding".[147] In themselves they are very profitable and they contribute to union, but they are not to be sought, for they would be sought in vain. God bestows such feelings when and to whom he wishes, and no human effort of the intellect can ever avail to produce them; rather, that would destroy the "delectable supernatural understanding". Therefore it is the function of the virtue of faith to keep the soul humble and passively resigned to God.

Having reviewed the various "apprehensions" or revelations that provide the material for the active night of the spirit, we can now ask how all of this pertains to the virtue of faith. It is already clear that the active night of the spirit is proper to the virtue of faith. This is evident from the fact that all the "perceptions" and "apprehensions" that must be rejected in this night pertain to the intellect, either immediately and directly or

---

[146] Ibid., bk. II, chap. 30, no. 5.
[147] Ibid., bk. II, chap. 32, no. 2.

somehow related to the intellect. It is there, in the intellect, that they encounter faith; and then, as our analysis demonstrates, when compared with the nature and function of faith, it becomes evident how they are to be handled in relation to the goal of union with God. However, they are not always handled in the same way. As we also saw from our analysis of the text, faith sometimes demands that they be rejected outright; at other times that they be submitted to the authority of the Church or the judgment of the confessor or spiritual director; or, finally, that the soul simply keep itself in a state of humility and resignation when God bestows something that contributes to union.

There is, in fact, something mysterious in contrasting faith with supernatural apprehensions, with the virtue of faith as the term of comparison. These phenomena are always intellectual or are related in some way to the intellect; but the virtue of faith is the proper means of uniting the intellect with God, and it therefore implies an intimate relation between the intellect and divinity. Consequently, the operations of the virtue of faith reveal its constitutive role, for it is through them that all the elements of the dark night are arranged in proper order or separated and eliminated. It is true that it is not an easy task to discern and explain how all these aspects are intrinsically dependent on faith or how they proceed from faith. Nevertheless, it is necessary assiduously to glean from the text anything that will shed light on this question.

At the very outset it should be noted that we are not concerned here with only a purely objective comparison of faith with the intentional and intrinsic value of the various types of supernatural apprehensions. Sometimes an objective comparison is made, as in book II, chapters 16 and 29, but that is only incidental. What is really of interest is the activity or operation that is grounded in the virtue of faith and proceeds from the very exigencies of faith. That, indeed, is the reason it is called the *active* night of the spirit, as is clearly stated in the text. What is more difficult to discern in the text is the nature of its dependence on faith, for the Mystical Doctor did not write with the speculative precision of systematic theology.

Nevertheless, even from an objective comparison one can see that the various distinct "apprehensions" are opposed to faith, to which is ascribed in book II, chapter 10, a "confused, general and dark knowledge". And the opposition occurs in the intellect itself. We already know something of the nature of the opposition from our study of book II, chapter 3, where we saw that the intellect remains in darkness when confronted with the revealed truths. The intellect is incapable of penetrating divinity and seeing it clearly by its own natural power, which remains unchanged under the excessive infused light of faith. Hence, even as the intellect attains to God through faith, at the same time it necessarily lacks the desired clarity of vision. Faith effects an essential elevation of the intellect but does not supply for its native insufficiency. Thus, the intimate relationship or proportion of the human intellect to divinity in this life comprises elements that are psychologically contrary but essentially commensurate. Such is the virtue of faith as seen in the texts of St. John of the Cross.

During the active night many kinds of particular and distinct "apprehensions" (which for the Mystical Doctor means they are limited to a certain mode or form of species or image) that come to the intellect coincide with the natural capacity and exigency of the intellect; therefore they can be received and retained by the intellect (cf. book II, chapters 16 and 17). In this respect they have a natural modality or aspect. But they also have this characteristic, namely, that they come in an extraordinary way—a supernatural manner, according to the Mystical Doctor. He does not deny their supernatural origin, at least in some cases.

It is precisely in this conjunction of the supernatural origin of the apprehensions with their limited and connatural aspect as received by the intellect that the Mystical Doctor sees great danger. The danger is not so much to faith itself, perhaps, but certainly to faith as the proper means for the union of the intellect with God; to faith which, according to its interior dynamism, is capable of providing that "general and obscure knowledge" which is contemplation.

In view of the great good of "the divine and substantial union of God",[148] faith must always negate these apprehensions, or better still, must regulate them in accordance with the exigencies of the union of the intellect with God, since faith alone provides the essential proportion between the intellect and God in this life. But at the same time, the essential proportion connotes that divinity is communicated in darkness.

Such is the logic of the active night of the spirit, from which follow certain characteristics proper to faith. We see, for example, that faith provides the internal proportion between the subject and the divine, and we can also see how it manifests this proportion in performing its unifying function. But since the intimate proportion is effected by faith, it follows that God cannot be manifested clearly to the intellect in this life; what the intellect sees clearly is necessarily limited, and hence not divine.

Thus the interdependence between the active night of the spirit and the virtue of faith is clearly demonstrated. We shall now see what can be deduced from the text of St. John of the Cross concerning the operation of that dark night.

First of all, the text indicates that the merit of faith and the virtue itself are increased by acts of abnegation regarding the clear and distinct apprehensions. Thus, the Mystical Doctor states:

> For, although it is true that the memory of them stimulates the soul to a certain love of God and to contemplation, it is aroused and elevated much more by pure faith and by detachment from them all in darkness, without the soul's knowing how or whence it comes to it.[149]

[148] *The Ascent*, bk. II, chap. 23, no. 4.
[149] *The Ascent*, bk. II, chap. 24, no. 8.

He states further that faith contributes much more to contemplation than does any vision and then, a little later, he speaks of the increase of the virtue of faith:

> And so it was that when faith was more deeply rooted and infused in the soul by means of that emptiness and darkness and detachment from all things, or spiritual poverty, all of which may be described as one and the same thing, at the same time the charity of God is more deeply rooted and infused in the soul. Therefore, the more the soul seeks obscurity and annihilation with regard to all the outward or inward things that it is capable of receiving, the more it is infused with faith and, consequently, love and hope, since these three theological virtues go together.[150]

The text obviously refers to the common theological teaching concerning the simultaneous increase of all the elements of the supernatural organism. It refers specifically to the increase of the theological virtues, which are intimately related to each other, so that when faith is increased, there is also an increase in hope and charity and in all the elements that dispose the soul for union with God.

For our purposes the text that is of primary importance is the one in which St. John states that faith is increased by means of the active night, "by means of that emptiness and darkness and detachment from all things". In other words, the abnegation practiced in the active night of the spirit causes an increase of faith.

We already know how this abnegation functions: the intellect is emptied of all intentional forms, which are proper to it in accordance with its nature, and it is precisely through that privation or abnegation of the intellect that faith is able to grow. We can conclude from this that, in the mind of the Mystical Doctor, the acts of abnegation are operations proper to the virtue of faith. However, a premise is missing: a virtue is increased by its acts. We do not find this explicitly stated in the works of

---

[150] Ibid.

St. John of the Cross, any more than we find an explanation of the psychology of habits. The omission is easily explained, however, because considering the intent of his writings, we should not expect to find detailed, speculative explanations. It suffices, then, to note the explicit connection between the increase of faith and the activity of the dark night of the spirit. We can deduce from this that St. John of the Cross considers the abnegation in regard to the intellect to be an operation of the virtue of faith. This is something new added to the consideration of faith that we saw in book II, chapter 3, but it is not foreign to it.

There, in chapter 3, after considering the incapacity of the intellect in this life to penetrate clearly the divine reality and make it intelligible, even with the light of faith, the act of faith was reduced psychologically to a firm assent based on absolute certitude. This assent, as we have seen, is something positive, because of the certitude bestowed by the divine light, but also and especially because through that assent the intellect adheres to the unseen divinity. At the same time this implies the total insufficiency of the intellect to assimilate the divine reality. We conclude, therefore, that the assent spoken of in chapter 3 is an assent of the intellect to the unseen.

Now, similar acts can be found in the operation of the dark night of the spirit, not in the same sense as described in chapter 3, but for the same reason. The fundamental reason for the abnegation of all "clear and distinct apprehensions" is that they are something proper to the intellect according to its natural mode of operation. They are connatural to it in that respect. But the divine reality cannot be reduced to the natural level; it cannot be presented to the intellect in a particularized and distinct modality; and therefore the divine reality, so far as it can be present to the intellect in this life in an intentional mode, can never be there as something "seen".[151]

---

[151] The following text explains this matter more fully: "In the perception of these aforementioned forms, they are always represented, as we have said, in some limited mode and manner. But the wisdom of God, to which the intellect

This is the basic reason for the necessity of abnegation. The intellect in this life cannot adhere to divinity as something seen, and if it does adhere to something seen, that something is not God; it has left the path to union with God. But in all the distinct apprehensions, the intellect does adhere to something seen—in different ways according to the various types of apprehensions—and hence in order to keep to the path to union, the soul must negate all that is seen. Such is the interdependence between faith and the activity of the night of the spirit. Our analysis has shown why the active night of the spirit is attributed to the virtue of faith. Indeed, whatever abnegation occurs in that night is proper to faith, however many other elements may intervene.

On the other hand, since we are now certain that the activity of the active night of the spirit is properly attributed to the virtue of faith, we can now deduce some particulars concerning that activity. Faith consists essentially in the assent to that which is not seen, but there is another aspect to be considered. The very act of assent implies a resignation or submission of the intellect to the divine. It cannot penetrate the divine truths, but by reason of the excessive light infused with faith, the intellect assents to them. Such seems to be the explanation of faith's assent as given in book II, chapter 3.

Looked at from another angle, in the operation of the dark night of the spirit the excessive light of faith enables the intellect to overcome its natural tendency for particular and distinct

---

is to be united, has no mode or manner; it has no limitations, and it cannot be grasped in any distinct and particular knowledge, for it is utterly pure and simple. And since, in order that these two extremes, the soul and divine wisdom, may be united, they will have to have some degree of likeness between them. Hence it follows that the soul must also be pure and simple, not limited or attached to any particular kind of knowledge, nor modified by any limitation of form, species and image. As God is not contained in any image or form, nor in any particular kind of knowledge, so the soul, in order to be united with God, cannot be restricted to any form or distinct knowledge" (*The Ascent*, bk. II, chap. 16, no. 7).

knowledge so that it can rise above itself to a knowledge of divine things. This necessarily implies a severe abnegation, which is the chief characteristic of the dark night as described by St. John of the Cross in book I, chapter 3. Our previous analysis has already revealed to us the essential note of faith as an "assent to the unseen". But now the intrinsic proportion between faith and divinity shines forth amid the difficulties and dangers of the dark night of the spirit.

Although, we repeat, we can conclude nothing from the text as regards the other supernatural elements involved in the activity of the dark night of the spirit, we can be certain of their dependence on faith and their relation to faith. This gives us a new perspective on the operation of the virtue of faith. The text does not give us grounds for studying faith first as a habit and then to study the acts of faith, but it does allow us to draw some conclusions concerning the activity of faith.

As regards other questions to be investigated, such as the internal structure of the act of faith according to the Mystical Doctor, nothing definite can be drawn from the texts studied thus far. As to the question concerning the source of the abnegation of the dark night and the faculty in which it occurs, St. John of the Cross speaks only in general and vague terms, such as "not to desire", "not to admit", "to negate", "to darken" and so forth. However, when he begins his treatment of the dark night, the Mystical Doctor does fix certain limits. He says: "It must surely be like a temporal, natural and spiritual death and annihilation of the will's esteem for everything, for that is the source of all negation."[152] This shows that the highest and most intimate degree of abnegation of the dark night is that of the will, but this is far from describing the inner dynamism of the activity proper to faith or of that highly praised abnegation of the dark night of the spirit that proceeds from it. We know that the essential elements of the dark night of the spirit belong

---

[152] *The Ascent*, bk. II, chap. 7, no. 6.

to the virtue of faith, but we do not know enough about the other elements that function together with faith and what they contribute to the dark night. We know, of course, that the other elements are present and that they grow together with faith, as we saw in the text cited from book II, chapter 24, but what they do actively is something we cannot determine from the text.

One thing, however, we can affirm at this point: all of the activity of faith previously described is directed to charity. First of all, the active night of the spirit occurs on the path to union and leads to union, but the unifying power properly speaking—as we have frequently noted—is love. With all the influence that the virtue of faith exerts on union—an influence greatly emphasized in the works of St. John of the Cross—faith is a means of union only in relation to charity. This is evident from the first chapters of book I of *The Ascent*, where St. John states that faith is the means of union, a medium through which the soul must pass, wherein the soul "abides in faith alone, but not to the exclusion of charity".[153] This has not yet been sufficiently emphasized.

The descriptive title of chapter 9, book II, affirms more explicitly how "faith is the proximate and proportionate means for the intellect whereby the soul can attain to the divine union of love".[154] Each of these virtues—faith and charity—has its proper function in respect to union. The soul is united with God through charity, but faith is necessary in the intellect, serving as the proper and proportionate means of union for this faculty. Hence, the unifying power of faith, as a means of union, pertains properly to the intellect. But in the active night of the spirit, the intellect experiences the abnegation of its natural functions through the power and activity of faith vivified by charity. The effect of the abnegation redounds to love,

---

[153] *The Ascent*, bk. I, chap. 2, no. 3.
[154] Ibid., bk. II, chap. 9, title.

through which the soul is properly united with God and transformed into God by participation. It is therefore evident that as
the root and source of the abnegation of the intellect, the virtue
of faith contributes something to the virtue of charity. Thus, St.
John of the Cross says:

> However much value they have in themselves [referring to clear and
> distinct apprehensions], they cannot contribute as much to the love
> of God as the smallest act of living faith and hope performed in the
> emptiness and renunciation of all things.[155]

Note the phrase, "contribute to the love of God". It is certain
therefore that faith does help charity insofar as it is the root and
source of the abnegation of the intellect's natural tendency to
know the forms presented to it clearly and distinctly. This is
evident if we recall the meaning of the dark night in general—
night as abnegation—for we know that its motivation is related
to love. Indeed, love requires the dark night, lest any natural
object occupy the will so that love of self excludes divine love
and, as a result, the transforming union. It is in this sense, then,
so far as it connotes the renunciation of every species that can
naturally illumine the intellect, that faith helps charity in the
attainment of union.

It is also clear from the principles of St. John of the Cross
that the function of faith in abnegation depends ultimately on
the will. We already know from our general discussion of the
dark night as described in book I, chapters 3 and 4, that the
entire *raison d'être* of the dark night rests on that abnegation.
Moreover, we have an explicit statement of the Mystical Doctor to that effect: "The intellect and the other faculties cannot
admit or reject anything unless the will intervenes."[156]

The preceding text touches our investigation directly because
it portrays clearly the role of the will in the abnegation of the

---

[155] *The Ascent*, bk. III, chap. 8, no. 5.
[156] Ibid., bk. III, chap. 34, no. 1.

active night of the spirit. Moreover, it explains more fully the meaning of the passages previously cited; for example, how the act of abnegation, "performed in the emptiness and renunciation of all things", which is, however, an act of living faith, assists charity, which in turn leads to the union of likeness. Since the act of abnegation depends ultimately on the will and the will is operative through love, it is easy to see the connection between that which occurs in the intellect by way of the abnegation of particular species, which is the function of faith, and that which occurs in the will, where the negation of one form implies the affirmation of the opposite form. The dark night is thus necessary for union, for when the will effectively causes the abnegation of the particular species that is connatural to the intellect and to the natural appetite, the will itself is more deeply penetrated by the opposite form; it adheres to it more closely and is more radically informed by it. All this is implied in the phrase, "contribute to the love of God".[157]

All of this presupposes that one is acting with an informed or vivified faith, as St. John of the Cross observes in book III, chapter 8. As a matter of fact, it is always and only a vivified faith that is discussed in all his works, as he stated at the very beginning: "in faith, but not to the exclusion of charity".[158] This is something we should always keep in mind. Nevertheless, the texts already analyzed treat of faith alone—always informed or vivified faith, to be sure—because St. John was not discussing there (for example, book II, chapters 3, 8 and 9) how faith helps charity. Here, however, he treats this aspect *ex professo*. Previously he discussed faith vivified by charity; now it is a question of the life of faith through charity, and this necessarily involves the operation of the will.

---

[157] Perhaps we could apply here the explanation given in the famous text of *The Ascent*, bk. II, chap. 15, no. 4: "When the loving soul lacks the things of the natural order, then it is infused with divine things, on both the natural and supernatural levels, because there can be no vacuum in nature."

[158] *The Ascent*, bk. I, chap. 2, no. 3.

In this respect we should note a curious passage in *The Spiritual Canticle*, chapter 31, no. 10: "Faith, symbolized by the eye, is rooted in the intellect by faith and in the will by love."[159] Evidently this refers to faith that lives by charity, where love exercises an intimate and continuous influence and faith receives therein its mode of union with God. This should be carefully noted, for we shall not find any more texts that speak of faith vivified by charity, but only of the life of faith through charity.

From all the texts we have examined that refer to the function of faith in the active night of the spirit, can we conclude anything concerning the psychological structure of faith? It would seem not; first of all, because we have already shown that the active night of the spirit involves the virtue of faith to such an extent it consists essentially in the activity of faith. Secondly, the acts of faith in this instance are specifically acts of abnegation with respect to the intellect, in which faith is rooted. Thirdly, acts of abnegation in any faculty are dependent on the will, as the Mystical Doctor teaches. Therefore the acts of abnegation exercised in the intellect by faith during the dark night of the spirit depend ultimately on the will, because the intellect cannot reject or admit anything without the intervention of the will.

All of this relates to the subject of our study, and yet we cannot deduce from it any conclusions concerning the psychological structure of the act of faith. For example, we cannot determine what pertains to the intellect and what pertains to the will. All of these elements are contained in the doctrine of St. John of the Cross but only latently, so that we cannot deduce explicit conclusions based on this or that work. Moreover, it

---

[159] The passage is found only in the second redaction, Canticle B. E. Allison Peers points out that three manuscripts have a variant reading that seems to supply something omitted by a copyist: "For faith, signified by the eye, is rooted in the intellect, *and love, signified by the hair, in the will. Hence there is union in the intellect* by faith and in the will by love." (Tr.)

seems that the Mystical Doctor did not intend to treat of this particular aspect of faith. He surely intended to treat of the nature of faith, and even of its metaphysical aspects as well as faith as an obscure habit, but he did not discuss the psychological structure of the act of faith. There are, of course, many psychological overtones, but they relate to another question which we shall soon treat, namely, the intimate connection and mutual influence between faith and love in the path to union. It is from this perspective that St. John of the Cross comments on the role of the will in the abnegation of the intellect by faith. But most, if not all, the statements refer to love, and there is nothing that deals concretely and directly with the psychological structure of the act of faith.

Last of all it should be noted that there is no *ex professo* treatment of the act of faith as such in the works of St. John of the Cross, although we find constant mention of the activity of the virtue of faith. Yet the operation of faith is not always clearly distinguished from the acts of the other supernatural powers so that we can isolate its distinctive characteristics. This is certainly the case with his treatment of the active night of the spirit and also, but in a different way, with his discussion of contemplation. We can deduce from some particulars concerning the nature and activity of faith, but usually—and especially evident in the later works—the Mystical Doctor describes the operations of all the supernatural powers taken together so far as they relate to the path to union. For that reason our investigation is somewhat hampered.

NOTES

1. This lengthy analytical study of the dark night in the works of St. John of the Cross was necessary because, although the word "night" is used as a symbol and not always in exactly the same sense, nevertheless, the reality behind the symbol is of

utmost importance for understanding the mystical theology of St. John of the Cross. It also has a special bearing on the question we are investigating.

The "dark night" permeates the entire teaching of St. John of the Cross; it expresses his attitude toward all reality, both natural and supernatural; it is experienced by the soul tending to union with God and is in fact an indispensable requirement for union and for progress towards union. It is in regard to the last aspect that the dark night is intimately related to the virtue of faith; indeed, it is effected by faith, explained and justified by faith, and ultimately dissipated by faith. Consequently, without a precise analysis of the dark night as related directly to the virtue of faith, it would not be possible to proceed to a deeper study of faith itself. Therefore, after our lengthy consideration of the dark night, we wish to make some important observations that are pertinent to the matter at hand.

2. We have already stated that in the present texts we are not dealing with the virtue of faith vivified by charity but with faith as lived through charity. Some of the texts have already indicated the relationship between these two theological virtues, and we found a manifestation of it in the active night of the spirit. We know that faith intervenes in that night by a special type of abnegation of the intellect, which, in its natural state in the body-soul composite, tends to the limited species perceived through the senses and terminates in the essence of the material thing that is known. Faith, on the other hand, because of its intimate proportion of likeness to divinity, penetrates the intellect intimately but obscurely with an unlimited form or species and is therefore in opposition to the natural tendency of the intellect. In order that this opposition be effective, the privation of the intellect is necessary.

As we have already seen, the privation or abnegation of the intellect is properly the work of faith. It is effected by the divine form's being present to the intellect in a hidden manner, or better still, it is attained by the intellect in darkness. The privation is caused by the presence of divinity and the concomitant darkness. As an object of the intellect, the divine reality is incompatible with distinct, particular species because they are limited; and herein lies the reason for the darkness which during this life necessarily accompanies knowledge of infinite, unlimited divinity. Intellectual darkness prevails because it is in darkness that the divine reality is possessed.

The privation or abnegation of the intellect proceeds ultimately from the will; that is, the intellect does not perform any act of abnegation without the intervention of the will. But—and here is the heart of the matter—together with the negation of the clear, particular species received by the intellect, there is an affirmation of the divine form as known through faith in its unlimited darkness. Hence the will, which is operative in this abnegation, at the same time that it receives the divine form present in the intellect through faith in a hidden and obscure manner, also receives through faith the essential proportion to divinity and adheres to the divine reality through love. We are dealing here with vivified faith which, according to *The Spiritual Canticle*, "is rooted in the intellect by faith and in the will by love."[160] From this follows the entire process that is characteristic of love: the assimilation of the lover to the beloved and attainment of union.

We have tried to show how the text of St. John of the Cross describes with precision the mode or the mechanism, as it were, by which the participation in the divine is transferred from faith in the intellect to love in the will. It is true that the explanation directly touches only a few particular cases, such as those mentioned by the Mystical Doctor regarding the active night of the spirit, where faith intervenes in the abnegation of the intellect.

[160] *Spiritual Canticle*, chap. 31, no. 10. See footnote 159.

However, the mechanism by which the divine form is transferred from the intellect, where it is concealed in the obscurity
of faith, to the will, where it is received through love—thus
producing the effect of a union of likeness—can also be applied
to situations outside the dark night and abnegation.

We have seen that the precise reason why the participated
divine form is transferred from the intellect to the will is not
the abnegation as such, but abnegation as a function of the virtue of faith. Hence the positive function of faith is that in negating the particular and clear intentional species, it presents to the
intellect the divine form which is in darkness and obscurity.
And faith can do this because of the "essential likeness" or
supernatural participation in the excessive light that we have
discussed previously. Then the divine form attracts the movement of the will.

Such seems to be the explanation of the life of faith through
charity, not in its total content, but touching some of its elements or, we might say, its basic cell structure. To put it another way, it is a description of the mechanism by which the
divine form is transferred from faith to love. The explanation is
drawn from concrete cases of the night of the spirit and can
readily be deduced from his text, where it is implicit. It would
also appear that it can be applied to the entire path to union
because according to St. John of the Cross the whole path is
night and abnegation; therefore it requires the intervention of
the will, as he states in book III, chapter 34 of *The Ascent*.

The entire journey to union with God is enveloped in the
darkness of faith; darkness covers all the steps of the soul to
God, who is already possessed by the intellect in the darkness
of faith. All these elements are operative, although their mutual
relationship is not always as evident as in the active night of the
spirit; but they are always present. This is the sense in which
we should understand the words of the Mystical Doctor: "God
. . . by means of the second night, which is faith, continually
communicates himself to the soul in such a secret and intimate

manner that he becomes another night to the soul."[161] St. John is not speaking here about the dark night of faith, which is the active night of the spirit, but simply of the virtue of faith as such, whereby God comes to the intellect and is united to the soul. Such is the way in which the divine intimacy or interior communication of the divine through faith, ordained to the union of charity, is to be understood according to the principles stated in the text of St. John of the Cross.

3. We have already stated that the text of St. John of the Cross does not warrant our saying anything about the psychological structure of faith with complete evidence, but some things can be deduced from the text. Many of the passages that treat of the active night of the spirit say something about the psychological aspect of the virtue of faith. Actually, the activity attributed to the virtue of faith is very special. If we accept what is usually taught about faith, namely, that its external act is to *confess the faith* and its internal act is *to believe*, then we must necessarily state that the type of activity attributed to faith during the active night of the spirit is authentic and corresponds to the very nature of faith. For if faith consists in the excessive light that attains to the divine essence and to revealed truths, and is at the same time a darkness of the intellect caused by the excessive light in the natural faculty, then it would seem that there is no other activity that corresponds as well to the interior "proportion" of faith as the activity of the night of the spirit.

It is a question of the intellect's negating every limited species so that it may affirm the unlimited divinity. Therefore the acts of darkness—if we may so speak—or the acts of the dark night, are exercised precisely as proportionate to divinity, the light of which is shared through faith. Moreover, the active night of the spirit proceeds immediately from the interior adequation that the human intellect enjoys through faith in respect to the divin-

---

[161] *The Ascent*, bk. I, chap. 2, no. 4.

ity that is possessed essentially. Such activity pertains directly and immediately to the nature of the virtue of faith, but how it proceeds from faith and what is its psychological structure, this is not clearly explained in the text of the Mystical Doctor. But we can and should at least point out the fact of a close correlation.

4. Having studied the activity and function of the virtue of faith as seen from our analysis of the dark night, we shall now investigate the specific dimension of faith that is manifested there. According to the Mystical Doctor, faith dominates every [religious] experience; indeed, in a sense it is superior to every experience, even that which is attributed to union, of which faith is a part. Faith does not negate or reject the experience, but on the other hand one should not desire the experience. Why? Because then it would become something that is the object of a natural desire, and since the measure of faith is participation in divinity, such a desire is alien to the virtue of faith.

It is here that faith is especially manifested as possessing an "essential likeness" to God, not merely as a metaphysical constitutive of faith, but as a dynamic element that is truly operative in faith, indicating a precise mode of action for the soul tending toward union through faith. Then the "essential likeness" is not only predicated of the virtue of faith, but one experiences the fact that through faith the soul participates to some degree in the divine reality that can be compared to no created or natural thing. And this divine reality, existing in faith, establishes the norm for the unifying power of faith so that the virtue of faith, participating as it does in the divine reality, is capable of leading the soul to union with God. All this is evident not only from the text and from the nonrepugnance of the terms, but from the very activity that is an exigency of faith.

The properly divine aspect of faith, which is clearly stated in *The Ascent*, book II, chapters 4, 16, 29 and elsewhere, is a distinctive characteristic of the teaching of St. John of the Cross.

We have frequently described it as the intimate "proportion" that exists between the intellect and the divine because that term expresses very well the substantially supernatural nature of faith and at the same time its habitual darkness in relation to the intellect. This is especially evident in the activity of the dark night.

5. We wish also to refer to some points that are not explicitly treated in the writings of the Mystical Doctor but are implied in his overall treatment of the active night of the spirit. We refer to the basis for the distinction between supernatural entities. And once again, we should note that the distinctions are not deduced *a priori* but are drawn from experience.

The question is asked: why must one reject the clear and particular apprehensions that are supernatural in origin? St. John of the Cross replies that in their intentional modality they correspond to a natural faculty and are therefore connatural to the human faculty.[162]

We then ask: what is to be said of the virtue of faith in this respect? St. John of the Cross answers throughout all of these chapters that there is no proportion or connaturality between that which faith represents in the intentional order and the intellect or any other human faculty. Consequently, he speaks of the essential "excess" that characterizes faith, for faith consists in a divine communication, an impression of divinity on the intellect. This is the substance of faith, which is supernatural; but the mode of expression is that of darkness to the intellect, and in that respect faith transcends the natural powers.

Is there not contained in this opposition and comparison that we have seen so clearly in the course of our analysis the classical distinction between the supernatural *quoad modum* and the supernatural *quoad essentiam*? It would seem so, and this beyond any doubt. But the Mystical Doctor never mentions the distinction

---

[162] Cf. *The Ascent*, bk. II, chap. 16, no. 7; chap. 4.

explicitly, and perhaps for this reason his testimony has greater value. Without using any technical terminology, but relying exclusively on experience and practice, the virtue of faith is placed on the level of the supernatural *quoad substantiam*; that is, it is substantially a supernatural power, but it works through the human intellect in a natural way.

6. In view of the foregoing explanation, it is clear why the Mystical Doctor states repeatedly that faith is inaccessible to the influence of the devil. That is why he says in book II, chapter 1 of *The Ascent* that the soul goes forth "by the secret ladder, disguised"—that is, by faith—and that the soul therefore cannot be impeded by temporal things or by the devil. But when it is a question of "apprehensions", there is always danger of the devil's intervention. In faith there is something to which the devil, for all his intelligence, has no access; and it is this element that can infallibly lead the soul to union with God. "Going forth beyond every limit of nature and reason in order to ascend by this divine ladder of faith, which reaches and penetrates even the heights of God."[163]

"The obscure and general knowledge, which is contemplation that is given in faith"

It should be noted at the outset that it is not now a question of faith alone. The treatment of contemplation introduces the operation of other supernatural virtues by which contemplation is experienced. They are intimately connected with contemplation and actively cooperate in it; therefore it is not easy to isolate the virtue of faith from the other virtues and consider it separately. In doing so one would always run the risk of attributing to faith the work of another virtue, or vice versa. Moreover, the

[163] Ibid., bk. II, chap. 1, no. 1.

general description given above does not help much here. The Mystical Doctor gives a description of contemplation that is vivid, penetrating and authentic, but precisely because of that, it does not lend itself to a strictly scientific analysis. But from what we already know about the virtue of faith we are able to investigate the "contemplation that is given in faith", and for the very reason that it is given in faith. From this point of view our investigation may give us some new insights concerning the nature of faith and at the same time corroborate our previous conclusions.

The first thing we must say is that we are now entering into the discussion of prayer properly speaking and not as formerly, where it was a question of the faith that lives by charity or some aspect of the role of faith in the dark night of the spirit. We are here speaking of interior prayer or meditation, which, according to St. John of the Cross, eventually yields to contemplation. For the latter, the Mystical Doctor uses various descriptions: "obscure and general type of knowledge"; "loving attentiveness upon God"; "loving general knowledge of God"; "contemplation". Terms such as these are found in various places throughout his works, but we are particularly interested in the relationship between contemplation and the virtue of faith, repeated constantly by St. John of the Cross. Sometimes, in fact, he identifies contemplation with faith, as when he speaks of "this dark and loving knowledge, which is faith."[164] Perhaps we should also note the adjectives that he most often uses to describe contemplative knowledge: obscure, general, confused and loving. It is under these aspects that we must seek the role of faith in contemplation.

In book II, chapter 12 of *The Ascent*, the Mystical Doctor treats in general of discursive prayer or meditation, wherein the soul uses the inferior faculties: the senses, the imagination and the fantasy. In the succeeding chapters (13–15), he discusses the

[164] *The Ascent*, bk. II, chap. 24, no. 4.

transition from meditation to contemplation and gives three signs by which the transition is indicated. These signs also serve as a key to understanding his doctrine on contemplation and will perhaps throw some light on the role of faith. The three signs are as follows:

> 1) The first sign is the realization that one can no longer meditate or discurse with the imagination nor take pleasure therein as he did formerly; rather, he finds aridity in that which formerly captivated the senses and brought him sweetness.
>
> 2) The second sign is a realization that one has no desire to fix his meditation or his senses on other particular objects, exterior or interior. I do not mean that the imagination neither comes nor goes— for even during deep recollection it usually moves freely—but that the soul has no pleasure in deliberately fixing it on other objects.
>
> 3) The third and surest sign is that the soul takes pleasure in being alone, with loving attentiveness upon God, without any particular consideration but with inward peace, quiet and rest, and without any acts and exercises of the faculties of memory, intellect and will—or at least without discursive acts, that is, without passing from one thing to another. The soul is alone, with an attentiveness and the general, loving knowledge we mentioned, but without any particular knowledge or understanding of the object.
>
> These three signs, at least, the spiritual person should observe in himself simultaneously before he can safely abandon the state of meditation and sense and enter that of contemplation and spirit.[165]

We can readily detect in these signs certain elements we have already noted. They can be classified into two groups. The first group comprises those which pertain to the intellect and knowledge. Here the Mystical Doctor insists on the disappearance of the concrete, particular elements that pertain to the senses and their replacement by that general knowledge which is "without any particular knowledge or understanding of the object."

[165] *The Ascent*, bk. II, chap. 13, nos. 2–5.

The last words clearly describe the condition of both the subject and the object. In that general knowledge the intellect does not perceive the object, since it lacks any particular understanding. We are once again faced with the problem noted previously, namely, the connaturality of the intellect in relation to the particular, limited form as known. This is the natural proportion of the human intellect in this life, and if the particular intentional form is lacking, the object of knowledge necessarily disappears. The same principles apply here as we have seen previously.

The second group of elements that are significant in the transition from meditation to contemplation pertain to the affective or appetitive order. The soul no longer finds any satisfaction in discursus and in particular considerations; therefore it can no longer meditate. Rather, its love is centered on a general attentiveness to God, accompanied by a general knowledge that is permeated with love. Here, for the first time, we see that the transition is marked by elements that we have already analyzed in relation to faith. But now they are manifested with a subtle difference, related as they are to interior prayer, where the elements most connatural to the faculties and arising for the most part from the sensate order are replaced by others that lack that connaturality. Nevertheless, they are something objective that can occupy the faculties. The Mystical Doctor insists very much on this replacement or substitution as the soul passes from meditation to contemplation.

Consequently, all three signs must be present simultaneously, and not just one or the other, to justify the transition from meditation to contemplation, but the third sign is the most important. The reason is obvious; it is precisely there that the previous elements disappear and the new ones take their place. Unless this happens, there can be no transition to contemplation. The first and second signs refer to the elements that have disappeared, but if the third sign is not verified, the soul would remain in a vacuum.

And this could happen, as we shall see in *The Dark Night*; therefore the soul must be vigilant lest this occur through its own fault. In that case it would be seriously deceiving itself, mistaking indolence for the activity of God.

In chapter 14 the Mystical Doctor explains the fittingness and, indeed, the necessity of the three signs, giving reasons why they should be discernible in the passage from meditation to contemplation. As regards the first sign, there is a twofold reason for its necessity. First of all, "the soul has received all the spiritual good that it can from the things of God by way of meditation and discursus." The spiritual good derived from the things of God seems to refer to the order of knowledge and also to the order of love. This is evident if we take into account the passage in book III, chapter 13, where "substance and spirit" unite with the faculties of the soul in "true understanding and love", whereas the faculties previously acted upon the "rind and accident" which must be abandoned.[166] Ultimately, when the operations of the faculties cease, the soul "receives the substance known and loved beneath those forms."

Similarly, in the text under consideration, discursive meditation consists in acts of knowledge and of love wherein the intellect and will function with the aid of the lower sense faculties. Meditation is thus characterized by the activity of the senses, and when it is directed to the consideration of revealed truths, the soul receives them so far as they are perceptible to the senses and imagination. The "spiritual good" received by the soul will be in proportion to the means used. Hence the soul acquires a certain knowledge as well as a certain delight in the revealed truths, for delight usually accompanies such knowledge, but in the measure that corresponds to the activity of the sense faculties. Such is the way in which the Mystical Doctor explains the first reason for the necessity of the first sign.

[166] Cf. *The Ascent*, bk. III, chap. 13, no. 4.

The second reason touches a more technical aspect of mental prayer. Through the repetition of acts of prayer, of "loving knowledge"—of the sensible order, to be sure—the soul has acquired the habit of interior prayer, the habit of "loving knowledge". As the Mystical Doctor says: "The soul at this time possesses the spirit of meditation both substantially and as a habit."[167]

The two reasons for the first sign are not of equal significance for our study. The first one refers to the objective content of that which is received through meditation; the second pertains to an acquired subjective disposition, namely, the facility in making acts of loving knowledge. Both reasons help us understand why the soul can no longer meditate as it was wont to do formerly.[168] It has now received all the benefits it can from the practice of meditation. We exclude from the general norm those exceptional cases in which suddenly and without any effort on their part, souls have received from God the grace of infused contemplation.

St. John of the Cross does not give a lengthy explanation of the second sign. He does, however, point out a curious detail in the transition from meditation to contemplation. Although the imagination still functions and produces its phantasms, the will finds no pleasure in them; rather it is "troubled thereby, because its peace and joy are disturbed." This is indicative of a disproportion between the superior and inferior parts of the soul and the will's displeasure is explained by the disjunction that suddenly occurs between the sense faculties and the higher, rational powers. Previously the rational part of the soul obtained satisfaction and pleasure through the exercise of the lower sense faculties, and it adjusted itself to their mode of

[167] Ibid., bk. II, chap. 14, no. 2.

[168] It should be noted that the texts we have been studying provide the basis for the assertion by the Carmelite school that St. John of the Cross taught the possibility of an acquired contemplation. This, however, does not pertain to our study except remotely.

operation; now it suddenly experiences dissatisfaction with the sensitive faculties because their mode of operation no longer suffices.

The type of pleasure experienced is always dependent on the type of knowledge acquired. Therefore, the soul does experience some pleasure when it receives a spiritual good, as the Mystical Doctor states in chapter 14, and when this happens, the intellect begins to transcend the particular species presented to it by the imagination. As a result, the will no longer finds pleasure in the material provided by the imagination.

The result is that the intellect, and by consequence the will also, begins to find difficulty in accommodating itself to the operations of the sense faculties; both faculties begin to rise above the material offered by the senses as regards revealed truths. Then it is that the first sign is clearly manifested: the individual can no longer meditate or think discursively. The intellect has, to some extent, lost its power or facility for utilizing sense knowledge. The soul can no longer meditate or discurse as before and now finds no sweetness or pleasure in meditation as it did previously. Why is this so? St. John of the Cross replies: "Because up to that time [the soul] had not arrived at the spiritual reality that was reserved for it."[169]

In other words, up to this time the soul had not attained to the spiritual substance, to the very essence, although it had been occupied with spiritual things. Meditation with the use of the senses and the imagination had kept the soul on the periphery of revealed truths, and all its previous efforts were spent on adapting those truths to the medium of sense knowledge. That such is the meaning of the passage under consideration is evident from a reading of chapter 12, where St. John explains the role of the imagination in discursive meditation. There one will see how the revealed truths are adapted to perception by the

---

[169] Cf. The Ascent, bk. II, chap. 14, no. 1.

sense faculties. Moreover the passage quoted helps to explain the objective content or the "spiritual good" that the soul received through its meditations and discursus.

However, it is the subjective aspect that is significant, for the soul has now acquired a certain facility in the practice of meditation, for now it always results in a loving knowledge. Yet the meditation still involves the operation of the senses, and the knowledge of revealed truths acquired by use of the imagination arouses a sensible love regarding those truths. The words of the Mystical Doctor still apply here, and they are of great significance for our study: "Because up to that time [the soul] had not arrived at the spiritual reality that was reserved for it."

Thus, an examination of the first and second signs reveals the following: in the transition from meditation to contemplation there is a disjunction between the higher and lower faculties of the soul due to the different mode of knowing and considering revealed truths in one's interior prayer. The former sensate mode is suddenly lacking to the intellect and, consequently, to the will. As a result the higher faculties no longer experience the accustomed quietness and pleasure but are conscious of a disorientation.

Having considered the first two signs, we shall now investigate the third, which, according to St. John of the Cross, is the most important for verifying the transition from meditation to contemplation. It is necessary in order that the deficiencies on the sense level can be replaced by new and more profound elements. The third sign consists in the general, confused, obscure and loving knowledge that is now the object of our investigation. St. John of the Cross states that he does not think it necessary to say a great deal about the third sign in chapter 14 because he will treat of it later, when discussing the various kinds of supernatural knowledge. He refers to a part of *The Ascent* that he never actually completed, and as a result we do not find any *ex professo* treatment of contemplation. Nevertheless, there are many places in which he treats of contemplation in passing, and from these references we can learn a great deal about his doctrine.

St. John of the Cross begins his explanation of the third sign by distinguishing the operations of the higher faculties in meditation and in contemplation. In the former, they utilize the sense faculties and engage in discursus; in the latter, the intellect, memory and will are all united in the general knowledge that characterizes the third sign. The knowledge resulting from the union of all three faculties working together produces a certain fruition or pleasure, a kind of quietude and satisfaction due to the fact that the operations of the lower faculties have ceased and do not intervene. This is the first characteristic of that "loving knowledge" as seen from the superior faculties that enjoy it. Here also the difference between meditation and contemplation is seen as a distinction between the effort to achieve something and "that which has already been received and effected in the spiritual faculties."[170]

St. John of the Cross states later that the general knowledge can be received by the soul in greater or less degree, but its perfection consists in its independence from any particular knowledge. When it is more "clothed in, mingled with or enveloped in certain intelligible forms", it is more compatible with and reduced to man's natural mode of knowing and loving. It is more readily perceived by the intellect and impressed upon the senses, but by the same token it is least pure and simple. All this is illustrated in the well-known example of the ray of sunlight passing through a window.[171]

At the very outset, therefore, contemplation is seen as a concentration of the higher faculties on a given object, resulting in knowledge or awareness, but the knowledge of the object is not clear and distinct; rather, it is an obscure, general and confused

---

[170] *The Ascent*, bk. II, chap. 14, no. 7.
[171] Cf. *The Ascent*, bk. II, chap. 14, no. 9.

knowledge. But it is precisely the obscurity and vagueness that constitute contemplative knowledge on the part of the subject.

As regards the object contemplated, there is some knowledge of it, but it is also obscure, confused and general; in fact the perfection of contemplation is measured by the imperceptibility of the object, its lack of any particular form in which the intellect can naturally come to rest. The intellect and the other powers must concentrate on the object in a purely supernatural manner, that is, without any natural intermediary. It is natural to the intellect to know and rest in the object in a manner connatural to itself, but if this occurs in contemplation, the perfection of contemplation is diminished.

Nevertheless, the intellect and the other superior faculties do find rest and satisfaction in the general contemplative knowledge that is not obtained or maintained by their own natural powers. As we have just stated, to the extent that the faculties intervene by their own natural power, the contemplation is less perfect. The perfection of contemplation requires complete darkness of the intellect in the sense that it does not perceive any particular, limited form naturally knowable. Nevertheless, given that obscure and vague knowledge, the intellect, the memory and the will, united in the contemplative act, enjoy complete quietude.

We have here the fundamental doctrine on contemplation in both its objective and subjective aspects and the relation between the two. As to the relation, however, we have merely indicated it in general, without studying its psychological structure. The following passage summarizes all the points we have been discussing:

> The same thing happens in the realm of spiritual light with respect to the sight of the soul, which is the intellect. This general knowledge or the light we describe as supernatural strikes the soul so purely and simply, and the soul itself is so despoiled of and detached from all the intelligible species that are objects of the intellect, that the intellect does not perceive it or advert to it. Rather, at times

(when it is purest), it casts the intellect into darkness, because it withdraws the intellect from its accustomed lights, species and phantasms, and then the darkness is clearly perceived and realized. But, when this divine light strikes the soul with less force, the soul neither experiences darkness nor sees any light nor perceives anything that it knows, from whatever source.[172]

Then, in the totally dark perception of that light and in the high point of mental prayer, the soul can testify that it "has been united in pure knowledge" and in "heavenly knowledge". The soul then "knows God without knowing how."[173]

What can we deduce from all this relative to our study? In the first place, we find some elements with which we are already familiar. When St. John of the Cross speaks of the contact between the supernatural light and the intellect, he states that the perfection of the divine light in the intellect consists in its being there without any species that is connatural to the intellect. But the intellect tends naturally to an intentional species so that it may find rest therein. We already saw this in our analysis of the active night of the spirit, where the fundamental distinction between the natural and the supernatural was applied. But now, in contemplation, the supernatural element is seen as a spiritual light or, under another aspect, as general and vague knowledge. Both of these elements apply to the virtue of faith, as we saw in our analysis of chapter 3, book II of *The Ascent*, where faith is treated explicitly.

Having made the foregoing observations, we can conclude that in the Mystical Doctor's teaching on the transition from meditation to contemplation—which is a general, obscure and dark knowledge given in faith—we find many elements already known to us from our analysis of faith; they form a nucleus of the doctrine on the virtue of faith. Moreover, the teaching on the transition follows the same intrinsic logic and the same principles that we found in the Mystical Doctor's treatment of

[172] *The Ascent*, bk. II, chap. 14, no. 10.
[173] Ibid., bk. II, chap. 14, no. 11.

the virtue of faith. This is the sum total of what we can conclude from the texts already studied; later we shall see more precisely what is the function of faith. For the time being we shall state as much as the previous texts allow.

First of all, contemplation, which is a general, vague and dark but loving knowledge that "is given in faith", is by its very definition something intimately connected with the virtue of faith. But when the general, loving knowledge was given as the third sign of the soul's transition to contemplation, where new elements replace what was lost with meditation, it was manifested as a convergence of all the higher faculties of the soul under the supernatural light. That light is already known to us from the teaching on faith, where it is described as a communication of divine knowledge to the intellect, in which knowledge the intellect participates through the virtue of faith. It is, indeed, the basic reason why the intellect is able to attain to the essence of revelation. We also noted that the infusion of supernatural light in faith terminates in the union of the intellect with the divine essence, although in darkness. The intellect attains to divinity, but it does not possess divinity in an intentional form or species; therefore it remains in darkness. That is why the intellect does not rest in faith alone; it still experiences the impetus to tend toward God.

As regards the last point, several things should be noted that pertain to our further investigation of the nature of faith. First, the tendency of the intellect toward the essence of revelation is clearly manifested in the first two signs. This is evident from our analysis of those two signs, where we concluded that there is a disjunction between the higher and lower faculties or, to put it another way, the intellect perceives a disproportion in the manner in which revealed truths had been perceived previously by the sense faculties. This point should be carefully noted.

The practice of mental prayer presupposes that the soul is tending toward union with God and is in the state of grace, where charity is operative and faith is vivified by charity.

Moreover, in discursive meditation the soul applies itself to the truths of revelation by acts of knowledge and love. Consequently, it is to be expected that in its mental prayer the soul will experience the hidden tension proper to faith, which the Mystical Doctor treats in book II, chapter 3 of *The Ascent*. Essentially, faith is an assent of the intellect to revealed truths, but now, in mental prayer, the intellect endowed with the virtue of faith is considering those same revealed truths. We know that the intellect of the believer still retains its natural tendency to the essence of revealed truths. Faith does not destroy that tendency but adapts to it, so to speak, and in a certain measure satisfies it. There is an essential satisfaction, a basic union of the intellect with the divine essence, achieved through faith, but it lacks clarity and any particular species. Rather, as we have stated previously, there is an experience of darkness because the divine reality far exceeds the intellect's natural capacity.

When the first and second signs make the intellect aware of the disproportion in its sensate mode of perceiving revealed truths and finding satisfaction in them, this seems to me to illustrate the primary function of faith in mental prayer. For St. John of the Cross the virtue of faith not only bespeaks an essential adherence of the intellect to divinity without an intentional species; it also affects the mode of this adherence. Without destroying the intellect's human mode of operation, it modifies this mode during the journey to union so that although human—and precisely as human—it is better proportioned for essential contact with divinity. We saw all of this clearly in our analysis of the active night of the spirit. All things considered, it appears that the first and second signs are intimately connected with the nature and operation of faith. It is the virtue of faith that causes the intellect to break away from meditation and discursus with the help of the sense faculties. As a consequence, the will, whose love is essentially supernatural as the virtue of charity, must conform its operation to the new mode of apprehension.

We can summarize the first two signs as follows: following its natural tendency to know the essence of revealed truths, the intellect is made more aware of the transcendence of that essence and its own disproportion to it, and this happens in an experiential and vital manner. There is a feeling of discontent and an awareness of the soul's incapacity to meditate on revealed truths through the use of the sense faculties, as it was wont to do. And this is the effect of the virtue of faith on the intellect, for it not only enables the intellect to unite with the divine essence, but it tends to produce in the intellect an ever more perfect psychological proportion to the divine by making it break away from its sensate manner of adhering to revealed truths.

NOTES

1. The operation of faith in the first and second signs of the transition to contemplation is implicit in the teaching of St. John of the Cross; he never describes it explicitly. Nevertheless, we arrived at our conclusions through a careful analysis of the text. Our analysis is not a conclusive proof of the function of faith in the first two signs, but it can be supported by the words of the Mystical Doctor: "Because up to that time [the soul] had not arrived at the spiritual reality that was reserved for it."[174] These words refer to the tendency of the intellect to know the essence of revealed truths, and this is the meaning of "spiritual reality" in the text cited and of "spiritual good" in book III, chapter 13 of *The Ascent*. This tendency to the essence of revealed truths is something proper to the virtue of faith; indeed, the culmination of faith consists in the fact that the intellect, aware of divine truths through revelation, tends toward them effectively through the intervention of the excessive supernatural light. Moreover, the context of all the passages previously cited indicates that the intellect, restricted until now to meditation on divine truths through the medium of the sense faculties, now breaks away from that exercise. The break cannot be explained in any other way than as an operation of the

[174] *The Ascent*, bk. II, chap. 14, no. 1.

virtue of faith, for we have already seen in our analysis of the active night of the spirit that it is the proper function of faith to transcend all particular intentional species. Something similar occurs here and can be explained only by the intimate proportion of the intellect to the divine reality, effected in the intellect by the virtue of faith.

2. The virtue of faith we are discussing here is a faith informed by charity. This is evident because, in producing the first and second signs, it does so as a vivified faith operating under the impulse of charity. Nevertheless, we are inclined to attribute the effects especially to faith because what is distinctive about the two signs seems to correspond in a particular way to the nature and function of faith as we understand them from the text of St. John of the Cross.

Until now, the soul "had not arrived at the spiritual reality that was reserved for it." Now, however, it begins to move toward that spiritual reality, with less satisfaction to the senses, to be sure, but disposing the soul for a more intense light.

But it is with the third sign that the soul effectively moves forward. We have already stated that this sign operates under the same logistics as the virtue of faith, which consists in the communication of divine light in which the intellect shares. This can be explained more precisely by considering how this communication occurs, is constituted and operates.

The manner is the same both as regards the third sign and the virtue of faith. The supernatural light focuses on its object with a great intensity which the intellect and the other spiritual faculties cannot diminish unless they interject some species which is connatural to those faculties. It is now a question of their actual and intense participation in the divine light and in its tendency to its proper object. Nevertheless, that object never appears clearly to the faculties that are now united in their orientation to the divine object. This demonstrates that the fundamental law and the essential proportion of faith are valid and that they apply strictly. Moreover, all contemplative knowledge evolves along the lines of the virtue of faith, has its foundation in faith, and is intrinsically measured by faith. We can see therefore why the Mystical Doctor says that knowledge "is given in faith".

But there is also a certain extrinsic aspect of contemplation that is not explained by faith. In the first place, we saw that all the higher faculties of the soul are united in the obscure knowledge of contemplation, but this conjunction of the faculties is not the work of the virtue of faith. St. John of the Cross attributes no more to the operation of faith than the union of the intellect with the divine essence by means of the participated supernatural light. Therefore the convergence of the other faculties in this obscure knowledge is not the work of faith. Moreover, the other faculties retain their own proper modality and function, and the convergence itself is animated by love, as is the knowledge that ensues. The virtue of faith does not suffice of itself to account for all these particulars.

Moreover, there is something given on the part of the intellect alone that cannot be attributed to faith. We refer to the quietude or satisfaction of the intellect that St. John of the Cross considers a necessary consequence of the reception of the species or intentional form by the possible intellect.[175] Does this mean that the intellect actually receives a species or form of the divine? Not at all, for contemplation is an "obscure knowledge" and is the more perfect as it is more obscure. Consequently, the communication of the divine light would seem to be greater and participation in it more perfect in the measure that the intellect and other faculties are more submerged in darkness. Their participation in the divine light is in direct proportion to their insufficiency and incapacity on the natural level. It is obvious that this would not produce the quietude and satisfaction of the intellect. The virtue of faith dominates everything here, and the intellect in contemplation does not

[175] Cf. *The Ascent*, bk. II, chap. 14, nos. 6–7 and also bk. III, chap. 13, no. 4.

have the privilege of receiving an intentional species of the divine, any more than does any act of faith.

The virtue of faith, therefore, is operative in the intellect in contemplation, but something more is given than can be attributed to faith. We saw in book II, chapter 3 of *The Ascent* that faith produces a union with God in an essential sense, but the union lacks perfection because of the lack of a clear intentional species of divinity. In other words, faith causes some degree of union between the agent intellect and divinity, for the agent intellect tends to the essence of those things that it knows through hearing (*ex auditu*); but lacking an intentional species of divinity, faith does not provide the quiet and satisfaction that pertain to the possible intellect. Hence, the obscurity or darkness primarily affects the possible intellect, which is deprived of rest in an intentional species.

For this reason the virtue of faith likewise causes a constant tension in the agent intellect, given the essential relationship that exists between the agent intellect and the possible intellect. And because of the interrelation of the two functions of the intellect, faith is said to unite the entire intellect to God. As regards the agent intellect, faith fulfills its function immediately, uniting it with the essence of revealed truths. But the agent intellect always operates in relation to the possible intellect. Consequently, the tension of faith perdures throughout the entire journey to union and is not terminated until the beatific vision in glory.

But it is said that all the higher faculties are united and find rest in contemplation. How does this happen? And how is it explained in reference to the operations of the intellect? This lies outside our investigation because it touches the nature and function of mystical contemplation. We are interested only in the role of faith in contemplation and, having described it, to investigate it more deeply.

However, we can say that the delight that accompanies contemplation in faith is not a perfect delight that proceeds from the activity itself but is something received passively. It derives from the virtue of faith, to which the intellect adheres in its journey toward union as the proper and proportionate means to that union. St. John of the Cross treats of this passive joy in book III, chapter 17 of *The Ascent*, where he distinguishes it from the active joy of the will consequent upon the clear and distinct knowledge of an object in which it finds fruition. Passive joy, on the other hand, does not demand such knowledge; rather, "the will may find itself experiencing delight without understanding clearly and distinctly . . . the reason for its delight, but it is not in the soul's power to experience it or not to experience it."[176]

So much for the delight of the will; what about the intellect? As we have just seen, when it is a question of the passive joy of the will, the intellect does not possess perfectly the "substance as understood" in the intentional order. Hence it is evident that in this respect faith is surpassed in contemplation. It gave the intellect the power of operation, but since faith is an "obscure habit", it needs assistance so that the intellect that tends to divinity in faith may somehow even in this life rejoice in divinity and find rest therein, though never transcending the limits of the virtue of faith.

St. John of the Cross explains all of this in the splendid passage in book II, chapter 29 of *The Ascent*. But before quoting the text in question, we should note that it is part of the chapter in which St. John of the Cross discusses locutions. The recollected soul receives an illumination from the Holy Spirit concerning the truth being pondered, though the locution as received may be defective. We treated of some of these defects when we discussed the active night of the spirit. But there is a great difference between the recollection accompanied by locutions and the recollection practiced in faith, wherein the Holy Spirit grants illumination according to the perfection of the virtue of faith. St. John of the Cross explains it this way:

[176] *The Ascent*, bk. III, chap. 17, no. 1.

The Holy Spirit illumines the recollected intellect and enlightens it according to its manner of recollection, and . . . the intellect cannot find any other and greater recollection than in faith; and therefore the Holy Spirit will not illumine it in anything else more than in faith. For the purer and more refined the soul is in faith, the more it has of the charity infused by God; and the more charity it has, the more is it illumined and the more the gifts of the Holy Spirit are communicated to it, for charity is the cause and the means by which they are communicated to it. And although it is true that, in the other illumination of truths, the Holy Spirit communicates a certain light to the soul, the light given in faith, where there is no clear understanding, is as different as is the most precious gold from the basest metal, and quantitatively, as the sea exceeds a drop of water. For in the first way wisdom concerning one or two or three truths, etc., is communicated, but in the other all God's wisdom in general is communicated, which is the Son of God, who is communicated to the soul in faith.[177]

The foregoing passage is weighty with meaning and doctrine. Perhaps in no other place has St. John of the Cross explained so precisely all the elements that intervene in contemplation. First of all, the virtue of faith is the foundation of all the other elements—faith taken in a subjective sense as it effects the purgation of the soul, and evidently in the active night of the spirit. The Mystical Doctor then states that in that way faith causes an increase in charity; in other words, the greater the vivified faith, the greater the charity. This teaching was also found in book II, chapter 4 of *The Ascent*. But in this text he states that the communication of the gifts of the Holy Spirit depends on the degree of charity in the soul. (We should note that St. John of the Cross does not treat explicitly of the gifts of the Holy Spirit, nor does he enumerate them or mention any of them in particular. However, we frequently find many elements in his works that in theology are usually attributed to the gifts of the Holy Spirit. But St. John never makes any specific

[177] *The Ascent*, bk. II, chap. 29, no. 6.

applications to the gifts of the Holy Spirit. The text we have quoted is exceptional in this regard.)

The text we are studying asserts the dependence of the gifts of the Holy Spirit on charity. The greater the degree of charity in the soul, the more active is the Holy Spirit through his gifts. This is the traditional doctrine. The illumination of the soul recollected in faith by the Holy Spirit operating through the gifts produces the obscure and general knowledge of divine things that, qualitatively and quantitatively, is a very lofty knowledge of God. It is, indeed, a participation in the very wisdom of God, in the Son of God communicated to us through faith. The last words signify that through contemplation in faith, actuated by the gifts of the Holy Spirit, the intellect shares in the essential knowledge of God and, moreover, the knowledge that terminates in the Word. But more of this later.

Up to this point we have seen that the virtue of faith intervenes in the lofty contemplation of divine wisdom as its efficient cause. However, the causality is indirect. The acts of vivified faith increase charity, in which all the gifts converge; and it is through the gifts that the Holy Spirit operates. He is the direct cause of contemplation by his illuminating action. We have in the preceding text, therefore, a description of the "*fieri*" or process of contemplation considered from the efficient cause.

But there is another aspect of faith that is more clearly and fully portrayed in the text. The Mystical Doctor first spoke of the recollection of the intellect in faith and stated that it differs greatly from the recollection of any particular truths, including revealed truth, the truth of faith. What does he mean when he distinguishes the latter from recollection in faith? To answer this question, we must keep in mind all that has been said previously throughout the text, going back to book II, chapter 10 of *The Ascent*. There, the recollection directed to a distinct truth, if ordained to the elucidation of that truth, comes under the classification of "distinct and particular knowledge". Recollection in faith, on the other hand, signifies the adherence of the intellect to the essence of revealed truths but without any particular intentional form, without any distinction of truths in themselves. Such an adhesion of the human intellect to the divine essence in faith results in darkness for that faculty, and any attempt at particular clarity is excluded.

But when the illumination of the Holy Spirit comes to the recollected intellect by means of his gifts, which are connected in charity, then that which is communicated to and united with the intellect under this illumination in a new mode—redounding from the motion of the Holy Spirit, but still without any essential clarity or any intentional species—is what the Mystical Doctor calls the "contemplation that is given in faith". It is a confused, general, obscure and total contemplation, which means that it encompasses the divinity, which is attained essentially through faith and in darkness. Hence this contemplation effects a participation in the wisdom of God so far as is possible in faith. It also produces the closest relationship with the Word that is possible through faith.

3. The objective extension of faith is explained in the last text cited. Since the Mystical Doctor attributes to faith the intrinsic communication of the divine light, as we saw in our analysis of book II, chapter 3 of *The Ascent*, he also attributes to faith the intrinsic participation in that light. According to his teaching, then, the participation in divine knowledge by means of that light pertains essentially to the virtue of faith. But the intellect shares the more perfectly in the light of divine knowledge as it experiences the greater darkness in its natural operation. Thus, St. John of the Cross says: "As Aristotle and the theologians say, the higher and more sublime the divine light, the darker it is to our intellect."[178]

This is the proportion that is proper to faith, and hence, the greater the natural darkness, the more perfect the faith and, as a

[178] *The Ascent*, bk. II, chap. 14, no. 13.

consequence, the greater the participation in the light of divine knowledge. But since the darkness of faith implies an abnegation for the intellect, it involves the will and thereby touches the virtue of charity. And as charity increases, so also do the gifts of the Holy Spirit and his illuminating influence. This comprises the dynamism of infused contemplation in the order of efficient causality.

From the foregoing we can deduce the efficient causality of faith in contemplation, and although it functions somewhat remotely in this respect, the virtue of faith is nevertheless intimately involved in the very substance of contemplation. For it is in faith and only in faith, according to St. John of the Cross, that the communication of divine knowledge in this life is verified. This being so, every increase in this knowledge is essentially related to the evolution and growth of faith. Thus it is that because of its participation in the excessive light, faith contains in its internal structure the very substance of all the degrees of contemplation possible in this life. It does not possess it in act, to be sure, but virtually; that is, as a potentiality to be realized and reduced to act by the illumination of the Holy Spirit, who is the true efficient cause of contemplation through his gifts.

Moreover, it is always understood that the orientation of the soul to contemplation is directed by charity, and so far as faith exercises an efficient causality in contemplation, it is ordained to charity. Objectively, however, considering the constitutive elements of contemplation, faith intervenes, not precisely as a virtue but so far as through faith the intellect participates in the light of divine knowledge which is actuated more and more in contemplation, but always characterized by the obscurity proper to faith.

4. At the same time the text in book II, chapter 29 of *The Ascent* and the analysis of the transition from meditation to contemplation reveal clearly the deficiency of faith as an efficient cause of contemplation. It is evident, therefore, that faith alone does not

suffice for contemplation. Although it is a constitutive objective element of contemplation and although it imparts to contemplation its own obscure manner of participating in the divine light, when we consider the efficient causality of faith in contemplation it becomes apparent that the contribution of faith is very limited.

This seems to be the mind of St. John of the Cross, for he describes the virtue of faith psychologically as an obscure habit, as the adherence of the intellect to the divine essence by assenting to the revealed truths whose essence remains hidden. From this point of view it is not evident how an active contribution to contemplation can be attributed to faith except remotely, so far as its activity is ordained to charity. Whatever efficient causality there is in faith comes to it from the impetus of the Holy Spirit, and for that reason it is more exact to say that faith becomes contemplative than that it causes contemplation.

The profound disproportion between faith as an intimate participation in the divine light and faith as a habit or the operative power of that participation is already well known to us. These are two distinct aspects of the virtue of faith, namely, faith as a sharing in divine knowledge—an aspect that transcends every grade of contemplation—and faith as an intellectual habit—an aspect that reveals the weakness and insufficiency of faith for actuating and using the divine light that it possesses by participation.

5. The foregoing material has been the object of many discussions, articles and books, especially so far as it pertains to the problem of contemplation, the transition from meditation to contemplation, the distinction between infused and acquired contemplation, and so forth. All of these questions have relevance to our investigation only so far as they can contribute something to our study of the nature of the virtue of faith. It is from this perspective that we have read and analyzed those studies, and here we offer some observations that pertain to our investigation.

In studying the three signs given by St. John of the Cross for discerning the transition from meditation to contemplation, Fr. Labourdette finds both a continuity and a discontinuity, but under different aspects. He says:

> The discontinuity that separates meditation from that type of knowledge which will serve as a proximate means is found on the level of its mode of operation and not in the substance of the profound spiritual knowledge that it should attain. That is why the Saint does not appeal directly to faith for the replacement of meditation, as he did when treating of visions and revelations. Rather, he refers to the activity of supernatural knowledge that he calls "contemplation", which shares with faith the common characteristic of a "proximate means" for the attainment of divine union by the intellect. This is in reality the positive side of "naked faith". . . . Faith is always the substance and, as it were, the body of our knowledge of God. The form of this knowledge may change, but faith always remains its source and foundation.[179]

And now, a quotation from Fr. Crisógono de Jesús Sacramentado: "General and obscure knowledge is not a pure negation any more than is the being of God; it is unlimited and undetermined, whereas limitation implies negation; and to the extent that specification signifies perfection, that knowledge cannot be described as undetermined. It has the same meaning as predication of the being of God."[180]

Lastly, Fr. Efrén de la Madre de Dios writes: "Contemplation is a loving knowledge because its *raison d'être* is charity, and since it is a knowledge of God that is given to us through faith, it has its roots in theological faith; and because the possession in faith tends to the full possession in charity, it increases likewise in hope."[181]

---

[179] M. Labourdette, art. cit., *Revue Thomiste* (1937) 45 ff.

[180] Crisógono de Jesús Sacramentado, op. cit., 27; cf. also vol. I, 323.

[181] Efrén de la Madre de Dios, *San Juan de la Cruz y el misterio de la Santísima Trinidad en la vida espiritual* (Zaragoza, 1947) 443.

"The Son of God, who is
communicated to the soul in faith"

These words are taken from the famous text in book II, chapter 29, of *The Ascent*, which we have used frequently to explain the function of faith in contemplation in the line of efficient and formal causality. They refer to a mystery that we should strive somehow to understand. Taken in context, they state that the Word is communicated to the intellect in faith because through faith the intellect shares in a knowledge that is essentially divine. But in the passage cited, the Word appears as the terminus of the knowledge in which God, knowing himself exhaustively and comprehensively, expresses his own infinite perfection in the person of the Word. Such seems to be the meaning of the Mystical Doctor: sharing through faith in a knowledge that is essentially divine—the wisdom of God—the intellect in some way likewise shares through faith in the generation of the Word. Since the divine knowledge essentially shared through faith is actuated by the impetus of the Holy Spirit in contemplation—originating in faith and always with the obscurity of faith—then *a fortiori* the intellect shares in the generation of the divine Word. We have here the nucleus of the Trinitarian doctrine that is developed explicitly in *The Spiritual Canticle* and *The Living Flame*, but it was necessary to make note of it here.

Expressions similar to those above are frequently found in *The Ascent*. We shall analyze some of them in order to probe more deeply into the nature of faith. In chapter 22 of book II of *The Ascent*, St. John of the Cross asks why it was lawful under the Old Law—and sometimes commanded—to ask God for a response by supernatural means, whereas it is forbidden under the New Law. He answers that at that time faith was not firmly established (in the objective sense of truths to be believed), and the law of the Gospel had not yet been promulgated. In other words, God had not yet revealed himself in his intimate life to the extent that he intended to do. Hence, there was a good reason why God should be queried by certain persons and why they could rightfully expect a reply. This was abolished under the New Law. Why? Let us note the response:

> But now that the faith is founded in Christ and the law of the Gospel has been made known in this era of grace, there is no reason to inquire of God in that manner, nor for him to speak or to answer as he did then. For, in giving us, as he did, his Son, which is his Word—and he has no other—he spoke to us once and for all in this single Word, and he has nothing more to tell us.[182]

Thus, the precise reason why it is no longer lawful to seek answers from God in a supernatural way is because God has manifested himself fully and definitively in his incarnate Word. Added to this reason are the words of the Apostle: "In times past, God spoke in fragmentary and varied ways to our fathers through the prophets; in this, the final age, he has spoken to us through his Son" (Heb 1:1).

The explanations that follow show that God revealed to men everything that was to be revealed about himself. Therefore, to seek anything further by way of a particular private revelation would be equivalent to asking for the incarnate Word a second time and seeking more revelation and more faith, as if the revelation already given were not sufficient. This would constitute a grave offense against God and against the incarnate Word. As St. John of the Cross says, it would be like "finding fault with God for not having given us everything we need in his Son. . . . Since all the faith has been revealed to us in Christ, there is no more faith to be revealed, nor will there ever be."[183]

St. John of the Cross directs his remarks to those impatient seekers after novelties who were certainly numerous in his day, but there is also a deeper meaning to his words. On the one

---

[182] *The Ascent*, bk. II, chap. 22, no. 3.
[183] *The Ascent*, bk. II, chap. 22, no. 7.

hand, he indicates the order of the revelation of truths pertaining to the intimate life of God, which constitute the object of
faith; on the other hand, he insists on the personal manifestation
of God in the person of Jesus Christ.[184] If in the first case objective revelation consists of the body of specific revealed truths
beyond which one is not to seek for more, in the second case
the personal revelation of God in Christ can never be ex-
hausted. There will always be an infinite number of ways to
imitate Christ and to know him more intimately, and through
the knowledge gained by love and imitation of Christ, there
will always be more revealed. In him one can learn more and
more of the hidden and profound mysteries of divinity. "Fix
your eyes on him and you will find the most secret mysteries,
and wisdom and wondrous things of God that are hidden in
him."[185]

Such is the basis of the mystical doctrine of St. John of the
Cross. Revealed truths are given to the intellect, but Christ
himself is given as the life of Christians. In him is found the
revelation of God to men, both in himself and as the exemplar
that all should imitate and, through love, reproduce in themselves. In this way, and not in the eager scrutiny of revealed
truths, the manifestation of God is attained and shared by each
one. For St. John of the Cross the revelation of God consists
much more in personal witness than in the purely intellectual
knowledge of revealed truths.

God has manifested himself intimately in revelation and, in a
sense, has done so completely. Consequently, there is nothing
more to be proposed for belief. And it should be noted that in
the very structure of faith, which consists objectively in the
manifestation of divinity by means of revelation, the divine
Word intervenes directly as personally manifesting divinity.
The thought of the Mystical Doctor can be stated as follows:
God expresses all that he is in the Word. He reveals himself to

[184] Cf. Pierre Blanchard, "*Le Christ Jésus dans la spiritualité de Saint Jean de la
Croix*", in *La Vie Spirituelle* (1945) no. 2, 131–43.
[185] *The Ascent*, bk. II, chap. 22, no. 6.

all men, not only through the preaching of the incarnate Word, but in the very Incarnation of the Word. All these things are made known through revelation; they are accepted and preserved in faith. And since the manifestation of God culminates in the Word, through faith we possess the divinity in its entirety.

St. John of the Cross does not raise the question of a distinction between divinity as received subjectively by the intellect and as contained in the body of particular truths proposed for belief. He simply states that faith considered objectively as the Incarnation of the Word, or better, as the Word incarnate, brings us the total divinity. For that reason the incarnate Word is the basis of the "general and dark knowledge" that brings us the wisdom of God, the entire divinity communicated in the Word.

All the preceding statements apply to faith considered objectively. As regards the subjective aspect, we already know that it consists in the communication of divine light to the intellect. This was evident from our analysis of chapter 3 in book II of *The Ascent*, where we saw that the excessive light that pervades the human intellect enables it to adhere firmly and with certitude, in spite of the obscurity, to the truths revealed concerning God. Moreover, we saw that the infused light causes the intellect to attain to the essence of revealed truth because in that light "God manifests himself to the soul".[186]

Later we saw also the much-cited text which states that in the dark contemplation that is given in faith, the wisdom of God is communicated to the soul in a general way and this is the Son of God communicated to the soul in faith.[187] Is this to be understood in an objective sense or subjectively as the light in which the intellect shares through faith? It would seem to be taken in an objective sense, as an expression of all that subsists in God and in the knowledge that God has of himself. But this knowledge is communicated to man in faith, and hence man by

---

[186] *The Ascent*, bk. II, chap. 9, no. 1.
[187] Cf. ibid., bk. II, chap. 29, no. 6.

participation can be said to share in that knowledge which is the generation of the Word.

Now we can see the nexus between faith and the Son of God in the teaching of St. John of the Cross: the objective faith of the New Law consists in the definitive revelation of God that culminated in the Incarnation of the Word. Therefore, faith is identified with the knowledge that God has in himself and of himself and to which he gives expression, not so much by reason of the revealed truths precisely as received by the intellect, but by reason of the person of the Word revealed in the Incarnation. Subjectively, however, faith as a virtue that consists essentially in the participation in the light of divine knowledge enables the human intellect to participate in the mystery of the generation of the Word. It is in this sense that we can explain the statement of St. John of the Cross that the "Son of God is communicated to the soul in faith". The generative light of the Word, shared through faith, causes the human intellect in this life to attain to the very reality of revealed truths, and this reality is the divine person of the Word, in whom divinity has manifested itself to men in order to be seen as the incarnate Word and to be believed in the mystery of the Incarnation.

Such seems to be the mind of the Mystical Doctor concerning the relationship between faith and the Son of God. Applying all that we touched upon in the previous consideration regarding the obscure knowledge that is given in faith, the following text becomes more clear:

> When the soul has completely purified and emptied itself of all forms and images that can be apprehended, it will remain in this pure and simple light, being transformed therein into a state of perfection. This light is never lacking to the soul, but because of the created forms and veils wherewith the soul is covered and entangled, the light is not infused into it. But if these impediments and veils were entirely removed (as will be said hereafter), leaving the soul in pure nakedness and poverty of spirit, then the soul, now simple and pure, would be transformed into simple and pure wis-

dom that is the Son of God. For when the loving soul lacks the things of the natural order, then it is infused with divine things, on both the natural and supernatural levels, because there can be no vacuum in nature.[188]

This text presupposes and connotes many other elements in the doctrine of St. John of the Cross, and it should be interpreted with them in mind. It refers, for example, to the obscure and loving contemplation in which, as we know from a preceding analysis, a special movement of the Holy Spirit illumines the soul.[189] But now we ask whether that illumination implies the infusion of a new essential light. It would seem not, because the illuminating action of the Holy Spirit simply actuates the excessive light that the intellect already has through faith. However, since this actuation by the Holy Spirit necessarily presupposes an intense degree of charity, it produces the special effect of concentrating all the superior spiritual faculties in that light.[190]

We also know from our previous analysis that the intensity of the participated divine light prevents the informing of the intellect and other higher faculties by any particular intentional species abstracted from created things. Hence the Mystical Doctor is presuming that the soul is actually free of all those things so that only the divine light, the divine knowledge participated by the intellect, is operative there. The intellect then does nothing more than share in the divine knowledge obscurely through faith, but presupposing an intense actuation of charity, for he speaks of the "loving soul". Moreover, the intensity of charity at this point is indicated by the absence of particulars, for, as we saw in our analysis of the active night of the spirit, this is the consequence of a profound abnegation in which charity was exercised and increased.

[188] *The Ascent*, bk. II, chap. 15, no. 4.
[189] Cf. *The Ascent*, bk. II, chap. 29, no. 6.
[190] Cf. *The Ascent*, bk. II, chap. 14, no. 6.

Together with the intense act of charity, we must presuppose a profound influence of the Holy Spirit, who is ultimately the efficient cause of infused contemplation. At this point, all other conditions being fulfilled, the soul, and especially the intellect, is occupied with nothing else but its participation in divine knowledge according to the obscure and general manner of faith. Then, according to the principle stated by the Mystical Doctor in book II, chapter 5 of *The Ascent*, one can say that the soul is transformed into divine wisdom by participation and shares in the generative light of the Word.

The preceding considerations on faith give a better understanding of the excessive light of faith and, as a consequence, of the lofty concept of faith that is presented in the works of St. John of the Cross. But they also lead us to something that is related to the foregoing and better manifests the relation between faith and the Church.

We already discovered something pertaining to this question in that fundamental chapter 3 of book II of *The Ascent*. After explaining the doctrine on the darkness of faith, the Mystical Doctor concludes: "For man, who is in darkness, could not fittingly be enlightened except by another darkness." He then quotes Psalm 18:3 and interprets it as follows:

> The day, which is God in beatitude, where it is day to the blessed angels and souls who are now day, communicates and speaks to them the Word, which is his Son, that they may know him and enjoy him. And the night, which is faith in the Church Militant, where it is still night, manifests knowledge to the Church, and consequently to each soul, which knowledge is night to it, since it is without clear beatific wisdom; and, in the presence of faith, it is blind as to its natural light.[191]

The text evidently refers to a twofold participation in divine knowledge: the clear knowledge of the Church Triumphant, where the angels and the blessed see the divine essence, and the

[191] *The Ascent*, bk. II, chap. 3, no. 5.

THE ASCENT OF MOUNT CARMEL

dark knowledge of the Church Militant, which is through faith. But the Mystical Doctor retains the concept of the manifestation of the Word, stating that in glory God "speaks" the Word which is his Son. This means that without any veil or darkness, God admits the angels and the blessed to the knowledge that he has of himself, which knowledge terminates *ad intra* as the Word. Such is the way in which God reveals himself to the blessed in glory.

In the Church Militant, however, it is still night, and that night is illumined by another night, which is faith. This means that essentially the same participation in the divine excessive light is effected here on earth by faith and in a dark manner. How does this happen? Through the intervention of the Church, as the Mystical Doctor has stated: "And the night, which is faith in the Church Militant, . . . manifests knowledge to the Church, and consequently to each soul." To all who are still travellers in this life, the participation in divine knowledge is given through faith in the Church and to each according to his capacity.

This is the first thing that the Mystical Doctor notes regarding the role of the Church in relation to faith. Later, in book II, chapter 22, where we find his teaching on faith as manifested in the Incarnation of the Word, he makes the following observation:

> And therefore we must be guided in everything by the law of Christ made man and by that of his Church, and of his ministers, in a human and visible manner; and in this way we must remedy our spiritual weaknesses and ignorances. . . . Nothing is to be believed in a supernatural way except that which is the teaching of Christ made man, as I say, and of his ministers, who are men. [192]

This doctrine on the mediation of the humanity of Christ and of other men in the supernatural act of faith, which is confirmed by the words of the Apostle in Galatians 1:8 and

[192] Ibid., bk. II, chap. 22, no. 7.

illustrated by examples from the Old Testament, is based on the following principle: God wills that everything supernaturally communicated to us should be received through other men so that we may perform a true act of faith, which would be lacking if we were to accept those things through a private and personal revelation.

But we may ask how this mediating human authority, which truly functions in place of divine authority, intervenes in the supernatural act of belief, according to St. John of the Cross. The answer is given in chapter 27 of book II of *The Ascent*, where he treats of private revelations and quotes St. Paul: "For even if we, or an angel from heaven, should preach to you a gospel not in accord with the one we delivered to you, let a curse be upon him!" (Gal 1:8). Then the Mystical Doctor concludes:

> Since there are no more articles to be revealed concerning the substance of our faith than those that have already been revealed to the Church, not only must anything new that may be revealed to the soul concerning this be rejected, but as a safeguard one should reject any other kinds of knowledge contained therein. And for the purity of faith that the soul should have, even if truths already revealed be revealed again, one should not believe them because they are now revealed anew, but because they have already been sufficiently revealed to the Church. Closing his mind to them, he should hold simply to the doctrine of the Church and to its faith, which, as St. Paul says, comes through hearing.[193]

The Mystical Doctor has answered the question with admirable precision. As we have already seen, the body of revealed truth is concentrated principally in Christ, to whom is attributed the personal manifestation of divinity. The same body of truth is likewise concentrated in the Church, especially when it is a question of the clarifications demanded by historical contingencies. Thus, the authority of the Church intervenes in

[193] *The Ascent*, bk. II, chap. 27, no. 4.

every act of faith. And the act of faith does not consist in adhering to a revealed truth because of some private revelation wherein that truth was presented anew, but precisely on the authority of the Church, which alone has received the total revelation to which the intellect must assent by believing. Faith, therefore, is for St. John of the Cross not simply the assent to the truths revealed by God without clear perception by the intellect; it is also, as we have seen, an assent to the truths revealed by God and proposed by the Church. It is in this way that the Church intervenes in every act of faith.

NOTES

1. Is there a distinction between "dogmatic faith" and "mystical faith"? Such was the opinion of Baruzi,[194] but for St. John of the Cross faith, which is the basis of mystical knowledge, consists objectively in the truths revealed by God and proposed for belief by the Church. Adherence to the revealed truths involves essentially the same supernatural impulse that produces the loftiest mystical experience. This is clearly seen in chapter 3, book II of *The Ascent*, where he states that the excessive divine light that is participated through faith is operative in the assent to revealed truths. The height of "mystical faith" does not consist in anything else but that same communicated light, now raised to an incomparably higher degree of intensity by the motion of the Holy Spirit. Therefore, no essential difference can be postulated on the basis of the texts of the Mystical Doctor. Indeed, it would seem that the nature of the revealed data—*donné théologique*—is such that it necessarily requires the intervention

---

[194] Cf. J. Baruzi, op. cit., 19. On p. 458 he speaks of "a submission of mystical faith to dogmatic faith", and on p. 456 he says: "And thus are combined the most gross submission to an external authority and an interior elaboration for which there is no preexisting material."

of the excessive light, that is, the intervention of faith, with the same essentially supernatural power that is operative in the loftiest contemplative knowledge.

2. There is another question concerning submission to external authority, but the texts of the Mystical Doctor show that this enters into every act of faith that is truly an act of faith. There is no basis for a distinction or opposition here, as can be seen from the following references to the texts:

1) God wills that the virtue of faith be exercised through submission even to human authority to whom the revelation was made and committed (*The Ascent*, book II, chapter 22, no. 9).

2) As depository of revelation, the Church, in proclaiming the revealed truths, makes the faithful in this life sharers in the same knowledge through faith that the blessed enjoy in glory by the full and clear manifestation of the Word (*The Ascent*, book II, chapter 3, no. 5).

3) For St. John of the Cross, submission to external authority is seen as an act of abnegation of the intellect and of spiritual poverty, which, in his opinion, should never be lacking in the virtue of faith (*The Ascent*, book II, chapter 22, no. 17).

THE DARK NIGHT OF THE SOUL

We should state at the outset that the *ex professo* treatment of the virtue of faith by St. John of the Cross is completed in *The Ascent*. In the works that follow there are only a few passages here and there that pertain to faith. Our first task, then, will be to locate and investigate those texts in order to see whether they can offer us any new insights. Our second task will be to see how each and all of the texts compare with the passages already analyzed as regards the nature of faith, in order to determine how they pertain to the question of faith and how faith is treated in them. The second task must be performed with great care, and the results can be stated only after an examination of the nature and concept of faith in all the works of St. John of the Cross. In this part of our investigation we shall simply propose the questions; the answers will be given in the synthesis at the end of our study.

Beginning with *The Dark Night*, we shall describe the scope of the entire work in order to see how the Mystical Doctor leads us along the path to union. Then we shall cite particular passages in which there is explicit reference to faith.

The word "night", whose exact meaning we already know from *The Ascent*, expresses the title and the theme of this work, but the application is different. In *The Ascent* the Mystical Doctor treated the *active* night; here it is a question of the *passive* night. St. John of the Cross describes the passive night:

> This night, which we say is contemplation, produces two kinds of darkness or purgation in spiritual persons, corresponding to the two parts of man's nature, namely, the sensate and the spiritual. And thus the one night or purgation will be sensate, wherein the soul is purged according to sense by subjecting it to the spirit; and the other is a spiritual night or purgation, wherein the soul is purged

183

and stripped according to the spirit by subjecting it and disposing it for union with God.[1]

The nature of the passive night is immediately evident: it is a certain type of contemplation that produces successive purifications in the lower and higher parts of the soul. They occur on the path to union and are ordained to the goal of union with God. Book I of *The Dark Night* treats of the first of the passive nights; book II treats of the second. Such is the structure and division of the work.

The explanation of the passive night of the senses is preceded by a description of the ways in which beginners are deficient, and it is a passage held in high esteem by spiritual writers. To correct those deficiencies, which human effort cannot do—it is understood that the active night is now completed—the passive night of the senses must come into play. The signs of the advent of the passive night are three in number, just as three signs were given for the transition from meditation to contemplation.[2] But whereas the signs in *The Ascent* pertain only to interior prayer, those in *The Dark Night* have special significance for the whole interior life, since they reflect a more intimate dialogue between the soul and God, greater progress toward union with God, and consequently interior detachment from created things and adhesion to God. This is especially evident in the first of the three signs.

Adherence to God touches the spiritual person most intimately; it is reflected in the individual and has its own particular modality. Formerly adhesion to God was experienced in a sensible way, but now "God transfers the good things and the strength of the senses to the spirit."[3] As a result, the soul ex-

---

[1] *Dark Night*, bk. I, chap. 8, no. 1.

[2] Cf. *Dark Night*, bk. I, chap. 9. Fr. Eugenio de San José gives a detailed comparison of the two sets of signs in his article, "*La contemplación de fe, según La Subida del Monte Carmelo*", in *El Monte Carmelo* (Burgos, 1928) 152–62.

[3] *Dark Night*, bk. I, chap. 9, no. 4.

periences aridity, which, however, does not impede its constant remembrance of God and its zeal, and this is the second sign.

The third sign, however, directly relates to interior prayer, and hence it implies the signs of transition given in *The Ascent*, although the first and second signs in *The Ascent* correspond properly to the second sign in *The Dark Night*. The difference lies in the fact that *The Ascent* allows for an effective replacement of the discursive element, which ceases (the first and second signs), by a new element that is contemplation properly speaking or a dark and loving knowledge (the third sign).

The Dark Night, on the other hand, states that this replacement does not actually occur as quickly as one might think. For a long period of time the infused light wavers, as it were, and it is not sufficiently intense so that the soul can leave discursus definitively. It may be able to use discursus sometimes and at other times not, but even when unable to practice discursive meditation, the soul does not necessarily experience the infusion of light, since the light is as yet weak and almost dark. St. John of the Cross states that the contemplation is "dark and hidden"; it is "so delicate . . . that ordinarily, if one desires or tries to experience it, he does not experience it."[4]

In other words, the faculties are not yet sufficiently adapted to the contemplative experience because they are not yet sufficiently purged of their connatural species. It is then, as St. John of the Cross teaches, that the purgation is effected by the very act of contemplation, by its infusion into the corresponding faculties, and precisely because up to this time the indisposition of the subject prevented it from experiencing the supernatural infusion. He affirms that when all three signs are verified, "when [the soul] leaves discursive meditation for the state of the advanced, then it is God who works in the soul."[5] And this divine work must not be disturbed by any strong effort on the part of a natural faculty, for it would be of no avail. It

---

[4] *Dark Night*, bk. I, chap. 9, no. 6.
[5] *Dark Night*, bk. I, chap. 9, no. 7.

would do nothing but "impede inward peace and the work that God is accomplishing in the spirit by means of aridity of sense."[6]

We understand from this text that the replacement of the previous manner of prayer, which was meditation, is not effected suddenly, though there may be exceptions, as was stated in book II, chapter 14 of *The Ascent.* Normally, however, it is a more or less gradual substitution in which contemplation moves through the successive stages to psychological plenitude. This much is evident from the text, but we repeat that as regards the psychological effects in the faculties in which infused contemplation is experienced, psychological plenitude is not yet attained in the passive night of the senses; rather, the contrary is true. But that contrary, if taken formally, is true contemplation according to St. John of the Cross, because an infused, supernatural modality replaces the human, natural modality, although as yet the soul lacks the capacity to experience it. Hence, the passive night of the senses would seem to be more of a contemplation *in fieri* or an incipient contemplation rather than fully actuated contemplation. Nevertheless, the essential elements of contemplation are already present, and it is precisely this fact that accounts for the passive purgation of the senses. Thus, the Mystical Doctor states:

> For God now begins to communicate himself to [the soul], no longer through sense, as he did before, by means of discursive reflections that joined and divided concepts, but through pure spirit, in which there is no successive discursus, communicating himself by an act of simple contemplation, to which neither the exterior nor the interior senses of the lower part of the soul can attain.[7]

It is true that there is communication with God in discursive meditation. It is experienced as an affective adherence through the virtue of faith to that which is revealed. But now the com-

[6] Ibid.   [7] Ibid., no. 8.

munication is one of "pure spirit" received in the act of contemplation which surpasses all discursus. The pure spirit refers to the essence of revealed truth to which faith tends and in which the intellect is absorbed through contemplation in faith.

Such, briefly, is the first of the passive nights. We have seen that it is a night of incipient contemplation, and, indeed, the night itself is an inchoate contemplation. The contemplation that occurs, however, is contemplation in the sense that we saw it in *The Ascent*: an illuminating motion of the Holy Spirit, revealing through faith the participated divine light and concentrating all the spiritual faculties on the object of that light through the virtue of faith. Thus does the passive night of the senses manifest the beginnings of infused contemplation, taking into account the weakness and incapacity of the subject. The relationship of all this to the virtue of faith is not described in detail but treated in only a general way:

> The narrow gate is this night of sense, from which the soul detaches and strips itself so that it may enter this gate, grounding itself in faith, which is foreign to all the things of sense, so that afterwards it may journey by the narrow way, which is the other night of the spirit wherein the soul afterwards enters in order to journey to God in pure faith, which is the means whereby the soul is united to God.[8]

Thus, we have only the general statement that asserts that faith is the foundation of all the soul's progress, but there is no explanation of how or why. There is also a reference to "pure faith", which pertains to the following night—the passive night of the spirit. The passive night of the senses is a preparatory stage on the path to union, but it is not the night of union properly speaking. St. John of the Cross states as much:

> The purgation of sense is only the gate and beginning of contemplation leading to the purgation of the spirit, and, as we have also said,

[8] *Dark Night*, bk. I, chap. 11, no. 4.

it serves rather to subject sense to the spirit than to unite the spirit with God.[9]

So the dimensions of the passive night of the senses are confined to bestowing on the soul a predisposition for union rather than effectively causing union with God. For that reason the passive night of the senses "can and should be called a kind of correction and control of desire rather than a purgation."[10] The passive night of the spirit "bears no comparison with it, for it is horrible and frightful to the spirit."[11] The Mystical Doctor explains:

In [the passive night of the spirit] the two parts of the soul, the spiritual and the sensual, must be completely purged, since the one is never totally purged without the other. . . . The reason is that all the imperfections and disorders of the sensate part have their strength and root in the spirit, where all habits, both good and bad, reside, and thus, until these are purged, the rebellions and perversity of sense cannot be purged thoroughly.[12]

Once again contemplation is described as the means of achieving purgation: "The Lord effects all this in [the soul] by means of a pure and dark contemplation."[13] In another passage it is stated even more explicitly:

This dark night is an action of God on the soul, which purges it from its ignorances and imperfections—habitual, natural and spiritual—and which contemplatives call infused contemplation or mystical theology. In it God secretly teaches the soul and instructs it in perfection of love, without its doing anything or understanding how this infused contemplation occurs. Since it is the loving wisdom of God, God produces important effects in the soul; by purging and enlightening it, he prepares it for the union of love with

---

[9] *Dark Night*, bk. II, chap. 2, no. 1.
[10] Ibid., bk. II, chap. 3, no. 1.
[11] Ibid., bk. I, chap. 8, no. 2.
[12] Ibid., bk. II, chap. 3, no. 1.
[13] Ibid., bk. II, chap. 3, no. 3.

God. Therefore the same loving wisdom that purges the blessed spirits by enlightening them is that which here purges and enlightens the soul.[14]

The preceding text is of great importance, for it reveals to us a type of contemplation in the dark night of the spirit that is of a lofty degree—comparable in some way to contemplation in glory. We already know from book II, chapter 14 of *The Ascent* that the light of contemplation admits of higher and lower degrees, depending on the illumination received from the Holy Spirit, as was stated in book II, chapter 29 of *The Ascent*. Materially, however, the degree of contemplation corresponds to the degree of purgation of the subject, as can be seen in chapter 14 of book II of *The Ascent*.

But now, in the passive night of the spirit, the degree of contemplative light is compared to that of glory, though it is always marked by the obscurity of faith. The sudden elevation of the subject, who is still in this life, causes a most painful purgation, but the soul understands at the same time that this purgation is disposing it for the transforming union, which is now seen as the perfection of glory anticipated here on earth under the darkness of faith. At the same time, one understands why the passive night of the spirit is compared to purgatory in *The Dark Night*, book II, chapters 7 and 10. All these elements help to explain the nature of the transforming union, which is truly the terminus of union in this life, a sharing in the divine light similar to that in glory. All that remains is to remove the veil of faith by separating the soul from the body; then the beatific vision will be granted. We cannot help but admire the logic of St. John's theological reasoning.

What is of special interest for our investigation is a more precise understanding of the light or "loving wisdom" that is experienced so painfully in the passive night of the spirit. It is the

---

[14] *Dark Night*, bk. II, chap. 5, no. 1.

same light as that which "purges the blessed spirits by enlightening them and of which the Mystical Doctor says: "The
same light and loving wisdom that must unite and transform
the soul are what purge and prepare it at the beginning."[15]

When that statement is compared with the text in book I,
chapter 9 of *The Ascent*, where the Mystical Doctor speaks of
the "wisdom of God" that is communicated to the soul in the
general and dark knowledge of contemplation, the unity and
continuity of his doctrine are readily seen. The same formal
cause is present in any contemplation—it is a sharing in the
knowledge of God himself, under the impetus of the Holy
Spirit. Consequently, contemplation increases in degree with
the intensification of the illuminating motion of the Holy
Spirit, as was stated in book II, chapter 29 of *The Ascent*.

But the motion of the Holy Spirit is related to the degree of
charity, according to which "the gifts of the Holy Spirit are
communicated to a greater or less degree", as stated in the same
chapter 29. As this impetus of the Holy Spirit that produces
contemplation increases, there is a concomitant increase of the
degree of "loving wisdom" or of participated divine knowledge. The increase can reach the same essential grade that is
proper to glory, as was stated in chapter 5 of book II of *The
Dark Night*. But since this communication is in no way connatural to anything in the soul or its faculties, it causes a profound purgation and the terrible sufferings of the passive night
of the spirit. And it is precisely through those sufferings that
the degree of definitive union with God is attained—the transforming union, which is not only definitive in this life but, all
things considered, is essentially identical with the degree of
union in glory. It needs only to be completed and crowned by
the beatific vision.

We can deduce from all this an important contribution to our
investigation of faith in *The Dark Night*. We have already seen

---

[15] *Dark Night*, bk. II, chap. 10, no. 3.

in our previous analysis that the obscure and general knowledge of contemplation is attributed to faith by the Mystical
Doctor; it is "given in faith". Moreover, chapter 29 of book II
of *The Ascent* stated that what is communicated to the soul is
"all the wisdom of God in general, which is the Son of God,
who is communicated to the soul in faith."

What is communicated to the soul in faith is therefore an
essentially divine knowledge in which the intellect is able to
share through faith. Faith, in effect, is the divine light by whose
power the intellect adheres to revealed truths, penetrating their
essence in an obscure manner. All of these elements are of the
same category, for our analysis has shown that the "divine
light" or "excessive light" communicated by faith is the same
as that "wisdom of God" which is communicated in contemplation—the contemplation "given in faith". There is only a
difference in names. Speaking of faith, the Mystical Doctor uses
the word "light"; for contemplation, "the wisdom of God" or
"loving wisdom", also expressed as "the Son of God"; but the
wisdom is always "given in faith" or "communicated in faith".

All these terms, as we have said, signify the same thing essentially. The divine light of faith and the wisdom of God that is
contemplation designate the same communication of knowledge that is given in faith and shared through faith. The difference in words—light and wisdom—is readily explained by the
distinction between the virtue of faith in itself and faith operating through contemplation. As to the rest, we already know the
difference between faith and contemplation by reason of the
efficient cause.

All things considered, we can assert the unity and continuity
of the general theme that runs through all the works of St. John
of the Cross. It is one and the same communication of divine
knowledge—whether light or wisdom—and this knowledge is
given essentially in faith as long as the soul is still tending
toward God in this life. But the reception of the light and
wisdom increases—indeed, it can surpass the power of faith

alone—and through the impetus of the Holy Spirit, it can increase even more, far surpassing the limits of faith as a virtue and a remote efficient cause of the participation in divine wisdom. It can, as we have stated repeatedly, attain a degree of contemplation proper to glory, but always characterized by the darkness of faith.

But is contemplation always involved somehow with the virtue of faith? It would seem so, even though it takes on the characteristic of a loving knowledge or loving wisdom. And why is this so? Because on the level of efficient causality, it depends much more on the operation of charity than on that of faith, as was stated in book II, chapter 29, of *The Ascent*. Nevertheless, so far as contemplation is a type of knowledge, it is always rooted in faith and always involves faith. Hence the Mystical Doctor says that it "is given in faith" or "is communicated in faith". Yet he adds that it is a loving knowledge or wisdom because charity gives it its affective character.

This would seem to be all that pertains to our investigation as a result of the comparison of *The Dark Night* with *The Ascent*. But the comparison and interpretation also reveal a continuity of doctrine in St. John of the Cross, going back to book II, chapter 9 of *The Ascent* and touching his comparison between faith and vision, which are distinguished as "believing" and "seeing". This is especially evident from the following statements:

> Just so does faith, which is symbolized by those pitchers, contain divine light within itself; and when it is finished and broken, at the ending and breaking of this mortal life, the glory and light of the divinity contained in it will appear.[16]

> When the pitchers of this life, which alone impedes the light of faith, are broken, [the soul] can see God face to face in glory.[17]

---

[16] *The Ascent*, bk. II, chap. 9, no. 3.
[17] Ibid., bk. II, chap. 9, no. 4.

If we keep in mind the basic unity and continuity of doctrine in *The Ascent* and *The Dark Night*, we can better understand the basis and meaning of the symbols used. The immediate transition from faith to vision is possible because of the soul's essential participation in communicated divine knowledge. However, the immediacy of the change cannot be properly understood unless one grasps the total doctrine of St. John of the Cross on the definitive perfection of the transforming union. Thus, in book II, chapter 5 of *The Dark Night* we find the basic reason for the possibility of the immediate transfer to vision: in the transforming union the degree of participation in divine knowledge is comparable to the degree in glory; faith, therefore, since it tends towards vision, can reach the same degree of participation. All that is required now is to die, so that one may enjoy the face-to-face vision.

The degree of participation comparable to glory, called "loving wisdom", implies not only an increase in faith by reason of a greater participation in the divine light, but also an increase in charity and the gifts of the Holy Spirit, as is evident from book II, chapter 29 of *The Ascent*. This point, however, does not pertain to our study. We are interested, rather, in the text of book II, chapter 5 of *The Dark Night*, which treats of an increase in the essential participation in divine knowledge, an increase that is equivalent to the degree proper to glory. Although the efficient cause of this participation in divine knowledge is the motion of the Holy Spirit, operating through charity and the gifts, it consists formally in faith, according to chapter 29 in book II of *The Ascent*. The reason is that it belongs to faith to unite the intellect with God, which means to share in the divine knowledge.

This doctrine, considered in its entirety and also in its particulars, is not found explicitly and in systematic form in St. John of the Cross. It is deduced from the relationship and interdependence of various texts. But the doctrine is certainly contained there, and it becomes evident when one passage is used to interpret another. Indeed, one passage cannot be adequately understood in many cases without reference to another. In this way the various texts manifest the doctrinal unity and the logic of the theological system of St. John of the Cross.

Similarly, admitting the conceptual coherence of the various texts, we can appreciate the importance of other texts already cited in relation to the virtue of faith. The following serve as examples:

> God, who, by means of the second night, which is faith, communicates himself to the soul in such a secret and intimate manner that he becomes another night to the soul. . . . When this third night has passed, which is the completion of the communication of God in the spirit, usually effected in great darkness of the soul, there follows its union with the spouse, which is the wisdom of God.[18]

> Although it is true that, naturally speaking, God is as dark a night to the soul as is faith, nevertheless, when these three parts of the night that are naturally night to the soul are over, God illumines the soul supernaturally with the ray of his divine light, which is the beginning of the perfect union that follows when the third night is past.[19]

But we repeat that our conclusions are latent in the text and must be drawn out by comparing various passages.

There is something else that is very useful for our investigation, although it does not pertain explicitly to faith. We already saw in *The Ascent*, book II, chapter 6 the relation between the three theological virtues and the three higher faculties of the soul. Now we want to look at that relationship after the purgation of the nights.

> My intellect departed from itself, being changed from human and natural to something divine; for, when united with God by means of this purgation, it no longer understands by its own natural power

[18] *The Ascent*, bk. I, chap. 2, no. 4.
[19] *The Ascent*, bk. II, chap. 2, no. 1.

and light, but by the divine wisdom with which it has been united. And my will departed from itself, becoming divine; for, united with divine love, it no longer loves with its natural power after a lowly manner, but with the power and purity of the Holy Spirit; and so the will, which is now near to God, does not operate in a human manner, and in the same way the memory has become transformed into eternal presentiments of glory. And finally, by means of this night and purgation of the old man, all the powers and affections of the soul are totally renewed with divine qualities and delights.[20]

With this text before us, let us recall the passage in book II, chapter 6 of *The Ascent*, where the three theological virtues are described as the means of uniting the faculties with God, but they do so through the emptiness and darkness of the faculties. In the passage quoted above, it is stated that the theological virtues have completed their functions as a means to union. Our question now is: what does the passage from book II, chapter 4 of *The Dark Night* tell us about the three theological virtues and in particular about the role of the virtue of faith in uniting the intellect with God?

We already answered these questions to some extent in our analysis of various texts, and we shall have more to say later about the terminus of union with God. What we want to note in particular in the text under discussion, where the Mystical Doctor speaks of the union of the intellect with God, is the change or substitution in the means of knowing. Formerly the soul knew by its native power and natural light, but now in union it knows by the "divine wisdom".

These words connote two things: first, the medium of knowledge has been changed. The natural light of the intellect, which makes its proper object intelligible—that is, the essence of material things—has been transformed into the light of divine knowledge in which the intellect shares and by which it now knows. From being human, it has become divine, and so

[20] *Dark Night*, bk. II, chap. 4, no. 2.

far as it knows by means of the participated light, its knowledge has a participated divine modality. Now, is this the virtue of faith?

We already know from book II, chapter 3 of *The Ascent* that the excessive divine light is shed upon the intellect in faith and, indeed, that it constitutes faith. However, the divine light "overwhelms and conquers" the natural light of the intellect lest, tending to its connatural operation, it would be stifled by the incomprehensibility of revealed truths. The infused light leads the intellect to the very heart of revealed truths, but without the clarity to which the intellect is accustomed. Such is the operation of faith and such is the proper proportion effected by faith between the natural intellect and the infused divine light.

In *The Dark Night*, book II, chapter 4, however, the divine light no longer overwhelms and conquers, and this is the second thing we can deduce from the passage quoted. The intellect does not understand "by its natural power and light, but by the divine wisdom with which it has been united." As a result of the change of proportion between the natural light and the divine light, there is also a change in the manner of knowing: through faith alone or in the contemplation that is "given in faith".

We already know that the operation of the divine light in contemplation proceeds from the impulse of the Holy Spirit. We have clear testimony of this, not only in book II, chapter 29 of *The Ascent*, but also in *The Dark Night*:

> First, it describes this dark contemplation as "secret", since, as we have indicated above, this is mystical theology, which theologians call secret wisdom, and, as St. Thomas says, it is communicated and infused into the soul through love. This happens secretly, hidden from the work of the intellect and of other faculties. Therefore, since the aforementioned faculties do not attain to it, but the Holy Spirit infuses and orders it in the soul, . . . it is called secret.[21]

[21] *Dark Night*, bk. II, chap. 17, no. 2.

This is the same teaching as in chapter 29, book II of *The Ascent*: the power that produces contemplation is the impulse of the Holy Spirit, working through charity. In *The Ascent*, specific reference is made to the virtue of faith, but in the quotation from *The Dark Night* there is no mention of faith. Nevertheless, the doctrine is the same.

Now we can understand the new proportion that exists between the infused divine light and the natural light in the operation of the virtue of faith in contemplation. It is explained by the impulse or moving power. We already saw the intrinsic disproportion of faith in our study of chapter 3, book II of *The Ascent*. God is manifested to the soul through the excessive light that is given in faith, as stated in chapter 9, book II of *The Ascent*. That same light enables the intellect to believe, to adhere to revealed truths and to attain to their essence, but without a clear vision of the divine reality that is received.

On the other hand, the divine light is excessive for the intellect because it surpasses the natural capacity of that faculty. From this we can see the interplay of two elements: the intellect is overwhelmed and conquered—not in a violent sense, but by an excess—and at the same time the intellect is united and adheres to revealed truths through the power of the divine light.

St. John of the Cross affirms that the intellect attains to the essence of revealed truths; otherwise faith would not be a light to the intellect—which naturally tends to the essence of things perceived by the senses—and the expression "faith is by hearing" (*fides ex auditu*) would be words without meaning. But, we repeat, the essence of revealed truths is attained without any intentional species.

Considering the intrinsic proportion or relation between the infused light and the natural subject, the virtue of faith, in itself, does not manifest the operative power we see at work in contemplation. Faith seems to be limited to the retention of revealed truths received through the infused light and, through them, of the divine reality presented to the intellect, but lacking an intentional species. It is the infused divine light that enables us through faith to hold constantly to the revealed truths. Any disproportion comes from the human subject.

When the intellect is overwhelmed and conquered—but again, not by violence—it can do nothing of itself. Moreover, the infused light received through faith is excessive for the intellect. Faith, therefore, if left to itself, has all the characteristics of being powerless and inoperative in relation to the intellect. But St. John of the Cross asserts repeatedly that faith is the means of union. Where does faith get this power?

First of all, the Mystical Doctor is referring to a living faith, a faith animated by charity and, through charity, relating to the gifts of the Holy Spirit, as we saw in chapter 29, book II of *The Ascent*. For that reason it is receptive of the movement by the Holy Spirit. Secondly, the Mystical Doctor identifies the essential element of union in faith and in contemplation as the infused light, which is excessive in relation to the natural power of the intellect but is connatural in relation to the influence and impulse of the Holy Spirit. That is the basis of his concept of contemplation. The motion of the Holy Spirit energizes the light that is essentially present in faith and is the formal element in knowledge of the divine. As a result, the soul experiences this knowledge in faith, but as a general, vague and dark knowledge subject to all the limitations of faith and yet as a sharing in the "wisdom of God".

Such seems to me to be the explanation of the general, vague and dark knowledge according to St. John of the Cross. But it is also a loving knowledge, and this designates the intervention of charity and—it would seem—the intimate union of that participation. All this can be deduced from numerous other texts, but that particular point is beyond the scope of our investigation. Nevertheless, it is necessary to stress the primary function of love in contemplation and in union with God, lest we lose the total view of the doctrine of St. John of the Cross, although our concern is primarily with the virtue of faith.[22]

It is evident from the foregoing explanation that the impulse of the Holy Spirit seems to change the intrinsic proportion between the intellect and the infused power of faith that unites the intellect with God. And this change of intrinsic proportion produces the dark knowledge of contemplation. It could also be called a delineation, in the sense that the Holy Spirit places in relief the divine knowledge that is already present in faith. Then the intellect no longer functions "by its own natural power and light, but by the divine wisdom with which it has been united", as was cited above from book II, chapter 5 of *The Dark Night*.

All of this, we repeat, is implicit in the text of the Mystical Doctor, but to make it evident, it was necessary to compare numerous passages and by doing so to see also the organic cohesion of the various passages. But perhaps we can find another application of the proportion between the excessive light and the intellect in the terrible suffering of the passive night of the spirit, which, says the Mystical Doctor, is "horrible and frightening". For this purpose we quote the following texts:

> The third kind of pain and suffering that the soul endures here is caused by the other two extremes, namely, the divine and the human, that are united here. The divine is this purgative contemplation, and the human is the subject of the soul.[23]

> As the philosopher says, whatever is received is received according to the mode of the recipient. Therefore, since these natural faculties do not have the purity or strength or capacity to receive and enjoy

[22] The capital importance of love appears clearly in this passage: "Contemplation is the science of love. This, as we have said, is an infused and loving knowledge of God, which enlightens and stimulates love in the soul until it raises it, step by step, to God its Creator." (*Dark Night*, bk. II, chap. 18, no. 5.) Thus, charity or love is the subjective efficient cause of contemplation, but formally it is a "knowledge that is given in faith".

[23] *Dark Night*, bk. II, chap. 6, no. 1.

supernatural things according to their modality, which is divine, but can do so only according to their own modality, which is human and base, as we have said, it is proper that they be in darkness also concerning these divine things.[24]

In texts such as the foregoing, we find the same logic that the Mystical Doctor applied to the explanation of the correlation between the excessive light and the subject that remains in darkness, when he discussed the nature of faith. The integration of the two elements, which further requires a divine mode of operation that corresponds to the supernatural infused element, is effected in contemplation, but always through the medium of the dark nights. The logic that applies to faith, to contemplation and to the dark nights is based ultimately on the "essential likeness" and the "proportion of likeness" that were discussed by the Mystical Doctor in book II, chapter 8 of *The Ascent*. Those key concepts are developed and applied throughout all the works of the Mystical Doctor.

If, finally, we ask what the Mystical Doctor says explicitly about the virtue of faith in *The Dark Night*, we would have to quote the following symbolic passage:

> Thus the livery which [the soul] wears is of three principal colors—white, green and purple—signifying the three theological virtues of faith, hope and charity. . . . Faith is an inner tunic of a whiteness so pure that it blinds the vision of the intellect. And thus, when the soul journeys in its vestment of faith, the devil can neither see it nor succeed in harming it, since it is well protected by faith—more so than by all the other virtues—against the devil, who is the most powerful and the most cunning of enemies.[25]

The Mystical Doctor always asserts the same thing, namely, that the virtue of faith conceals the soul from the gaze of the devil, as was stated in book II, chapter 1 of *The Ascent*. The

[24] *Dark Night*, bk. II, chap. 16, no. 4.
[25] *Dark Night*, bk. II, chap. 21, no. 3.

content of faith exceeds the devil's grasp. But now let us continue with the Mystical Doctor's description in *The Dark Night*:

> This white garment of faith was worn by the soul on its going forth
> from this dark night, when, walking in interior constraint and dark-
> ness, as we have said before, receiving no comfort of light from its
> intellect—neither from above, since heaven seemed to be closed to it
> and God was hidden from it, nor from below, since those that
> taught it satisfied it not—it suffered with constancy and persevered,
> passing through those trials without fainting or failing the Beloved,
> who in trials and tribulations proves the faith of his spouse.[26]

Such is the description of "naked faith" that perhaps best exemplifies the fundamental concept of the virtue of faith according to St. John of the Cross. It is a faith that lacks all consolation and is without any light from above or below. It is a faith that is manifested as the unwavering constancy of the intellect in its adherence to God. But a faith like this is much better understood by experience than by abstract concepts.

[26] *Dark Night*, bk. II, chap. 21, no. 5.

SPIRITUAL CANTICLE

The analytical study of the *Spiritual Canticle* should always be prefaced by a word of caution, due to the argument concerning the authenticity of the various redactions of this work. We already referred to this in our Introduction, and there we stated our method of procedure.

Moreover, it should be noted that both the *Spiritual Canticle* and the *Living Flame of Love* are more descriptions of the mystical experience than they are systematic studies; certainly they are much less speculative than *The Ascent* or *The Dark Night*. Nevertheless they do contain something of value for our particular investigation, and this is especially true as regards the *Spiritual Canticle*.

St. John of the Cross states in the prologue: "Mystical wisdom, which comes through love and is the subject matter of the present stanzas, does not have to be understood distinctly in order to produce love and affection in the soul, for it is similar to faith, whereby we love God without understanding him."[1]

The role of love in mystical knowledge is primary. But love does not need distinct knowledge of the object; the mode of faith suffices, wherein God is loved without clear knowledge. Such is the function of faith; it disposes the soul for divine love but without any species of the divine clearly presented to the intellect. The modality of faith, as we have stated repeatedly, is that of an obscure and general knowledge. And the key to the doctrine on faith as expounded in the *Spiritual Canticle* is found in the commentary on stanza 11, which is preceded by the following verses of the poem:

---

[1] *Spiritual Canticle*, Prologue, no. 2.

O crystal fountain,
If on that your silver surface
You would suddenly form
The eyes that I desire
Which I bear outlined in my inmost parts!

Then follows the Exposition:

Since the soul so ardently desires union with the Spouse, and sees that there is no relief nor any means to that end in any creature, she speaks again to faith as that which can most vividly provide light concerning her Beloved and takes it as a means to that end. Indeed, there is no other means by which a soul can come to true union with God, as is indicated by Hosea: "I will espouse you to me in faith" (Hos 2:22). Then with ardent desire she says to faith: O faith of Christ my Spouse! If you would but show forth clearly the truths concerning my Beloved that you have infused into my soul obscurely and darkly, so that what you contain in faith, which is unformed knowledge, you would suddenly manifest and reveal formally and completely by separating yourself from [that unformed knowledge] and turning it into a manifestation of glory! The verse, then, says:

O crystal fountain![2]

Exegesis. It is immediately evident that redaction B is more precise than redaction A, but the doctrine is substantially the same. Moreover, this doctrine is already known to us, at least in general. Faith, not creatures, is the means of union. This was the fundamental teaching of *The Ascent*. There is a reference to

---

[2] *Spiritual Canticle*, stanza 11, no. 1. In redaction B, however, this is stanza 12, and we note the following additions in the commentary: "Indeed there is no other means by which a soul can come to true union *and spiritual betrothal* with God . . . as *the Spouse declares* through Hosea. . . . If you would but show forth clearly the truths infused into my soul obscurely and darkly—*for faith, as the theologians say, is an obscure habit*—so that what you contain in faith . . . *separating yourself from those truths—because faith is a covering and veil over the truths* of God—and turning it into a manifestation of glory. (Tr.)

the relation between faith and vision, which is also found in *The Ascent*. What should be noted, however, is the manner in which the doctrine is expressed: the truths revealed by God are possessed in faith as "unformed knowledge", which means knowledge without an intentional species. This certainly follows from the context, because later he contrasts it with the formal and complete knowledge that is the "manifestation of glory". The unformed knowledge gives faith its characteristic obscurity and darkness—expressions already familiar to us— while the words "formally and completely" signify the clear manifestation of vision. It seems to me that the thought of the Mystical Doctor is the same here as in book II, chapter 3 of *The Ascent*, where he stated that faith is not knowledge, and not because of the lack of a demonstration, but simply because there is no intentional species of the object known. That is why faith is darkness, a dark habit and a night. And now, to continue with the text of stanza 11:

> She calls faith "crystal" for two reasons: the first, because it is from Christ, her Spouse; and the second, because it has the properties of crystal in being pure in its truths, and strong and clear, cleansed of errors and natural forms. And she calls it "fountain" because from it flow to the soul the waters of all spiritual goods. Therefore Christ our Lord, speaking with the Samaritan woman, called faith a fountain, saying that in those who would believe in him he would make a fountain whose water would spring up into life everlasting. And this water was the spirit believers would receive in their faith.[3]

Exegesis. The text is descriptive and poetic, and the words of greatest importance to us are the following: faith is "pure in its truths, and strong and clear"—the objective aspect—and faith is "cleansed of errors and natural forms", which would seem to pertain to the subjective aspect of the dark night. Faith is not only free from errors in the propositions of revealed truths that

---

[3] *Spiritual Canticle*, stanza 11, no. 2.

it presents to us, but subjectively it has the power of rejecting all natural intentional forms. It seems to me that here the Mystical Doctor is thinking of faith as a theological virtue that unites our intellect to the divine essence without any clear intentional species of the divine essence, and at the same time is able to renounce all particular and distinct intentional forms, as we saw in our analysis of the active night of the spirit. To return, now, to the text:

If on that your silver surface

The propositions and articles that faith sets before us she calls a "silver surface". To understand this and the other verses, it should be noted that faith is compared to silver with respect to the propositions it teaches us, and the truths and substance that they contain are compared to gold; for that same substance that we now believe, clothed and covered with the silver of faith, we shall see and enjoy in the next life, when the gold of faith is revealed and laid bare. Therefore David, speaking this, says thus: "Though you rested among the sheepfolds, the wings of the dove shone with silver, and her pinions with a golden hue" (Ps 68:14). He means that if we close the eyes of the intellect to things above and below—which he calls "to rest among the sheepfolds"—we shall remain alone in faith, which he calls a dove, whose feathers, which are the truths that [faith] tells us, will be silvered, because in this life faith proposes them to us obscurely and veiled, for which reason the soul here calls them a silver surface. But when this faith comes to an end, which will be when it terminates in the clear vision of God, the substance of faith, now stripped of this veil of silver, will have the color of gold. Thus, faith gives and communicates to us God himself, but covered with the silver of faith; but it does not on that account fail to give him to us in truth, just as one who gives a vessel of silver-plated gold gives none the less a golden vessel, though covered with silver. Therefore, when the bride in the Song of Songs desired this possession of God, as he had promised it to her so far as possible in this life, he said that he would make her earrings of gold, but plated with silver (Song 1:10). In these words he promised to give himself to her, veiled by faith. So the soul now says to faith: "Oh, if on that your silver surface", by which she means the articles aforementioned, wherewith you have covered the gold of the divine rays, which are the "eyes that I desire", whereof she next speaks, saying: You would suddenly form the eyes that I desire[4]

Exegesis. Part of the foregoing text can be taken as a more detailed explanation of the commentary on stanza 11, paragraph 5. It can also be seen as a valuable commentary on some of the points briefly suggested in chapter 3, book II of *The Ascent,* but from another aspect. The lengthy text quoted above explains only the objective aspect of faith, that is, the relationship between the concept of faith and the divine reality contained in faith. There is no reference to the "excessive light" or the "dark but certain habit" of faith; thus, the subjective aspect, touching faith precisely as a virtue, is absent. In its propositions or formulas, faith is compared to silver, and the formulas as stated in conceptual form contain within themselves the truth and substance in an intentional mode. In this life they are the objects of belief, but in glory the intellect will see them clearly. Hence the word "substance" in the passage cited refers to the intentional order so far as it relates to the knowing intellect, and perhaps nowhere does the Mystical Doctor speak so clearly of the intentional mode of the presence of divinity in faith as when he states: "For that same substance that we now believe, . . . we shall see and enjoy in the next life."

In the same way one should understand the words, "faith gives and communicates to us God himself." Propositions and concepts concerning revealed truth give God to the intellect and at the same time hide him from the intellect. We repeat that they hide God in the intentional order and yet, the Mystical Doctor insists, they truly give God to the intellect. Then he explains this by an example: the gold vessel does not cease to be gold if plated with silver, and, if given to someone, it is truly gold that is given. Likewise, although the revealed truths and

---

[4] *Spiritual Canticle,* stanza 11, no. 3. The differences between redaction A and B are minimal. (Tr.)

concepts conceal the divine "substance", nevertheless, they truly give divinity to the intellect, and what they give is nothing other than the divine substance, but received in an intentional mode. This applies, of course, to the intentional order, for the divine substance can be thus hidden only in its relation to the intellect. It can be expressed in certain particular revealed concepts and, thus expressed, can retain its intentional identity with the divine reality—an identity of the intentional form contained in those concepts with the form of the divine reality as it is in itself.

Therefore the word "substance" is qualified as "substance as understood", meaning the intelligible essence of things, to which the intellect normally attains by abstraction from the sense perceptions that come to it.[5] The "substance" taken in its intentional mode is hidden in the propositions of faith because the conceptual expression of these propositions, in keeping with the operation of the intellect in this life, hides the divine substance from the intellect even as it gives it to the intellect. Yet, that which it gives is truly the divine substance.

We shall now compare the foregoing exegesis with what we have said in our analysis of chapter 3, book II of *The Ascent*. First of all, we note the incapacity of the intellect to penetrate the revealed propositions in the manner that is connatural to it, whereby it would arrive at the essence or "substance" of the revealed truths presented to it by faith. Then the "excessive light" of faith intervenes, and, by reason of its ontological proportion to the divine and as the proportionate means of union, it unites the intellect to the divine substance that is hidden beneath the concepts of the propositions revealed to the intellect. Thus, through faith the human intellect is united with the "substance" of revealed truths ontologically, but not psychologically, because the excessive light of faith in no way changes the nature and mode of operation of the intellect. Consequently, faith does no more psychologically than enable the

[5] Cf. *The Ascent*, bk. II, chap. 8, no. 5; bk. III, chap. 13, no. 4.

intellect to give its assent to those things which it does not see. In one and the same act of faith both things are realized: the union of the intellect with the "substance" of revealed truths, thanks to the "excessive light", and the assent of the intellect which, for St. John of the Cross, excludes the attainment of the "substance" by the intellect, psychologically speaking.

The foregoing consideration shows more clearly the meaning of the "darkness" of faith and why faith is a dark or obscure habit. The revealed propositions are presented to the intellect, and it adheres to them through the power of the excessive light. The propositions come from hearing (*ex auditu*), but they contain a substance, as does anything perceived by the senses. Hence, the intellect naturally tends to penetrate to the substance and unite with it in an intelligible way. However, although the intellect is aided by the excessive light, it does not attain to the substance as it normally would with those things perceived by the senses. Hence the reason for the darkness.

One should not, therefore, try to explain it as some mysterious thrust of the intellect toward the essence of God under the power of an infused light, from which, blinded, it recedes into darkness. The explanation of the darkness of the intellect is simply this: the divine substance is truly present in the revealed concepts in an intentional mode; the intellect adheres to those concepts, and through the power of the divine infused light it also adheres to the "substance" contained in those concepts, but in an intentional mode of adherence. However, never in this life can the possible intellect be united to the divine substance in an intentional mode that is clear and evident. The reason for the darkness lies in the inability of the intellect to penetrate the revealed truths to their substance on the intentional level. In other words, it is a question of the intellect's incapacity to make the divine essence intelligible from the revealed truths.

It is this notion of darkness that is fully explained when the text of the *Spiritual Canticle* is compared with chapter 3, book II of *The Ascent*. Here also is a verification of our conclusion based on the analysis of that same chapter 3, namely, that the "dark habit" of faith is opposed to knowledge not because of the lack of a demonstration but the lack of a form or species. And now we continue with the text of stanza 11.

> By the eyes are meant, as we said, the divine truths and rays, which, as we have also said, faith proposes to us in its formless and hidden articles. And so it is as if [the soul] were to say: Oh, if those truths that you give me formlessly and darkly, veiled in your articles of faith, you would now give me clearly and formally as revealed in them, as my desire begs. And [the soul] calls these truths eyes because of the great presence of the Beloved that she experiences, so that it seems that he is always gazing at her. Therefore she says:
> Which I bear outlined in my inmost parts![6]

Exegesis. This text offers some further precisions. First of all, the propositions of faith, which conceal divine truth in themselves—that is, the very substance of God as related to the intellect as an object of knowledge—coincide in the text as articles of faith. They are the immediate object of belief, and through them the intellect adheres directly to that which corresponds to those articles, so far as the state of the present life allows.

Secondly, the continued "presence of the Beloved" is noteworthy. It does not do away with the unseen quality (*de non visis*) of faith, but, granted this condition, it stimulates a vehement desire to see as soon as possible. This point is important for our later investigation, but now we shall continue with the text.

> [The soul] says that she bears these truths outlined in her inmost parts, that is, in her soul, in the intellect and the will, for it is by means of the intellect that she possesses these truths infused into her soul by faith. And, because her knowledge of them is not perfect, she says that they are outlined; for even as a sketch is not a perfect

---

[6] *Spiritual Canticle*, stanza 11, no. 5.

painting, so the knowledge of faith is not perfect knowledge. Therefore the truths infused into the soul through faith are like a sketch, and when they are clearly visible they will be in the soul like a perfect and finished painting, according to the words of the Apostle: where he says: "*Cum autem venerit quod perfectum est, evacuabitur quod ex perte est*" (1 Cor 13:10). This means: When that which is perfect is come—namely, clear vision—then that which is in part—namely, the knowledge of faith—will pass away.[7]

Exegesis. Taken as a whole, the text makes a comparison between faith and vision on the basis of the imperfection and the perfection of the soul's knowledge of the divine object in the two states. Moreover, the text strongly suggests the existence of some kind of intelligible species, which Father Crisógono excludes from the Mystical Doctor's theory of knowledge. Certainly the text under consideration could never be used to prove that hypothesis. However, the comparison made by St. John of the Cross is of interest to us because he contrasts the imperfection of faith as regards the intentional form with the intellect's perfect possession of the divine form in glory. "Outline" and "painting" are used to designate faith and vision. Just as the outline or rough sketch is very primitive as compared to the lines and colors of a painting, which is a perfection in its own order, so faith as compared to vision is an imperfect impression or realization of the divine form in the intellect. Its imperfection is in the order of cognition or knowledge, for which reason the attainment of divinity through faith is not perfect knowledge, as is vision. Or, to follow the example given, the impression of the divine form that is received through faith does not constitute a source of perfect knowledge; that is achieved only through the complete and full knowledge of vision.

The text also states that the material element of this "outline" is the truths proposed as articles of faith. The same truths,

[7] *Spiritual Canticle*, stanza 11, no. 6.

without the silver plating referred to in paragraph 4, will constitute the perfect "painting". But then, in vision, they will no longer be covered by the veil of "articles of faith".

Lastly, the text asserts that the impression of divinity, still imperfect in the intentional order, is received by the soul through the intellect and the will. But how does each of these faculties function as a medium? As regards the intellect, the Mystical Doctor teaches that the revealed truths are presented to the intellect and thus are impressed on the soul. As regards the will, the Mystical Doctor is silent concerning its function in the adhesion of the soul to the "substance" of truths revealed through faith. We return to the text.

> But over this outline of faith there is another outline in the soul of the lover, which is of love, and this is according to the will, where the image of the Beloved is sketched in such a way and so completely and vividly drawn when there is union of love, that it is true to say that the Beloved lives in the lover and the lover in the Beloved. And in the transformation of the lovers, love causes such a likeness that it can be said that each is the other and that both are one. The reason is that in the union and transformation of love the one gives possession of itself to the other, and each one surrenders and exchanges itself for the other. Thus, each one lives in the other, and the one is the other, and both are one through the transformation of love. This is what St. Paul meant when he said: "*Vivo autem, jam non ego, vivit vero in me Christus*" (Gal 2:20). [I live now, not I, but Christ lives in me.][8]

Exegesis. Our commentary on stanza 11 will end with the text just cited. It is stated here that beyond the imperfect impression of divinity in an intentional manner, given to the soul through faith, there is another impression or "realization" of the divine in the soul which is greatly superior and much more vivid, namely, the one effected through love. With this we are touching the core of the mystical doctrine of St. John of the

---

[8] *Spiritual Canticle*, stanza 11, no. 7.

Cross, which we have frequently expressed as follows: the divine union or transformation of the soul by participation pertains directly and immediately to charity, and to faith as subordinated and joined to charity. The Mystical Doctor teaches that not only is there an intentional but imperfect possession of the divine object in the intellect through faith, but there is a vital, transforming union so intimate that it can be said that the Beloved lives in the lover and the lover in the Beloved.

It is no longer a question of any intellectual or intentional likeness, but of an identity of life, a mutual possession, a unity that truly merits the name "union". We saw in book I, chapter 4 of *The Ascent* that love creates likeness; now we see that love has a transforming power that is proper to itself. This power not only enables the intellect to acquire an intentional likeness, but the whole soul is made to resemble the divine in the transforming union of love. The manner in which all of this is realized is something that lies outside the scope of our study, however.

Our analysis of the *Spiritual Canticle* now moves on to stanza 13 (or stanza 14 in redaction B). The text we are going to study does not pertain directly to the question of faith, but it will clarify for us the nature of contemplative knowledge. The Mystical Doctor here describes how the soul in the unitive way is led to the lofty state of the mystical espousal. In that degree of union the soul receives various sublime communications from the Spouse, which St. John of the Cross describes in metaphorical terms. The last verse of stanza 13 and the accompanying commentary are of particular significance for our investigation.

The whistling of the amorous breezes,

The soul mentions two things in this present verse, namely, breezes and whistling. By the amorous breezes are here understood the virtues and graces of the Beloved, which, by means of the said union of the Spouse, assail the soul, communicate themselves most lovingly and touch it in its very substance. And the whistling of these breezes signifies a most lofty knowledge of God and of his virtues, which redounds to the intellect at the touch that these virtues of God impress on the substance of the soul; and this is the greatest delight there is in anything that the soul here experiences.[9]

Exegesis. The text is clear, but it requires some previous explanation. When St. John of the Cross distinguishes between "breezes" and "whistling", he describes the former as the divine communication to the soul in the spiritual espousal; the latter is the redounding of this communication to the intellect by way of a lofty and most delightful knowledge of God, which constitutes the satisfaction and fruition derived from this state. As regards the "breezes", two things should be noted. First of all, the Mystical Doctor had already stated a basic principle in *The Ascent*: "Although these visions of spiritual substances cannot be stripped and seen clearly in this life by the intellect, they can nevertheless be felt in the substance of the soul, by means of the sweetest touches and unions, all of which belongs to spiritual feelings."[10] He also devotes a special chapter to the discussion of spiritual feelings, where he describes their impact on the intellect: "apprehension and knowledge and understanding overflow from them to the intellect".[11]

Secondly, we should note Father Labourdette's remarks concerning the terminology of the Mystical Doctor. The expression "substance", according to Father Labourdette, does not have a philosophical meaning in the works of the Mystical Doctor, as opposed, for example, to "potencies" of the soul. It simply designates in a general way that part of the soul in which mystical knowledge and love are experienced and perfected.[12] Yet, in chapter 24 of *The Ascent*, the Mystical Doctor declared his intention of treating of the union of the soul with the divine substance:

[9] *Spiritual Canticle*, stanza 13, no. 8.
[10] *The Ascent*, bk. II. chap. 24, no. 4.
[11] Cf. ibid., bk. II, chap. 32.
[12] Cf. M. Labourdette, art. cit., *Revue Thomiste* (1937) 48.

Our pen is being directed and guided to these, that is, the divine joining and union of the soul with the divine substance. We shall speak of this when we treat of the dark or vague mystical knowledge that remains to be described. There we shall discuss how God is united with the soul in a lofty and divine degree by means of this dark and loving knowledge; for the dark and loving knowledge that is faith serves in some way as a means to divine union in this life, even as, in the next life, the light of glory serves as the means for the clear vision of God.[13]

The preceding text has great significance for our study, for it serves to link the section of the *Spiritual Canticle* we are analyzing with the doctrine explained above. The "joining and union of the soul with the divine substance", which can also be translated as a "touch" of the divine substance in the substance of the soul, is associated with the dark and loving knowledge, and this pertains ultimately to faith. That is why the text from stanza 13 merits our investigation. In the description of the touch of the divine perfections in the soul, we find the same doctrine that is expounded concerning the spiritual espousal, from which redounds to the intellect that "most lofty knowledge of God and of his virtues". It is, as we have seen, the same doctrine as in *The Ascent*, book II, chapters 24 and 32.

What is the "touch" of which the Mystical Doctor speaks? According to Father Gabriel of St. Mary Magdalen, it cannot be identified with the operation of the gifts of the Holy Spirit in producing the general, dark and loving knowledge[14] that we studied in book II, chapter 29 of *The Ascent* and in book II, chapter 17 of *The Dark Night*. The spiritual touch would seem to belong to another area of mystical experience. So far as the operation of the Holy Spirit through the gifts and charity is concerned, it is in the order of efficient causality; but here we

---

[13] *The Ascent*, bk. II, chap. 24, no. 4.
[14] Cf. Gabriele di S. Maria Maddalena, "*La mistica Teresiana*" (Firenze, 1934) 143.

are dealing rather with the material cause of the mystical experience.

In the next paragraph of the Mystical Doctor's commentary, we find a penetrating analysis of "the whistling of the amorous breezes". Just as we have two distinct sensations from the rushing wind, namely, the tactile sensation of the moving air and the sound of the wind's motion, so also, in the experience described by this metaphor: "The touch of the virtues of the Beloved is felt and enjoyed in the soul's power of touch, which is in its substance; and the knowledge of those virtues of God is perceived in the ear of the soul, which is in the intellect."[15]

Note that the intellect is described as the ear of the soul; this will be repeated later, where the intellect is related to hearing rather than seeing. The spiritual touch brings great satisfaction to the soul and for this reason is called "amorous breezes"; and because it also communicates the virtues of the Beloved, it is called the "whistling of knowledge", which the Mystical Doctor explains in paragraph 14 of stanza 13:

> It is called a whistling because even as the whistling caused by the wind enters subtly into the organ of hearing, so this most subtle and delicate knowledge enters with marvelous sweetness and delight into the inmost substance of the soul, and it is a delight far greater than any other. The reason is that substance as understood is given to it, stripped of accidents and phantasms because it is given to the intellect that the philosophers call "passive" or "possible", because it receives it passively, without doing anything of itself. This is the principal delight of the soul, because it is in the intellect where, as theologians say, there is fruition, which is to see God. . . . And the soul here calls it a whistling of amorous breezes because from the amorous communication of the virtues of her Beloved it overflows to her intellect.

Exegesis. We have already stated the basic cause of the overflow—the loving spiritual espousal or spiritual touch pro-

---

[15] *Spiritual Canticle*, stanza 13, no. 13.

duces in the intellect a subtle and loving knowledge. The present text makes further precisions concerning that knowledge. It penetrates to the inmost substance of the soul and there causes fruition and sweetness. Three reasons are given for this. In the first place, we are dealing with the "substance as understood, . . . stripped of accidents and phantasms". We know from chapter 13, book III of *The Ascent* that such is the proper goal of the intellect, namely, to attain to the essence of intelligible things.

The second reason is that the "substance as understood" is received into the possible intellect, which, according to the theologians, provides the fruition of the vision of the divine essence in glory. Similarly, when the substance as understood is infused into the possible intellect, the communication of divinity reaches to the very substance of the soul. The precise reason why this communication, which directly touches the substance of the soul, provides sweetness and delight is that the intellect receives it stripped of all accidents and imaginative forms. This is what constitutes its fruition, and in this lofty contemplation it is a fruition of the divine form received intentionally.

By referring back to paragraph 4 of stanza 11, we can see that the "substance as understood" signifies the intentional form of divinity that was hidden beneath the conceptualized propositions of faith but is now freed from them, separated from them and joined to the intellect. And now the intellect has completed its work, which up to this time was fruitless, as we saw in chapter 3, book II of *The Ascent*. The agent intellect had been unable to abstract the divine "substance" from the propositions of revealed truth that came to it through the senses (*ex auditu*). Consequently, the possible intellect was left without an intentional form of the divine object and, due to this privation, it remained in darkness. But now the deficiency is taken care of and the intellect is satisfied, for the "substance as understood" is communicated to the soul, not in the normal way of abstraction by the agent intellect, which is impossible, but by the redundance of love.

The third reason has to do with the phrase, "stripped of accidents and phantasms". In what does this consist? In paragraph 15, stanza 13 of the *Spiritual Canticle*, the Mystical Doctor states that it is not a question merely of the "substance as understood", but also of "the manifestation of truths concerning the divinity and the revelation of his hidden secrets". This refers certainly to a profound and penetrating knowledge of God that is purely spiritual and is a kind of spiritual "vision". But what is the relation between the "substance as understood" and revelations and visions? In the former, there is a general and simple intuition of divinity; in the latter, there is a knowledge of the truths that are in God. But in neither case is there a particularized intentional knowledge as could be obtained through the senses; there are no "distinct apprehensions", but simply a more profound intuition of the "substance as understood". These questions, however, lie outside the scope of our investigation.

There is, however, another statement in paragraph 15 of stanza 13 that does pertain to our study: "For just as faith, as St. Paul also says, comes through bodily hearing, so also what faith teaches us, which is the substance as understood, comes through spiritual hearing." Then, after referring to Job 42:5, the Mystical Doctor concludes: "There it is clearly stated that to hear [God] with the ear of the soul is to see him with the eye of the possible intellect of which we spoke."

We are already familiar with some of the doctrine, namely, the soul's twofold power of hearing: the external sense of hearing, through which the truths of faith proposed in revelation are received, and the spiritual hearing that receives what is contained in the propositions of faith—the "substance as understood" or the intentional form of God received into the intellect. The spiritual hearing, therefore, signifies the possible intellect, which receives the divine essence in an intentional form.[16]

[16] On this point Father Labourdette states: "The Saint also distinguishes in faith the two elements that we already know: the one contained in our natural process of knowledge, which necessarily comes through the senses and relates

But now, in paragraph 16 of stanza 13, the Mystical Doctor places a restriction on the "substance as understood" and received by the soul. It does not transcend the limitations of faith:

And it should not be understood that, because what the soul understands is naked substance, as we have said, it is perfect and clear fruition as in heaven. For although it is stripped of accidents, it is not for that reason clear; rather, it is dark, because it is contemplation, which, as St. Dionysius says, is in this life a "ray of darkness". Therefore we can say that it is a ray and image of fruition, inasmuch as it is in the intellect, where fruition is enjoyed. This substance as understood, which the soul here calls a whistling, is the "eyes that I desire", of which the soul said, when the Beloved revealed them to her, because she could not bear the experience of them: "Withdraw them, Beloved."

Thus does the Mystical Doctor define the nature of the "naked substance", the intentional form that the possible intellect enjoys in contemplation. It is free from accidents, but it is not clear. We are still on the path to union and to the beatific vision, and only in glory will there be clear vision, full fruition and the complete and intimate possession of the divine essence by the intellect. Whatever the intellect can attain in this life will never surpass the limits of faith.

It is true that faith can gradually divest the propositions of revealed truths of the distinct and particular intentional forms in which they are clothed, and this is part of the work of the active night of the spirit, but it is incapable of attaining a clear vision of divinity. This exceeds the limitations of the path to union, which is by faith, and therefore faith can never achieve it.

But what is the "substance as understood" that the possible intellect enjoys in contemplation? Considering all that we have seen from the various texts of stanza 13, it would seem to be

---

to the bodily ear. . . ; the other element is what faith speaks—the 'substance as understood', which pertains to the spiritual ear to which it is carried through the virtue of faith" (art. cit., *Revue Thomiste* [1937] 202).

nothing else but that which redounds to the possible intellect from the profound satisfaction of love in experiencing the divine perfections. The satisfaction overflows to an intellect that is now completely purified and liberated from all intentional species of the natural order. And at this point we should recall what was said in book II, chapter 14 of *The Ascent* concerning the perfection of the light of wisdom, which is attained when there are no more obstacles or impediments on the part of distinct and particular species—which are radically natural—and how and to what extent the human intellect can participate in the light of divine knowledge through faith. Yet, it must be remembered that since the light is participated through faith, it never attains the divine object clearly.

It would seem to follow from the foregoing consideration that the "substance as understood" that the intellect enjoys in contemplation is the satisfaction and fruition overflowing from love into the possible intellect that has been perfectly disposed through the virtue of faith; that is, it is free of all natural intentional species so that it can participate fully in the light of divine knowledge. When these two elements are combined—the overflow from love and the full participation in the divine light—one can understand what is meant by the "substance as understood" within the limitations of faith, that is to say, in darkness. (Note that the spiritual espousal occurs toward the end or at the completion of the passive night of the spirit, when the essential degree of participation in the divine light may equal that of glory, as we saw in book II, chapter 5 of *The Dark Night*.)

Consequently, there is more fruition in the possible intellect than there is apprehension of an intentional species. The fruition, as we have stated, is an overflow from love, and since the intellect cannot place any obstacles by way of distinct and particular species, the participation in the divine light can reach a very lofty degree under the impetus of the Holy Spirit. In this situation, the possible intellect enjoys fruition in nothing but divinity, though lacking clear apprehension and in spite of the fact that the possible intellect does not normally find fruition and satisfaction without a clear intentional form.

How should this be understood? The fruition can be communicated to the intellect by the will, but the "substance as understood" is something proper to the intellect. It cannot be communicated by the will. The "naked substance understood" designates the terminus of an operation proper to the intellect. Therefore, according to the text of paragraph 4 of stanza 11, this substance is truly impressed on the intellect, but it is hidden beneath the propositions of faith. Yet the intellect is actually united to it through faith. The fact that the substance is hidden is due to two things: first, from the nature of the intellect, which, united to the body in this life, cannot grasp the divine object clearly; secondly, from the manner in which the intellect functions in this life—dependent upon the senses.

However, the virtue of faith causes a modification in the operation of the intellect; not an essential one, for it does not change the nature of the intellect, but by way of negation, since it withdraws the intellect from its dependence on the sense order in its cognitive activity. The withdrawal or abnegation is in view of the divine object and is commensurate with the intrinsic proportion between the intellect and the divine essence effected by the virtue of faith. As a result, the divine object can never be confused with any purely natural element of cognition. This is evident in the active night of the spirit and, in a more passive way, in the transition from meditation to contemplation.

Moreover, the abnegation of the intellect can reach such a degree that the intellect never actually mixes any limited, particular and natural elements with its adhesion to revealed truths. Then it is characterized by that vacuum or emptiness referred to in book II, chapter 6 of *The Ascent*, and it experiences the darkness caused by the lack of any clear intentional species. Then, as we deduce from paragraph 4 of stanza 11, the "substance as understood", contained in the propositions of faith, is no longer subject to the natural limitations of the intellect, although it still remains obscure.

How do we explain this? Perhaps the following consideration will enable us to grasp better the role of the "substance as understood" in the contemplative phase. At the same time, we shall see the importance of the virtue of faith in the experience of union and in that "spiritual touch" that we are now discussing.

The intellect now functions in pure faith, purified and emptied of every natural intentional species. This postulates a suspension of the intellect's activity, for the agent intellect tends by its nature to abstract the essence of natural things; but this activity must be suspended. That is why there is an absence of all natural species in the intellect, while faith retains its essential adhesion to the "substance as understood" contained in revealed truths. And since the revealed truths are not translated into any particular and distinct intentional species by the agent intellect, the only thing present to the intellect is the "substance as understood". Then the possible intellect, as we have said, experiences the fruition that redounds from the touch of love.

When all these factors are understood, one can see why the Mystical Doctor asserts that the possible intellect finds fruition and satisfaction in the "substance as understood". The fruition does not proceed from the intellect's adhesion to the divine object, for fruition from that source would require clear apprehension. That is why the fruition is not an operation proper to the intellect but "borrowed", as it were, from the will. We can say, therefore, that the intellect participates in the fruition of vehement love caused by the spiritual "touch".

Together with the fruition, there is in the intellect such a psychological purity of faith that the intellect's adherence to revealed truths is not in any way connected with naturally acquired intentional species. And if the revealed truths truly contain the divine object, though not seen clearly, but darkly, then the intellect in its "borrowed" fruition is united with that divine object. Then the intellect is at rest, because the agent intellect ceases to operate; but there is no fruition of the intellect as such because there is no clear perception of the divine object.[17] Nevertheless, St. John of the Cross maintains that this perception produces a very lofty delight in the experiencing of the "touch".

The preceding explanation is not apodictic and completely evident, nor is it found explicitly in the works of St. John of the Cross. It is deduced from an analysis of numerous texts that treat of the various aspects of the virtue of faith. The subsequent comparison and compilation of the texts seem to justify our explanation of the "substance as understood" in which the intellect experiences fruition through the spiritual touch. We are near the end of our study of faith in the *Spiritual Canticle*, but we should note the following passage in which St. John of the Cross commments on Daniel's vision (Dan 10):

"There stood before me one whose countenance I knew not, an image before my eyes." The one who he says stood before him was God, who communicated himself after the manner described. And he says that he knew not his countenance, meaning that in that communication and vision, most lofty though it be, the face and the essence of God are neither known nor seen. And he says that it was an image before his eyes, for, as we have said, that knowledge of the hidden word was must sublime, like the image and trace of God, but it is not to be understood as an essential vision of God.[18]

---

[17] Cf. *Spiritual Canticle*, stanza 38, no. 9. In redaction B, stanza 39, no. 12, we read: "[the soul] calls it night, because the contemplation is dark, . . . wherein . . . God teaches the soul in a most hidden and secret manner, without her knowing how. This is what some spiritual men call 'to understand without understanding'. For this is not effected by the intellect that philosophers call the active intellect, which works on the species and phantasms and apprehensions of the bodily faculties; it takes place in the intellect so far as it is possible and passive. Without receiving such forms, etc., it receives passively only a knowledge, stripped of all images, which is given to it without any work or activity of its own."

[18] *Spiritual Canticle*, stanza 13, no. 20.

This is a synthesis of the whole doctrine, and we can also interpret the text with reference to the continual presence of the Beloved that the soul claims to have experienced in stanza 11.

A final observation should be made concerning an objection to which the Mystical Doctor responded. It is found in stanza 17, paragraph 6 of the *Spiritual Canticle* (in redaction B, stanza 26, paragraph 8). The objection states that the will cannot love anything unless the intellect first knows it. St. John of the Cross answers by saying that the objection is valid as regards the natural order of knowledge and love, but not as regards the supernatural order, for God can infuse love and increase it without any corresponding increase of knowledge in the intellect. He invokes the testimony of many spiritual persons, saying that they "can understand little and love much or understand much and love little." "Infused faith suffices for them instead of intellectual knowledge, and through faith God infuses charity into them and increases it together with the act of charity, which is to love more, even though their knowledge is not increased."[19]

It is evident, then, that an increase in the experience of love does not necessarily imply an increase in cognitive awareness. Faith alone suffices for the highest degree of charity in this life. And the reason why knowledge is not increased, explains the Mystical Doctor, is that we are not dealing with the natural order, which is subject to the norms of psychology; we are dealing with the supernatural order, the order of gratuitous infusion, and the principles of psychology do not suffice to explain this type of experience. The infusion of graces is determined primarily by the one who infuses them, and the experience of those graces in this or that way also depends on him. One thing is certain: the actual increase of charity necessarily presupposes the virtue of faith in the intellect and, in fact, a

---

[19] *Spiritual Canticle*, stanza 17, no. 6.

faith that is sufficiently intense and active, because every increase of charity occurs through the medium of faith.[20]

However, the actual experience of love in the will does not necessarily presuppose the experience of a correlative knowledge in the intellect. The reason, we know, is that the knowledge in this case depends on the Holy Spirit as the primary agent, and therefore it depends on him to regulate it. Also, the experience denotes passivity and an adequately receptive faculty on the part of the subject. A case in point is that of the passive nights, when we want to verify at a given time or phase of the path to union the relation of one element of the experience to another. We are then beyond the limits of purely psychological laws because then the soul is being led to union under the guidance of the interior Director, who is the Holy Spirit.

These reflections reveal to us incidentally something about the function of faith. The essential relationship of the intellect to God is through faith; therefore, faith is absolutely necessary for union and transformation, though immediately and directly they are effected by the will. It is essential, therefore, that the intellect remain in faith, as expounded so clearly and forcefully throughout *The Ascent* and mentioned specifically in the descriptive title of chapter 9 in book II: "How faith is the proximate and proportionate means for the intellect so that the soul may attain to the divine union of love."

[20] Cf. *The Ascent*, chap. 3, no. 1; *Living Flame*, stanza 2, no. 24.

THE LIVING FLAME OF LOVE

The last part of the tetrology of St. John of the Cross is dedicated to the height of union that is celebrated in the mystical marriage.[1] It likewise repeats many doctrinal elements taken from *The Ascent* and *The Dark Night*, such as the teaching on the dark night and on the transition from meditation to contemplation, found in stanza 3 of the *Living Flame*. We can easily find in those restatements some material that relates to the doctrine on faith. For example:

> God, toward whom the intellect is advancing, transcends the intellect, and therefore he is incomprehensible and inaccessible to it. For that reason when the intellect is understanding, it is not advancing toward God but is rather withdrawing from him. Therefore the intellect must depart from itself and its knowledge in order to reach God, walking in faith, believing and not understanding. In this way the intellect will reach perfection, because it is by faith and no other means that it is united with God. . . . The intellect goes forward by establishing itself more firmly in faith, and thus becoming more obscure, for faith is darkness for the intellect.[2]

The conclusion is that the intellect "should not be occupied with distinct kinds of knowledge." We see here many points already noted: faith as the means, the aspect of darkness and the abnegation of all distinct knowledge. The *Living Flame* presupposes all this doctrine; it does not add anything new or even explain in greater detail what we have already seen regarding faith.

---

[1] J. Baruzi says: "It is actually easy to discern in the *Flame* the highest point of the states already analyzed in the *Canticle*. . . . The expressions denoting spiritual espousal and marriage, which were predominant in the *Canticle*, play a very minor role in the *Flame* (op. cit., 684).

[2] *Living Flame*, stanza 3, no. 48.

Besides the doctrinal points that are repeated and appear here in a new light, the *Living Flame* contains a splendid and lofty doctrine concerning the transforming union, a doctrine that is eminently Trinitarian. We do not intend to explain it here, but we shall make some observations as the occasion offers. Father Gabriel of St. Mary Magdalen has already made a study and summary of the doctrine.[3] He maintains that the transforming union constitutes the perfection of the evolution of grace, the virtues and the gifts, and then he enumerates the elements that are found in the transforming union:

> It is perfect love, meriting the plenitude of grace. This seems to the Saint to connote confirmation in grace . . . peace and rest for the soul . . . the perfect subordination of the senses to the intellect and of the intellect to God, a subordination that is the effect of perfect virtues. Then follows the plenitude of the gifts of the Holy Spirit and the quasi-constant movement that pertains to them; from which it follows that God is the beginning and end of all the soul's actions. Then follows the habitual experience of the embrace . . . a divine experience that is usually characterized by a feeling of an intimate embrace, sometimes identified with a divine touch. And it is in the divine touch that mystical theology reaches its plenitude.[4]

We saw something of the various elements described above when we studied the *Spiritual Canticle*. The best way of speaking of this matter would be to quote the texts of the Mystical Doctor, but they are so numerous that it is difficult to make a selection.

In stanza 3 of the *Living Flame* the Mystical Doctor states:

> This is the great satisfaction and contentment of the soul, to see that it is giving to God more than it is in itself and is worth in itself,

---

[3] Cf. Gabriel de Ste. Marie-Madeleine, "*L'union transformante*", in: *La Vie Spirituelle* (1927), a volume dedicated entirely to St. John of the Cross; also "*L'union de transformation dans la doctrine de S. Jean de la Croix*", in: *La Vie Spirituelle* (1925) and the related sections in his book, *S. Giovanni della Croce: Dottore dell'Amore divino* (Firenze, 1937).

[4] Cf. Gabriel de Ste. Marie-Madeleine, art. cit., *La Vie Spirituelle* (1927).

with that same divine light and divine warmth that is given to it. This is caused in the next life by the light of glory, and in this life by most enlightened faith.[5]

What does the soul give to God through that "most enlightened faith"? We know from book II, chapter 29 of *The Ascent* that the illumination of faith comes from the Holy Spirit, but now faith has reached its highest point of perfection and enlightenment. So the Mystical Doctor says: "In this state the soul cannot perform any acts; the Holy Spirit performs them and moves the soul to perform them. Therefore, all the acts of the soul are divine because the soul is actuated and moved by God."[6]

The motion by the Holy Spirit is immediate and supernatural as to its substance and mode, as is indicated in the following statement:

Such is the operation of the Holy Spirit in the soul that is transformed in love, that the interior acts that he produces in it are like the enkindling of fire; they are inflammations of love whereby the soul's will is united and loves most deeply, transformed into love by that flame.[7]

The text explains sufficiently why faith is at this stage most enlightened, but what does the soul give to God, of whom it is now so intimately aware?

Since by means of this substantial transformation the soul is the shadow of God, it does in God and through God what he does through himself in the soul and in the same way as he does it, because the wills of both are one and hence the operation of God and that of the soul are one. Therefore, as God is giving himself to the soul with a free and gracious will, so also the soul, having a will that is the more free and more generous in the measure that it is more united in God, is giving God himself in God to God, and it is a true and total gift of the soul to God. For in this state the soul sees that

<hr>

[5] *Living Flame*, stanza 3, no. 80. [6] Ibid., stanza 1, no. 4.
[7] Ibid., stanza 1, no. 3.

God truly belongs to it, and that it possesses him as its inheritance, with the right of ownership, as an adopted child of God through the grace that God conferred on it in giving himself to the soul. And since he belongs to the soul, it may give and communicate him to whomsoever it desires of its own will. Thus it gives him to its Beloved, who is the very God that gave himself to it. In this way the soul pays to God all that it owes him, since it willingly gives him as much as it has received from him.[8]

The concept of the relationship between God and the soul, at once filial and conjugal, is based on two constant elements: the communication of grace of adoption and the power of love. The soul becomes "God by participation" and therefore by participation it possesses divinity itself. Then the will gives to the Beloved through love nothing less than that which it had received from him: the gift of participated divinity. Hence, the soul gives God to himself through himself because in the transforming union the motion of the Holy Spirit is practically continuous. Yet, the one who gives is the soul, which loves God in return to a supreme degree. Since its will is perfectly united with God, it cannot act otherwise than does the divine will. Consequently, because of the perfection of the transforming union, the will is constantly and solely occupied in the same thing as the divine will, namely, loving God and giving to him by its love that which it has by participation—God himself. Moreover, the soul does this not only with a loving will but in a divine mode, since it is under the impetus of the Holy Spirit.

With this, we reach the "Trinitarian" mysticism that was already mentioned in the *Spiritual Canticle*:

The Holy Spirit . . . with that his divine breathing elevates the soul most sublimely and informs and disposes her so that she may breathe in God the same spiration of love that the Father breathes in the Son and the Son in the Father, which is the same Holy Spirit who in this transformation breathes in the soul in the Father and the Son to unite her to himself.[9]

[8] Ibid., stanza 3, no. 78.
[9] *Spiritual Canticle*, stanza 38, no. 2.

These are the peaks whose foundations are firmly established in the doctrine of the Mystical Doctor on participation and the motion of the Holy Spirit. We shall not attempt to explain them here, but we merely mention them in order to show what is meant by "most enlightened faith" and how it operates in the soul. That enlightened faith is not only operative here, but it also enables the soul to see what is happening and to be more aware of the experience. None of the statements concerning the transforming union will cause any surprise to one who knows the doctrine of the Mystical Doctor concerning faith, its essential transcendence, the divine light that is operative in faith, and the "substance as understood" that is infused into the intellect through faith.

But once again, it should be noted that the statements on the transforming union do not further explain the doctrine on faith; they presuppose all the previous doctrine, present it in a new light, but always based on the same principles established by the Mystical Doctor. The following text exemplifies this:

> For the intellect, which before this union understood in a natural way with the power and strength of its natural light by means of the bodily senses, is now moved and informed by another and higher principle of the supernatural light of God, the senses having been left aside. It has thus been changed into something divine, because through union its intellect and that of God are both one.[10]

The preceding quotation is part of the lengthy text in which the Mystical Doctor describes the consummation of the transforming union so far as the intellect, memory and will—always the same threefold division—participate in it. But if we compare this text with the one we analyzed in chapter 4, book II of The Dark Night, the one from the Living Flame is much stronger. Actually, it speaks of the consummation of union of the intellect in this life and not merely its painful preparation for union in the purifying night. Nevertheless, we are still in this life and therefore still within the limits of faith. Hence, in

[10] Living Flame, stanza 2, no. 34.

order to understand rightly the words "its intellect and that of God are both one". it is necessary to apply all that was said in chapter 29, book II of *The Ascent* concerning the movement of the Holy Spirit and what was stated in stanza 13 of the *Spiritual Canticle* concerning the "substance as understood", where the possible intellect is at rest in the fruition redounding from love.

Lastly, we cite the text that speaks of the "deep caverns of sense":

> These caverns are the faculties of the soul—memory, intellect and will—and they are as deep as is their capacity for great blessings, for they cannot be filled with anything less than the infinite. And from what they suffer when they are empty, we can understand to some extent how much they rejoice and delight when they are filled with God, for one contrary can shed light on the other. In the first place, it should be noted that these caverns of the faculties, when they are not empty and purged and cleansed from all creature affection, are not aware of the great emptiness of their deep capacity.[11]

What an insight into the spiritual part of human nature! The infinite capacity of the higher faculties of the soul, their capacity for the infinite, is precisely the metaphysical reason and basis why they are the subjects or faculties of the theological virtues, for it is through the theological virtues that the soul is united with the infinite. However, union demands the purification of the faculties and their being emptied of everything finite, limited, particular and distinct. The purgation of the faculties is therefore a function of the theological virtues insofar as they must open the infinite capacity of the faculties; and thus they both open the capacity and fill it with participated divinity.

The doctrine of St. John of the Cross on the theological virtues, given in chapter 6, book II of *The Ascent*, corresponds perfectly with this concept of the higher faculties of the soul. The theological virtues must unite the soul with God and also purify it by placing the soul in "emptiness and darkness". And

---

[11] *Living Flame*, stanza 3, no. 18.

the second function is necessary in view of the first. Here also we can apply the principle stated in chapter 4, book I of *The Ascent*, concerning the impossibility of two different forms simultaneously informing the same subject.

We note, finally, that the first of the caverns is the intellect and is described as follows:

> Its emptiness is thirst for God and it is so intense when the intellect is disposed for God that David compares it to that of the hart. . . . This thirst is for the waters of the wisdom of God, which is the object of the intellect.[12]

[12] Ibid., stanza 3, no. 19.

PART TWO

SYNTHESIS

DOCTRINAL RESUMÉ

In this part of our study we intend to summarize in a series of conclusions the results of our previous investigation. But before doing that, it will be well to determine the precise aspect under which faith is treated in the works of St. John of the Cross. For the virtue of faith is treated differently in fundamental theology, in dogmatic and moral theology, in religious psychology and in mystical theology. It is from the point of view of mystical theology that St. John of the Cross treats of faith.

1. Nowhere in the works of the Mystical Doctor do we find a treatment of "unformed" faith taken in itself; he speaks always of a faith informed and vivified by charity. This was noted in chapter 2, book I of *The Ascent*, and it remains unchanged throughout all his works. It is always a question of faith vivified by charity and, indeed, of faith as the means of divine union by reason of its ordination to charity. This is the first point that needs to be emphasized.

2. Neither does St. John of the Cross treat of faith precisely as the assent to revealed truths by reason of the authority of the one revealing. He uses the word "assent" in chapter 3, book II of *The Ascent*, it is true, but this aspect of faith, however authentic, is not the subject matter of the texts of the Mystical Doctor. He presupposes it, as we can see from his use of the word "assent" and also from his reference to the function of the Church in proclaiming the revealed truths, thus affecting the act of faith of each believer.[1]

3. Faith is treated by St. John of the Cross as the means of union of the soul with God; more precisely, as the means proper to the intellect for uniting the soul with God in love.

[1] Cf. *The Ascent*, bk. II, chap. 27, no. 4.

237

Under this aspect faith is compared with vision, which unites the intellect perfectly with God in glory, and it is distinguished from vision because it deals with the unseen (*de non visis*). The comparison with vision and the distinction from vision on the basis of the unseen is characteristic of the works of St. John of the Cross. Vision effects perfect union of the intellect with God; faith joins the intellect to God on the path to perfect union. This constitutes the framework within which the Mystical Doctor develops his teaching on faith. Nor is it necessary to insist that it is a method that is especially suitable for mystical theology. And that suffices to show the precise aspect under which the Mystical Doctor treats the virtue of faith.

4. The entire teaching of the Mystical Doctor on faith is developed in an organic way and according to a strictly logical deduction from the one principle that is also the principle underlying all his mystical doctrine. The principle, stated in chapter 8, book II of *The Ascent*, can be designated as the principle of "essential likeness". The Mystical Doctor states that there is no essential likeness between God and any creature, for the divine essence infinitely transcends the essence of every creature, however perfect. From this follows another principle that is basic to all of his mystical doctrine: by reason of its essence or nature, no creature can serve as a proportionate means of union with God, because it lacks the proportion of likeness that is absolutely necessary for union with God.

These two principles—the metaphysical principle of essential likeness and the more practical principle that follows from it, that of proportionate means of union with God—influence the ultimate theoretical conclusions and the practical norms found in the mystical theology of St. John of the Cross. His entire doctrine on faith rests on those principles, as do his theoretical and practical conclusions concerning faith.

5. Faith is described as the proportionate means—and also the proper, proximate, accommodated, adequate and legitimate means—of the union of the intellect with God. With this asser-

tion and in comparison with the principles previously stated, the ontological aspect of faith is identified and the proper foundation is established for discussing the nature of faith.

a) *The ontological aspect.* For St. John of the Cross the concept of the proportionate means for union with God necessarily connotes the proportion of likeness with the divine essence, which proportion is lacking to all creatures as regards their nature. Faith, on the other hand, possesses a proportional likeness to divinity, and by that fact it is situated on a higher level and transcends every created nature, even the most perfect.

The radical elevation of faith above every creature is confirmed by the statement in chapter 5, book II of *The Ascent*, which treats of the nature of the union for which faith serves as a proportionate means. It is a supernatural union, a union consisting in the communication of divinity on the part of God and participation in God through grace and charity on the part of the soul. And through grace and charity the soul is capable of reaching the "transforming union", where it becomes "God by participation". Hence, faith as the proportionate means of union is something substantially supernatural. Further precisions will be made later.

b) *The proper foundation for discussing the nature of faith.* Likeness to God is denied of every creature, but it is predicated of the very essence of faith because faith is an "essential likeness" to God. The concept of likeness as applied to all essences separates the divine essence from all created essences, but when applied to faith, the concept of likeness is appropriated to its very essence. That is why it is possible to investigate the nature of faith in relation to union with God.

6. The essential likeness of faith to God is the basis for its proportion of likeness, which is, in turn, the reason why faith is the proportionate means of union with God. By reason of its essential likeness to God, faith is substantially supernatural; by reason of its proportion of likeness, faith is the proportionate means of union with God. From this it necessarily follows that

the intellect is proportioned to God through the virtue of faith, through the essential likeness to God that faith has by its very nature. Such is the progression from the metaphysical principle of "essential likeness" to the principle of "proportionate means of union", which also includes a proportion of likeness. But this necessarily postulates a point of origin (*terminus a quo*) and a goal or end (*terminus ad quem*) between which the means functions as such.

7. If divinity is proportionate to the intellect through faith, we want to ask immediately how this proportion should be understood. The response of St. John of the Cross is that the proportion is such that the virtue of faith is capable of uniting the intellect with God; or more precisely, it is capable of acting as the proper and proportionate means of union of the intellect with God. It can do this because of its essential likeness to divinity, and since it involves the intellect, the likeness must somehow be reduced to the intentional order.

We can ask further: what does it mean for St. John of the Cross to unite the intellect with something? He gives an explicit answer in chapter 12, book III of *The Ascent*, where he says that the intellect is united with anything when by its operation it grasps the essence of that thing in an intentional mode, that is, when it attains to the essence of the thing in an intelligible manner. This is described by St. John of the Cross as the "substance as understood".

8. From what has been said it is clear that the intellect will be united to God perfectly through the beatific vision of the divine essence, for then it will know the divine essence as the "substance as understood". This is the constant teaching of St. John of the Cross. But faith is described as the proper means of the union of the intellect with God in this life for essentially the same reason, but not so perfectly and not in the same way. The following text is to the point: "In some way this dark and loving knowledge, which is faith, serves as a means to divine

union in this life, as, in the next life, the light of glory serves as a means to the clear vision of God."[2]

The text immediately raises a question, however: St. John of the Cross is not speaking there of faith alone but of faith so far as it intervenes in contemplation. To answer the question, it is necessary to investigate the nature of faith and to explain how and in what sense faith constitutes a proper means of union with God in this life. Indeed, the entire teaching of St. John of the Cross on the nature of faith is contained in its function as a means of the union of the intellect with God. Its nature and its definition are based on its unifying function.

9. When faith is compared with vision as a means of the union of the intellect with God, a fundamental distinction emerges: God as seen and God as the object of belief. "God as seen" in the beatific vision is the definitive and perfect apprehension of the divine essence by the intellect; "God as the object of belief" lacks clarity in the apprehension. Yet, if the intellect is to be united with an object, it must attain to that object, as is evident from chapter 13, book III of *The Ascent*. So how can faith be called the proper means of union when there is no clear apprehension of the divine essence in the intentional order, no "substance as understood"?

The Mystical Doctor responds that the intellect does attain to the divine essence in the intentional order through faith, but without an intentional species. Consequently, faith is the means of union, though an imperfect one. And now we ask why this is so.

10. Faith is the means of union for the intellect in this life as vision is the means in glory because faith contains essential elements similar to those of vision, namely, the infused divine light and the divine object intimately united with the intellect through the infused light. But the Mystical Doctor states: "*Ab*

---

[2] *The Ascent*, bk. II, chap. 24, no. 4.

objecto et potentia paritur notitia; that is: from the object that is present and from the faculty, knowledge is born in the soul."[3]

Then why does this not happen in regard to faith? It is due entirely to the incapacity of the intellect to attain such knowledge of the divine object by means of an intentional species. And this point, which directly touches the nature and function of the intellect, opens up the whole question concerning faith, which is for St. John of the Cross a virtue localized in the intellect, a habit of the intellect. As such, it is affected by the natural incapacity of the intellect with respect to the divine essence, to which faith joins the intellect.

We stated above that in this life the intellect is essentially proportioned to divinity through the virtue of faith, but precisely because it is a virtue of the intellect in this life, the proportion is restricted by the natural function of the intellect. For that reason, faith as the proportionate means of union has some characteristics that pertain to the goal or *terminus ad quem* of union, and others that pertain to the point of origin or *terminus a quo*.

11. And now, what does the Mystical Doctor teach concerning the point of origin—the *terminus a quo*—of union?

a) According to St. John of the Cross, the intellect is one of the three faculties of the higher part of the soul, the part of the soul that is orientated to God and is capable of communicating with divinity as such, to the point of participating in the divine nature and life. Consequently, as a spiritual faculty the intellect has a capacity for the infinite, as the Mystical Doctor expressly states in stanza 3 of the *Living Flame*. Indeed, it cannot be satisfied and find rest in anything less than the infinite. Hence its natural desire for the divine object—to possess the divine essence in an intentional mode.

b) However, in the state of the union of body and soul, the intellect depends on the senses for its operation. The soul is

---

[3] *The Ascent*, bk. II, chap. 3, no. 2.

infused into the body as a smooth, blank board or a *tabula rasa*, according to chapter 3, book I of *The Ascent*, and it is informed by the species that are presented to it by the senses. The intellect has its own proper function in this information or reception of species. The active or agent intellect abstracts the intelligible form or essence of the object presented to it by the senses; then this form is received by the passive or possible intellect as the "substance as understood" or the substance as known. Such is the natural process of cognition which terminates in the rest and quiet of the intellect in the "substance as understood". Through this cognition the intellect is informed intentionally with the limited, particular and distinct species wherein it attains the natural perfection of cognition and has fruition in the "substance as understood" that is known with clarity.

At the same time the intellect as a spiritual faculty has a capacity for an unlimited and infinite form, but the capacity and natural desire for such a form is impeded by the mode of operation to which the intellect is restricted in the state of union between body and soul.

12. The intellect, therefore, by reason of its very nature, should unite with God, but perfect union with the infinite and unlimited form is attained only through the beatific vision, which requires a change in the subject, namely, the separation of the soul from the body. In this life, union with the divine and the infinite is attained through faith, but without changing the condition of the subject. At the same time, the work of faith is preparatory for the perfect union of the beatific vision.

From the notion of faith given us by the Mystical Doctor in chapter 6, book II of *The Ascent*, it would seem that the operation of the virtue of faith has a twofold function: first, to unite the intellect with God and, second, to produce "emptiness and darkness" in the intellect. These two functions express clearly the two ways in which faith transcends the natural order, as is necessary if the intellect is to attain to the divine object.

The first transcendence is ontological, and it postulates the elevation of the intellect from the natural order of knowledge to the supernatural order of the divine essence, as is explained in chapter 8, book II of *The Ascent*. Faith provides this ontological transcendence because it is supernatural in substance (*supernaturalis quoad substantiam*). The second transcendence pertains to the subject of faith—the intellect—and is therefore a psychological transcendence that requires a change in the intellect's natural mode of knowledge so that it can put aside the particular species received through the senses and open its spiritual capacity to the infinite form.

The second transcendence is deduced from the fundamental principle in the mystical doctrine of St. John of the Cross, stated in chapter 4, book I of *The Ascent*: two contraries cannot exist at the same time in the same subject. And since the Mystical Doctor considers that any natural created species is totally contrary and incompatible with the divine object, according to the principle of "essential likeness", which is lacking to created things, it is impossible for the divine form to co-exist in the intellect with any created species. As we have said, this impossibility refers to the psychological aspect, and it is in this sense that it constitutes the basis for the second type of transcendence that we are discussing here. The first kind of transcendence—the ontological—is verified with the very infusion of faith, while the psychological transcendence evolves successively throughout the entire path to union, preparing for the beatific vision of God, and with some brief pauses at the various degrees of contemplation.

13. It has been stated that the nature of faith as substantially supernatural can be deduced from its primary function, which is to unite the intellect with God, not so much in a psychological as in a metaphysical sense. How does it do this? First of all, the divine essence is presented to the intellect in the revealed truths, which are given in the form of words and therefore are received through hearing (*ex auditu*), reaching the intellect through the senses. The agent intellect then operates in its usual

fashion to abstract from the words the intelligible content so that the possible intellect may assimilate the "substance as understood" and thus enable the intellect to enjoy the natural fruition of understanding.

However, the normal operation of the intellect would seem to meet an impasse in the present case. The senses fail to form a species because that which is given in revelation is totally inaccessible to the senses. As a result, the agent intellect lacks material or sense species on which it can focus, so that the revealed truths seem doomed to remain only words or meaningless names of an unknown object. But the virtue of faith is infused into the intellect, and with faith the intellect receives the excessive light by which it is attracted to the revealed truths and united with them. This was explained in chapter 3, book II of *The Ascent*.

Now we must consider this attraction and union, and the first thing to note is that the revealed truths that come to the intellect through hearing (*ex auditu*) and through the conceptual species expressed in words contain in themselves the divine essence in an intentional mode, as we saw in stanza 11 of the *Spiritual Canticle*. This means that they contain the "substance" that is ordained to the intellect, just as any sense experience provides the intellect with the substance of things as material for cognition. And so the divine essence is presented to the intellect in this life by means of the revealed truths, wherein it is united to the intellect through the concepts expressed in words. And these words and concepts that come to the intellect through the senses (*ex auditu*) contain the divine essence as the proper object of intellection or as the "substance as understood".

However, as we have already stated, this intellection is not achieved because the human intellect is not capable of penetrating the veil of revealed truths to their "substance as understood". It is only by means of the excessive light that the intellect can adhere to revealed truths, and this light, as our analysis has shown, is the light of divine knowledge, shared by the intellect through faith. Thus, what the natural light of reason could not achieve is effected by the infused light whereby "God manifests himself to the soul."

The infused light, generally speaking, makes it possible for the intellect to adhere to revealed truths, which means the adherence of the intellect to the conceptual propositions of faith that both contain and conceal the divine substance from the intellect. We say, therefore, that in adhering to revealed truths, the intellect is united to the divine essence so far as it is contained in those revealed truths. In this way the intellect truly attains to the divine essence, to the "substance as understood" of revealed truths.

The foregoing conclusion seems to be certain when we consider the premises laid down by the Mystical Doctor, and there are three reasons for saying this. 1) The human intellect naturally tends to the intelligible essence of anything presented to it by the senses; 2) when it is a question of revealed truths, however, it is not able to attain to their essence by its own power, but the excessive light comes to its aid and enables it to do so; 3) faith, as the Mystical Doctor states repeatedly, is the means of union, but union with the object necessarily postulates the attainment of the essence of the object in some way.

The conclusion that follows from the foregoing statements is that in and through faith the intellect truly attains to the "substance" of revealed truths and hence is truly united with the divine essence in a manner corresponding to the exigencies of the intellect enlightened by faith. The conclusion is not found in this explicit form in St. John of the Cross, but it can be deduced from the principles expressly stated in his works. If such an interpretation is not admitted, then we cannot speak of faith as a means of union, because faith would be no more than the knowledge of certain words known through revelation. Therefore, in and through faith the intellect attains to the "substance as understood" of revealed truths and is thus united to the divine essence. This follows from the premises already established and is of importance on the metaphysical level.

The case is far different on the psychological level. Although the divine essence is truly united objectively to the intellect through faith as the "substance of revealed truths as understood", psychologically the intellect lacks that "substance as understood". It does not have a clear apprehension of the divine essence, and hence it lacks an intentional species of the divine. Psychologically speaking, therefore, faith is not knowledge, nor science, nor understanding—all of which signify for St. John of the Cross the full possession of an intentional species—but it is the assent of the intellect to revealed truths. Psychologically, this is most certain.

With this we have explained the first transcendence attributed to faith so that it can unite the intellect with God. Thereby we have also explained the first function of faith, namely, to make the intellect essentially proportioned to God by reason of the ontological transcendence that is based on faith's "essential likeness" to divinity. Thus faith is able to unite the intellect to God.

There still remains the psychological transcendence whereby the intellect can attain to God on the psychological level. However, before seeing the conclusions that follow from it, certain previous observations are necessary.

14. We saw that the union of the intellect with God is effected by the supernatural virtue of faith. The Mystical Doctor seems to refer to this union through faith vivified by charity when, in chapter 5, book II of *The Ascent*, he refers to the "permanent and total union according to the substance of the soul and its faculties with respect to the obscure habit of union." In this sense, faith is called an obscure but certain habit. It is called a habit insofar as the divine essence is possessed by the intellect and the intellect is united to the divine essence in faith. It is called obscure because the intellect lacks the intentional species of the divinity to which it is united in faith. It is called an obscure but certain habit to designate the constant assent of the intellect to revealed truths. However, assent of the intellect pertains to the study of faith from another point of

view, so far as it treats of the lack of evidence and demonstration in faith. This is not the approach of St. John of the Cross,
who does not discuss the lack of scientific demonstration and
proof, but the lack of a visible object. For that reason faith is
described much more frequently in his writings as an obscure
habit.

15. We have explained why faith is by its very nature the
proportionate means of union of the intellect with God. We
know also that such a union lacks the required psychological
perfection: the divine form possessed with clarity in the intentional order. Nevertheless, the Mystical Doctor attributes to
faith something of the psychological aspect, not as fully and
definitively realized, but as something preparatory and perfect-
ible by degrees. In other words, it is relatively perfect, to the
extent that the conditions of this life allow. Thus, the Mystical
Doctor is led to speak of that "confused, general and dark
knowledge" which is given in faith.[4] At that point it is no
longer a question simply of the virtue of faith as the means of
union, but of the union itself in its totality, comprising the
other supernatural virtues and the gifts of the Holy Spirit. This
we must also investigate in order to obtain a better understanding of our theme, which is the nature of faith.

16. We know the nature of the operation of the intellect as it
functions in the body-soul composite. And when the virtue of
faith is infused into the intellect and unites the intellect with the
divine essence, with the "substance" of revealed truths, this infusion does not change or destroy the intellect's natural mode
of operation in the acquisition of intentional species. It simply
enables the intellect to adhere to the divine essence, although as
compared with the psychologically clear and complete operations of the intellect in the natural order, this adhesion is psychologically imperfect so far as it is simply an assent or adhe-

---

[4] Cf. *The Ascent*, bk. II, chap. 10, no. 4.

sion to that which is not seen. The natural operations, on the other hand, normally terminate in the acquisition of distinct and particular intentional species.

If considered simply as the assent of the intellect, the virtue of faith would remain on the level of the natural operations of the intellect, though remaining substantially supernatural and psychologically imperfect, unless other powers were added to faith and together they could unite the soul to God. Then faith, while retaining its adhesion to the unseen (*de non visis*) will be extended, as it were, and acquire the psychological plenitude possible in this life. And since faith is rooted in an intellectual faculty, its plenitude is nothing other than a certain "understanding" or contemplation of divine things.

17. At this point it is necessary to state once again that for St. John of the Cross the virtue of faith is the proximate and proportionate means in the intellect so that the soul can attain to the divine union of love, as stated in book II, chapter 9 of *The Ascent*. The virtue that unites properly speaking is charity, says the Mystical Doctor, for love causes likeness. This means that the virtue of charity has an essential likeness to divinity not only in the ontological order, but it can produce and increase the likeness in the psychological order as well, causing a likeness between the lover and the beloved. And since the supernatural union is a union of likeness, tending even to the participated transformation of the lover into the Beloved, it is evident that the virtue that effects this transformation is the virtue of charity. Its primary operation is centered in the will, in which charity is rooted, but it likewise extends its influence to the other faculties, on which it impresses the psychological likeness of the Beloved.

Since love causes likeness, it also dispels dissimilarity. In other words, in turning to the object loved, as presented by the intellect, it expels all contrary forms. Such is the way in which St. John of the Cross understands the power of love to create likeness between lover and beloved in the psychological sense. Of its nature, love tends to ever greater and more perfect likeness and thus postulates the expulsion of all contrary objects.

It is, therefore, in love that we find exemplified the fundamental principle of the dark nights, due to the contrariety between the form of the divine and that of any creature. It is first an ontological contrariety because of the lack of "essential likeness", as stated in chapter 8, book II of *The Ascent*, and then an intentional or psychological contrariety, as stated in chapter 4, book I of *The Ascent*. But as a divine love that creates a likeness between the soul and God, charity tends by its very nature to expel all contrary forms, all forms that are created, natural and limited. It is a question of expelling all those created forms from the intentional order, lest they remain as objects of love, and also that God may be loved more and more. In this way the soul acquires more and more the form of the divine as an object of love and increases the supernatural union of likeness, ultimately to the point of a participated transformation in God.

18. The influence of love on the virtue of faith and on the intellect should now be evident. It should also be clear how faith vivified by charity is the proper means of union with God. It is true, of course, that charity first effects likeness to God in its own faculty of operation, namely, the will, and it seeks a progressively more intimate union with the divine object. But as the virtue that unifies the whole soul with God, charity likewise seeks the divine likeness in the other faculties and powers as well. This is particularly true of the intellect, for the simple reason that the divine object is presented to love and to the will by the intellect endowed with faith. It is through faith, as we have stated repeatedly, that the intellect attains to divinity, to the "substance as understood" of revealed truths and adheres to it, but without a clear intentional species. We likewise stated that this union is primarily of the ontological order, since it is psychologically imperfect, due to the lack of fullness and completion.

The relative perfection of the psychological order, always limited by the conditions of this life, comes to faith through charity. This requires that faith be vivified or informed by charity and, secondly, that it operate through charity.

19. We have stated that so far as love creates likeness, it must likewise expel all contrary forms. Love performs this function immediately and directly in the will, but from the moment that faith works through charity, love also produces this effect in the intellect.

The element of essential likeness attributed to faith—or better, the likeness in the intellect through faith vivified by charity—is the "substance as understood", which is united to the intellect through revealed truths but is also hidden beneath the revealed truths as regards the intentional form. The element of dissimilarity with divinity in the intellect is caused by any natural intentional species acquired by abstraction from the sense impressions; that is, any distinct and particular species, however perfect and complete in the intentional order. But St. John of the Cross does not discuss any and all intentional species, but only those that pertain to the revealed truths received by the intellect. Hence his consideration is restricted to the path to union and the fundamental means of attaining union, namely, interior mental prayer.

According to the Mystical Doctor, mental prayer involves acts of loving knowledge of God, acts that stem radically from faith and charity (and also from hope), acts which therefore have a markedly psychological character. Here we touch upon the core of our problem: the psychological development of faith. In observing the psychological evolution of faith, therefore, mental prayer is of capital importance, prescinding from the fact that in Carmelite spirituality great emphasis was placed on mental prayer in relation to union with God. For our purposes it suffices to look at it simply as an object of investigation.

20. Hence, the problem of faith operating through charity to

reach perfect psychological union with God, so far as is possible in this life, occurs especially in two areas, and they are discussed by St. John of the Cross: the transition from meditation to contemplation, treated in chapters 13–15 in book II of *The Ascent*, and the active night of the spirit, explained in chapters 16–32 of the same book of *The Ascent*.

The doctrine on faith is more explicit in the second reference because the active night of the spirit is more properly attributed to the virtue of faith. In what does it consist? A careful analysis reveals that there is always operative in the active night of the spirit some abnegation of the intellect; that is, the rejection of all natural, clear, distinct and particular intentional species. This is necessary in order that the intellect may adhere to the divine essence, to which it is united in the "substance" of revealed truths. But this occurs without any clear, particular and distinct intentional species because divinity cannot be united to the intellect in such species. The divine essence cannot be limited to an intentional species; it is general and not particular.

It follows that in the rejection of all particular intentional species, faith provides the intimate proportion between the intellect and the divine essence whereby the intellect adheres to the unlimited and general form of the divine essence but in an obscure manner, naturally speaking. The proportion provided the intellect by vivified faith is unifying not only in an ontological sense, but it admits of a certain psychological proportion as well, stemming from the metaphysical union through faith. It is precisely the psychological union of the intellect with the unlimited and obscure form that constitutes the "dark, general and loving knowledge" that is contemplation.

But before we discuss contemplation, we want to determine the role of faith in the active night of the spirit. It actually reveals to us something characteristic of faith. We are not referring now simply to the metaphysical aspect of the union of the intellect with God, but also to the psychological aspect, wherein the virtue of faith operates through charity and through charity produces psychological union with God, the divine and infinite object that is darkness to the intellect in the present life. But what is the function of faith in this operation and what is the function of charity?

According to the premises stated above, it is essentially the work of love to create a likeness with the beloved and to reject all that is dissimilar or contrary to the beloved. When, through faith vivified by charity, the operation of love touches the intellect, it produces a likeness to the Beloved in that obscure adhesion of the intellect to the essence of revealed truths. It is, we repeat, psychologically imperfect because it lacks a clear intentional form. At the same time, it produces the dissimilitude as regards any particular, distinct and naturally clear intentional form. Let us add that this type of adhesion of the intellect to revealed truths applies to the soul that is on the path to union.

Why is this so? Because the adhesion of the intellect to revealed truths without any clear and distinct understanding is the mode of adherence to the substance of revealed truths that is proper to the human intellect in this life. On the other hand, adherence to particular and clear truths introduces a natural element of knowledge that is psychologically satisfying, but precisely because of that, it lacks the required proportion to the substance of revealed truths.

To what "proportion" do we refer? First and evidently to metaphysical proportion, because the clear and particular intentional species is essentially of the natural order. Secondly, the psychological proportion, because this designates the point of origin (*terminus a quo*) of the proportion and not the end or goal (*terminus ad quem*). The true proportion between divinity and the intellect endowed with faith but working in its human mode is the absence of the distinct intentional form. We have already stated that the particular form is necessary for the intellect in its purely natural mode of knowledge, but this is absolutely incompatible with the unlimited form of God. It is only through faith that the intellect acquires a proportion to God, but from faith also comes the obscure and general knowledge.

Consequently, in producing the likeness to the Beloved, love strengthens in the intellect the obscure and general adhesion that lacks any clear intentional form and at the same time rejects any adhesion to particular and distinct species, since love expels anything that is dissimilar to the object loved. Such is the abnegation in the intellect, which tends naturally to intentionally clear species. And the greater the abnegation, the greater the activity of the will, for, as the Mystical Doctor states, the intellect and the other faculties cannot receive or reject anything without the intervention of the will. But in the will it is love that produces likeness to the Beloved; therefore it is love that moves the intellect to this abnegation, which is immediately an operation of the intellect and therefore of the virtue of faith.

Indeed, the whole work of intellectual abnegation is rooted in faith because faith provides the essential proportion between the intellect and divinity. We refer not only to the metaphysical proportion emanating from the union of the intellect with God in faith, but also to the psychological proportion, insofar as faith is an intellectual virtue that unites the intellect with God and seeks an intentional form or psychological likeness of divinity in the intellect. And here again faith relates to charity and is led by charity, for love seeks likeness in the psychological sense, while faith possesses the Beloved as the "substance as understood", as united to the intellect but lacking the power to possess an intentional likeness by means of a clear species. Faith is of things not seen (*de non visis*).

Such seems to be the contribution of faith and of charity as deduced from the study of the active night of the spirit. We shall now consider some of the conclusions that follow from the foregoing analysis.

21. Faith can be called the means of union of the intellect with God, but not the means of transformation. Faith considered in itself, even vivified by charity but not operating through charity, cannot be called the means of transformation. Can it even be called the means of union?

The answer is that St. John of the Cross never speaks about faith alone or unformed faith, but always about faith vivified by charity. That is the faith that is the means of union with God. But, then, what about dead or unformed faith? When we mention that kind of faith, we are outside the works of St. John of the Cross.

However, since we cannot speak of union with God without charity, there would still be the adherence to the truths of revelation by unformed faith—which is always present as long as there is faith—but that faith could never produce likeness to the Beloved. According to the principles laid down by St. John of the Cross, dead or unformed faith lacks the unifying power necessary for creating this likeness. Whatever unifying power faith has is because of its relation to charity, which is the unifying virtue properly speaking, and it works directly and immediately in the will and only then extends its power to the intellect. We may conclude, therefore, that dead or unformed faith possesses some elements of union, but it is not properly the means of union.

22. Faith is the means of union by reason of establishing an essential proportion to divinity in the intellect, but it does so only so far as it operates through charity. In this way faith's essential proportion to divinity passes from the purely ontological order to the psychological order, becoming more and more perfect through the abnegation of the intellect and tending to that obscure and loving knowledge of which we spoke. However, it is not now a question of faith alone, but more and more of charity. But as the psychological proportion of the intellect to divinity becomes more and more perfect under the impetus of charity, in the same measure does faith increase progressively as the proportionate means for uniting the intellect with God.

23. From the previous considerations on the active night of the spirit, we can readily conclude that faith is essentially or substantially supernatural, while the "distinct and particular apprehensions" are at most supernatural only in mode. The

essence of such apprehensions, or the intentional species, is something connatural to the knowing intellect. That is why the apprehension is clear and distinct. But in faith the intellect adheres to a form that surpasses its power, and it does so through the medium of the light that exceeds its natural light. And since faith adheres to the divine object by means of the excessive light, faith is essentially supernatural, for neither in the object nor the excessive light is there anything of the natural order.

24. The study of the function of faith in the active night of the spirit also reveals its function in the transition from meditation to contemplation. The difference consists in this, that in meditation the experience of faith is very explicit and deals with particulars, while in contemplation the experience of faith is blended with and hidden beneath the operation of the entire supernatural organism. But if one considers the three signs of transition from meditation to contemplation, it is easy to discern that, as in the active night of the spirit, the human mode of operation and the sensate adherence to revealed truths are being transcended. In other words, the particular and distinct intentional species are fading away, and the faculties are being placed in a natural void or in the "night".

Previously the adherence to revealed truths was more on the sense order; faith was operative, but through the natural modality of the faculties. Now the adhesion is empty as regards the senses, but it corresponds better to the nature of faith, for it better expresses the proper proportion between the intellect and the divine essence, the substance of revealed truths. Now there is more of faith, so to speak, both in the metaphysical and the psychological sense.

It should be noted, however, that in the transition from meditation to contemplation it is no longer a matter simply of the operation of faith vivified by charity, but of certain effects produced passively in the faculties. It is no longer the intellect operating through faith and charity operating in the will to rid itself of the distinct and natural species of the intentional order.

Now the intellect is purged of those natural forms and species by another power, which is that of the Holy Spirit, working through contemplation in the soul that is passive and receptive.

25. As regards the treatment of contemplation in the works of St. John of the Cross, we can distinguish a twofold order: the order of efficient causality and the objective order. The first pertains to the agent and power that causes contemplation, and the second refers to contemplation as an operation, or what contemplation is objectively.

In the order of efficient causality the virtue of charity plays a predominant role, for the gifts of the Holy Spirit are all united in charity, and through the gifts the Holy Spirit illumines the soul. This is stated in the famous text in chapter 29, book II of *The Ascent.* Consequently, the first mover in contemplation is this divine impetus, and this explains why contemplation transcends the human mode of operation. Faith plays a small role in contemplation as regards the efficient cause, and then only as impelled by charity and in the measure that its adhesion to the unseen increases the fervor of charity.

When it is a question of the objective order of contemplation, however, the role of faith is of great importance, according to St. John of the Cross. In this context also the nature of the virtue of faith is more clearly manifested. The illuminating motion of the Holy Spirit, working through his gifts, stimulates charity and then, through charity operative in faith, affects the adhesion of the intellect to the substance of revealed truths, which is exercised through faith. The ontological union of the intellect with divinity is presupposed in this adherence through faith, as is the abnegation of the distinct and natural knowledge of revealed truths on the psychological level, greater or less according to the degree of the psychological development of faith. Then the illuminating motion of the Holy Spirit, working through charity, penetrates the intellect recollected in faith[5] and

[5] Cf. *The Ascent,* bk. II, chap. 29, no. 6.

finds there the divine light whereby the soul, through faith, participates in the divine knowledge. The motion of the Holy Spirit intensifies the participation so that under his impetus the excessive light of faith becomes the light of divine wisdom. Then it is most true that the intellect knows no longer by its own light but with the participated light of divine knowledge.

But—and here we see the influence of faith greatly accentuated—the degree of intensification of the divine light, of the actual participation in the knowledge of God himself, will depend on the purity and purification of the intellect, which means the absence of any particular and natural species. The more the intellect is purged of such species, the fuller and more profound its purity, and hence the greater its participation in the divine knowledge under the impetus of the Holy Spirit. On the other hand, the less the purity of the intellect, the more the illuminating motion of the Holy Spirit is mingled with and involved in intelligible species of the natural order.[6]

We can see from this the important role of faith in contemplation, for the actual purity of the intellect by way of the absence of natural intentional species involves the work of faith in the intellect. It presupposes faith as the bond of union of the intellect with the substance of revealed truths, though in obscurity, and not only in a metaphysical sense, but in a psychological sense, but now greatly elevated. It presupposes that the intellect is now habitually occupied much more with the supernatural adhesion to the obscure and unseen truths than with clear apprehensions of the natural order. Together with that progressive perfection of faith, the participated light of divine knowledge is more and more intimately united to the intellect and intensified. Thus it is disposed for the movement of the Holy Spirit whereby the intellect is actually introduced into that divine but obscure knowledge that is contemplation.

---

[6] Cf. *The Ascent*, bk. II, chap. 14, no. 8.

26. Contemplation is given in faith, as the Mystical Doctor states in chapter 10, book II of *The Ascent*. This shows what he thinks of faith as the means of uniting the intellect with God. For him, the excessive light in which the soul shares habitually through faith is above all a participation in divine knowledge. It is precisely in and through this that it is possible for the intellect to enjoy actual union in contemplation under the impetus of the Holy Spirit. Moreover it is because of this that the soul can attain to the vision in glory, for St. John of the Cross teaches that under the motion of the Holy Spirit the participation in divine knowledge through faith and in the obscurity of faith can increase even to the beatific vision. Contemplation, therefore, normally marks the beginning of the passive night of the spirit and is a preparation for the transforming union.

27. Such is the objective aspect of contemplation, in which faith plays such an important part. But this does not exhaust the subject. We have seen that faith as a participation in divine knowledge is the means through which contemplation occurs, but what is it that is contemplated? The importance of faith will again be manifested in answering this question.

Through faith the intellect adheres to the "substance" of revealed truths, which means that the divine essence is united to the intellect in the intentional order. But the intellect cannot penetrate this substance through faith, cannot see it clearly and find rest and satisfaction for the possible intellect by means of an intentional species. Such is the nature of faith as an "obscure habit".

Nevertheless, the intellect tends by its very nature to grasp the intentional species, and this stimulates the agent intellect to ponder the revealed truths, as in discursive meditation. But because of its natural mode of operation, the intellect can apprehend the revealed truths only by means of particular and distinct intentional species. On the other hand, the effort of the intellect is restrained by the intrinsic proportion of faith, which consists, as we have seen, in an obscure adhesion to the essence of revealed truths that are not seen (*de non visis*). In other words, the obscure and unlimited apprehension given in faith gradually replaces the clear but limited apprehensions obtained by the agent intellect in a natural manner.

At this point the intellect is able to cease its natural and limited operations relating to revealed truths and concentrate all its energy on the "obedience of faith", on adhering to the obscure and unlimited intentional form, or the "substance" of revealed truths. This is not done, of course, in a natural mode but is effected supernaturally, for in contemplation the activity of the agent intellect is suspended. Concentrating on the revealed truths, the intellect admits no natural intentional species; it remains in a state of emptiness or psychological purity as regards its natural functions. In this state it adheres to the unlimited substance of revealed truths, and there is nothing from the natural operations to impede it. The possible intellect enjoys fruition in the loving "touch" of the divine substance, and now the intellect has truly attained to the "substance as understood"—the *substance*, because of the purity of the intellect, and *understood*, not through any intentional species of the divine, but through the redundance of love—understood through love. This is the height of the mystical experience possible in this life under the conditions of the obscurity of faith. This is also the high point of the union of the intellect with God, not only in the metaphysical sense, but in the psychological sense as well.

28. It follows from all that we have said that the intellect is not actually united with God except through faith in contemplation. The contemplative union is transient, however, for the only permanent and habitual union is through faith and in obscurity, as was stated in chapter 5, book II of *The Ascent*.

29. Thus we see in what sense faith can be called the root of contemplation, according to the teaching of St. John of the Cross. It is the root not only in an incipient sense but also as the

foundation or basis of contemplation, and the more intense the contemplation, the more extended is the influence of faith, always intervening in a more perfect form but unchanged in its nature as faith. It is capable of progressive perfection because of the constitutive element of its nature, namely, as a participated divine knowledge and because of the adhesion of the intellect to the "substance" of revealed truths. Psychologically, this adhesion to the substance of revealed truths admits of ever greater perfection.

THE NATURE OF FAITH

We have seen from our analysis and resumé how much doctrine on the virtue of faith can be found in the works of St. John of the Cross. However, he does not give us a formal and systematic treatise on faith but treats rather of certain special aspects of the virtue of faith. Thus, his discussion revolves around two principle questions: first, faith in its ontological aspect, namely, its supernatural quality, from which flows its capacity to unite the intellect with God; and secondly, following from the principles established in the first question, the psychological aspect, namely, the purifying power of faith operating in the intellect. These are the two major questions concerning faith treated by the Mystical Doctor, and they are referred to in chapter 6, book II of *The Ascent*, where he gives a quasi-definition of the virtue of faith.

What do these two special questions tell us concerning the nature of faith when compared with the common teaching of theologians? Because of the precision and detail with which the Mystical Doctor explains them, we should be able to find some important applications to the nature of faith in general.

It would seem that faith has more value as providing information to the intellect than as an operative virtue. It is in this sense also a means of uniting the intellect with God, for in adhering to revealed truths, the intellect receives something of the "substance as understood". And although it is not received as a distinct intentional species, it is nevertheless a type of information.

But if the intellect is not informed by means of an intentional species, how is it informed? Can we say that it is informed by darkness and obscurity? What precisely is meant by the darkness and obscurity of faith?

It would seem that the intellect is informed with an intrinsic proportion to God, but a proportion lacking any intentional species, because in this life the intellect cannot have a clear vision of the divine form. The Mystical Doctor asserts that in this life God is known more by not knowing than by knowing according to the natural mode of knowledge. That is why he insists on the rejection of the clear and particular knowledge of revealed truths, whether naturally acquired or supernatural in origin.

This shows that the union with the divine essence obtained in faith, though not expressed psychologically in the grasping of the form of the object, nevertheless manifests a psychological proportion of the intellect to the divine object. It is not an "intentional" identification with the divine object, but at best a preparatory disposition. The intellect does not attain to the divine form or species, but through faith it is habitually disposed psychologically to achieve this at some future time.

The proportion established through faith is of great value by way of psychological information, as is evident from the principle of the Mystical Doctor concerning the inability of two forms to exist at the same time in the same subject. Since faith rejects the opposite or contrary natural and particular forms and leaves the intellect in a state of emptiness and darkness, this proves that in the obscure proportion to divinity there is contained some psychological reality—not an intentional species of the divine object, but some "form" emanating from the intellect's intimate union with God and produced by the power of faith, but characterized by obscurity.

The "intentional proportion" is caused in the intellect by the infused light, that is, by the participation of the intellect in divine knowledge and by reason of the subsequent adhesion to the substance of revealed truths. The proportion thus constituted is something truly psychological and capable of a definite activity in the intellect, as we saw in the transition from meditation to contemplation and better yet in the active night of the spirit. And this psychological proportion coincides with that which we call the virtue of faith.

But what is the operative power or dynamism of faith? To answer this question it would be well to keep in mind the theory of habits as taught by St. Thomas Aquinas in the *Summa theologiae*, I-II, q. 50. He states that the perfection conferred on a faculty by a habit does not consist in a new operation added to the faculty, but in a perfective determination and modification of the faculty. The operative power is already contained in the faculty; the habit simply modifies that power and thereby also modifies and perfects the operation of the faculty. This doctrine is nowhere treated explicitly in St. John of the Cross, but it is helpful for understanding his teaching on the virtue of faith.

Faith is a supernatural virtue that operates in the intellect and has the power of uniting this faculty with God. The power of the virtue extends likewise to the purification of the intellect, which becomes "empty and dark". But what is this power of faith precisely? If one reads carefully chapter 3, book II of *The Ascent*, it will be seen that the power by which the virtue of faith unites the intellect to God is the "excessive light", which the Mystical Doctor describes as a participation in the divine knowledge.

But immediately a question arises concerning the degree and intensity of the participation in divine knowledge that is proper to faith. The answer is not given explicitly by the Mystical Doctor; all we find is that the excessive light conquers and overwhelms the intellect and, moreover, that the light extends to the assent of the intellect. In other words, the power of the light is such that it enables the intellect to assent to the revealed truths proposed by faith, in spite of the lack of clear apprehension of the object. Thus, through the medium of the excessive light, the intellect is united with the "substance" of revealed truth, a union more in a metaphysical than a psychological sense. All this is deducible from the text of the Mystical Doctor.

However, because of the lack of an intentional species, because of the obscurity of faith, it would seem that the intellect participating in that light does not cease to operate in the manner that is proper to it. Hence it tends to the essence of revealed truths, for the virtue of faith satisfies this tendency metaphysically but not psychologically. In other words, the intellect still operates in its natural mode. We discover this natural mode of operation throughout the works of the Mystical Doctor, for example, in treating of mental prayer and the active night of the spirit. The virtue of faith operates in a human mode (*modo humano*). Moreover, this natural mode of operation provides the material for the abnegation of the intellect, for its purification and transition to the psychological transcendence that we discussed previously.

It is in the human mode of operation, to which faith is restricted, that we find the deficiency in the operation of faith. Here also is the reason for the disproportion of faith that we noted in our analysis. The power of uniting the intellect to God is in the infused light, in the participation in the divine knowledge. Logically, this should be an operative power of the virtue of faith as a unifying virtue, but the participation in divine knowledge is limited to the *assent of faith to revealed truths*. But even with this limitation, the virtue of faith does effect a union of the intellect with the "substance" of revealed truths.

Yet precisely because of its limitation, faith is not able to produce the total psychological purification and the successive transitions that are proper to faith according to the doctrine of St. John of the Cross. The reason is that a more profound psychological purification requires a greater participation in the divine light through the impetus of the Holy Spirit, and that will also determine the function of faith as a means of union. Thus the union of the intellect with God through contemplation is now possible and the "intentional proportion" or likeness between the intellect and the divine object is more perfectly and deeply rooted, thus preparing for the ultimate reception of the divine form.

It would seem that it is at this point that there is a limitation on the operative power of faith and, consequently, on its ability to unite the intellect with God. And this pertains not only to faith as a habit but also to the act of faith in a psychological and experiential sense. But it is also here, at this same point, where the weakness and disproportion of faith are evident, that faith, according to St. John of the Cross, opens itself to the other virtues that comprise the total supernatural organism.

Indeed, if faith is to attain its plenitude and total possible perfection, it must open itself to the other virtues because it needs them. To be perfect, faith must be a living faith, vivified by charity and the gifts of the Holy Spirit. Its whole purpose is to unite the intellect with God, but it can do so only in a limited and habitual manner. Yet faith tends to the perfection proper to its nature, which already bestows on the intellect an essential likeness to God that is habitual (*per modum habitus*). Faith tends further to make that likeness an actual one (*per modum actus*), and the intellect itself is prompted by its natural tendency to seek the essence of revealed truths, and this tendency has great psychological significance.

Thus the two things coincide: the habitual union tends to be perfected as actual union, and the metaphysical union tends to be perfected as psychological union. But faith alone does not suffice for either one. It lacks the operative power, and that is why it must be open to the other virtues and powers that can effect the plenitude and perfection of union that is possible under the conditions of the present life. The very nature of faith demands this assistance, since only in that way can faith be extended and perfected. It is proper to faith to participate in the light of divine knowledge and thereby unite the intellect with the essence of revealed truths. And this participation in divine knowledge, as we have seen, is much more perfectly realized in contemplation, under the impetus of the Holy Spirit.

All things considered, it seems that rather than the virtue that causes union, faith, by reason of its intimate nature as a participation in the divine, functions as an infused power from which union with God and contemplation derive. But, as we have said, faith alone does not suffice for this; faith must be actualized and explored, as it were, by the other supernatural virtues. The operative power of faith is unable to explore the totality of the unifying participation that faith enjoys by its very essence, just as it cannot attain to the psychological union of the intellect with God that is experienced in this life through contemplation. This comes from infused faith vivified by charity and the impetus of the gifts of the Holy Spirit, especially the gifts of wisdom and understanding.

Thus, the teaching of St. John of the Cross is in accord with the doctrine of St. Thomas Aquinas, for the Angelic Doctor expressly affirms that the virtue of faith is substantially supernatural, and he writes at some length concerning the perfection of faith by charity and the gifts of the Holy Spirit.[1]

Speaking of infused prayer or of mystical experience, St. John of the Cross rarely mentions the gifts of the Holy Spirit, but he does speak of the gifts equivalently when treating of formed or vivified faith, for only through charity and the gifts is infused faith the proportionate means of intimate union with God.

---

[1] Cf. *Summa theologiae*, II–II, q. 1, a. 1; q. 2, a. 3; q. 6, aa. 1 and 2.

We have seen that St. John of the Cross discussed the virtue of faith under a particular aspect, namely, so far as it constitutes the proper and proportionate means for uniting the intellect with God. Within this context he provided an accurate and detailed analysis of faith. We now turn to the writings of St. Thomas Aquinas in order to see whether there are any passages in his works that treat the virtue of faith in a manner similar to that of St. John of the Cross.

St. Thomas composed a complete treatise on the virtue of faith; he did not limit himself to a specialized area as did St. John of the Cross. Nevertheless, we can say that in general there is a fundamental similarity of doctrine in both of these Doctors of the Church. But we shall seek further, in order to see if there are any passages in the works of St. Thomas in which the similarity in doctrine is even more explicit, and especially as regards faith as a means of union and as a virtue of purgation.

Faith as a means of union

In the *Summa theologiae*, at the very beginning of his treatment of faith, St. Thomas explains how this virtue unites the intellect to the object of faith:

> The object of faith may be considered in two ways: first, as regards that which is believed, and in this respect the object of faith is something simple, namely, the very reality which is believed; secondly, as regards the one believing, and in this respect the object of faith is complex, expressed in the form of a proposition (*Summa theologiae*, II-II, q. 1, a. 2).

The act of the believer does not terminate in the proposition, however, but in the reality, because we formulate propositions only that through them we may know the reality itself. This is true of knowledge and also of faith (Loc. cit., ad 2um).

We can say that the foregoing passages contain the nucleus of the doctrine of St. John of the Cross on faith as a means of union, so far as through the virtue of faith the intellect adheres to the reality of revealed truths. St. Thomas teaches the same doctrine in *De Veritate*:

The object of faith is divine truth, which in itself is most simple; but our intellect receives this truth according to its own manner of operating, that is, by formulating propositions. Thus, in giving its assent to the proposition formulated, the intellect tends to the First Truth as its object (*De Veritate*, q. 14, a. 8, ad 5um).

Faith does not terminate in the proposition but in the reality; and the reality is always the same, although the propositions are diverse (Loc. cit., q. 14, a. 12).

Similar statements can be found in St. Thomas' *Commentary on the Book of Sentences*:

Although First Truth is simple in itself, nevertheless a variety of things can be found in it because the human intellect forms various concepts concerning the one reality. Accordingly, the intellect can unite and divide those concepts and thus formulate a proposition concerning God (*In III Librum Sententiarum*, dist. 24, a. 1, q. 2, ad 1um).

The activity of the intellect in uniting and dividing tends toward an operation in which the intellect perceives something simple, because the essence of a thing (*quod quid est*) is the principle of demonstrating the existence of a thing (*an est*) and its existential reality (*quia est*). Similarly, that which follows faith and in which faith is completed is the vision of simple Truth (Loc. cit., ad 2um).

The object of charity is the good which, according to the Philosopher (*In VI Metaphys.*, 8), exists in external reality; but the object of faith is truth, which is attained by an operation of the mind. And since the formulation of propositions by composition and division is an operation of the mind, the object of faith is complex, while the object of charity is simple (Loc. cit., ad 3um).

Faith as a virtue of purgation

Also as regards the second problem of faith treated by St. John of the Cross—its purifying action on the intellect, discussed by St. John in *The Ascent of Mount Carmel* (book II, chapter 6) when explaining the active night of the spirit—we find parallel texts in the works of St. Thomas Aquinas. Thus, the Angelic Doctor asks whether purification of heart is an effect of the virtue of faith, and he replies:

> The rational creature is more excellent than all transitory and corporeal creatures; consequently it becomes impure by subjecting itself to transitory things by loving them. From this impurity the rational creature is cleansed by means of a contrary movement, namely, by tending to that which is above it, that is, to God. The first beginning of this movement is faith, since "anyone who comes to [God] must believe that he exists", according to Hebrews 11:6. Hence the first beginning of the purification of the heart is faith, and if this be perfected by being vivified by charity, the heart will be perfectly purified thereby (*Summa theologiae*, II-II, q. 7, a. 2).

> Even lifeless faith [faith without charity] excludes a certain impurity which is contrary to it, namely, that of error, which consists in the human intellect's adhering inordinately to things beneath itself through wishing to measure divine things by the rule of sensate objects (Ibid., a. 2, ad 2um).

The final words approach the teaching of St. John of the Cross very closely. Usually the purifying role attributed to the virtue of faith by St. Thomas consists in cleansing the intellect from error by adhering to the truth. Similar statements can be found in *De Veritate*, q. 28, a. 1, ad 6um.

However, when it is a question of the purification of the intellect which St. John of the Cross attributes to faith working through charity, St. Thomas, with greater theological precision, assigns this purifying action to the gift of understanding:

> There are two kinds of purity. The first is a dispositive purity that prepares for the vision of God, and this consists in the purgation of the affections from all inordinate attachments. This purity of heart is attained by means of the virtues and gifts that pertain to the affective powers.
>
> The second kind of purity of heart is quasi-perfect in relation to the vision of God. It is a purity of the mind purged of all phantasms and errors, so that the propositions concerning God are not received by means of corporeal images nor heretical distortions. This purity is effected by the gift of understanding.
>
> Similarly, the vision of God is twofold. One is perfect vision whereby the divine essence is seen; the other is imperfect, whereby although we do not see what God is, we see what he is not. And the more perfectly we know God in this life, the more we realize that he exceeds anything that the human intellect can comprehend.
>
> Both of these kinds of vision pertain to the gift of understanding; the first to the gift of understanding in its plenitude, as it will be in glory, and the other to the inchoate gift of understanding as it is experienced in this life (*Summa theologiae*, II-II, q. 8, a. 7).

In conclusion, we can say that the entire doctrine of St. John of the Cross on the purgative power of the virtue of faith, of the preparation of the intellect for the vision of God, and of the realization of God's incomprehensibility is synthesized in this passage from the *Summa theologiae*.

BIBLIOGRAPHY

SAN JUAN DE LA CRUZ, *Obras de* —, *Doctor de la Iglesia, editadas y anotadas por el P. Silverio de Santa Teresa:* t. 1: *Preliminares* (Burgos, Tipografía de El Monte Carmelo, 1929); t. 2: *Subida y Noche oscura* (1929); t. 3: *Cántico espiritual* (1930); t. 4: *Llama de amor viva. Cautelas. Avisos. Cartas. Poesías* (1931); t. 5: *Procesos de beatificación y canonización* (1931).

SAINT THOMAS AQUINAS, *Summa theologiae* (Taurini, Marietti, 1938); *Quaestiones disputate: De veritate; Scriptum super IV Libros Sententiarum Petri Lombardi.*

ARINTERO, O.P., Juan G., *Inanidad de la contemplación adquirida:* La Ciencia Tomista 29 (1924) 331–49; 30 (1924) 51–27.

BARUZI, Jean, *Saint Jean de la Croix et le problème de l'expérience mystique* (Paris 1924; 2d ed. 1929).

BOISSELOT, O.P., Pierre, *La lumière de la foi:* La Vie Spirituelle, Suppl. 41 (1934) 34–45.

———, *La foi, connaissance affective:* ibid., 81–94.

BRUNO DE JÉSUS-MARIE, O.C.D., *Saint Jean de la Croix* (Paris, Plon, 1929).

CARRO, O.P., Venancio D., *La naturaleza de la gracia y el realismo místico:* La Ciencia Tomista 25 (1922) 362–75.

———, *¿Hay más de una contemplación?:* ibid., 28 (1923) 185–216.

CHEVALIER, O.S.B., Philippe, *Le "Cantique spirituel" interpolé:* La Vie Spirituelle (1926–1930) (series of articles).

———, *Saint Jean de la Croix en Sorbonne:* ibid., 12 (1925) 188–212.

———, *La doctrina ascética de Saint Jean de la Croix:* ibid., 16 (1927) 175–96.

Connaissance de Dieu et union d'amour. Traité attribué à S. Jean de la Croix. Traduction et notes par le P. Théodore de Saint-Joseph (Bruges 1924).

CRISÓGONO DE JESÚS SACRAMENTADO, O.C.D., *San Juan de la Cruz. Su obra científica y su obra literaria,* 2 vols. (Madrid 1929).

————, *San Juan de la Cruz. El hombre. El doctor. El poeta* (Barcelona–Madrid 1935).

EFRÉN DE LA MADRE DE DIOS, O.C.D., *San Juan de la Cruz y el misterio de la Santísima Trinidad en la vida espiritual* (Zaragoza 1947).

EUGENIO DE SAN JOSÉ, O.C.D., *La contemplación de fe según la "Subida del monte Carmelo"* (Burgos, El Monte Carmelo, 1928).

FARGES, Albert, *La manière de poser la question mystique:* Revue d'Ascétique et de Mystique 3 (1922) 273–82.

————, *Point d'idées infuses dans la contemplation infuse:* La Vie Spirituelle 8 (1923) 193-207.

GABRIELE DI SANTA MARIA MADDELENA, O.C.D., *La mistica teresiana* (Firenze 1934).

————, *San Giovanni della Croce, Dottore dell'Amore Divino* (Firenze 1937).

————, *La contemplazione acquisita* (Firenze 1938).

————, *Visioni e rivelazioni nella vita spirituale* (Firenze 1941).

————, *La contemplation acquise chez les théologiens Carmes dé-chaussés:* La Vie Spirituelle, Suppl. 11 (1923) 277–303.

————, *L'union transformante selon Saint Jean de la Croix:* ibid., 16 (1927) 223–54.

GARDEIL, O.P., Ambroise, *La structure de l'âme et l'expérience mystique,* 2 vols. (Paris 1927).

——, *La contemplation mystique est-elle intentionnelle?:* Revue Thomiste N.S. 15 (1932) 226–50, 379–93.

GARRIGOU-LAGRANGE, O.P., Reginald, *Perfection chrétienne et contemplation,* 2 vols. (Saint-Maximin [Var], éd. de La Vie Spirituelle, 1923).

——, *Les trois âges de la vie intérieure, prélude de celle du ciel* (Paris, éd. du Cerf, 1938).

——, *La mystique et la doctrine de S. Thomas sur la foi:* La Vie Spirituelle 1 (1920) 361–82.

——, *La contemplation mystique requiert-elle des idées infuses?:* ibid., Suppl. 7 (1922) 1–21.

——, *Les vertus théologales et la nuit d'esprit:* ibid., 17 (1927) 269–90.

——, *Saint Thomas et Saint Jean de la Croix:* ibid., Suppl. 49 (1936) 357–76.

——, *L'illumination spéciale du don de sagesse suffit à la contemplation infuse?:* ibid., Suppl. 50 (1937) 115–20.

GROULT, Pierre, *S. Jean de la Croix. Sa doctrine mystique:* Nouvelle Revue Théologique 54 (1927) 561–91.

HAPPIG, S.J., Bernhard, *Die Theologie der Mystik nach dem hl. Johannes vom Kreuz:* Scholastik 12 (1937) 481–97.

HOORNART, Rodolphe, *L'âme ardente de S. Jean de la Croix* (Paris 1928).

JÉRÔME DE LA MÈRE DE DIEU, O.C.D., *La tradition mystique du Carmel:* La Vie Spirituelle, Suppl. 9 (1924) 61–92, 133–63. 133–63.

JORET, O.P., F. D., *L'intuition obscure de Dieu:* ibid., 5 (1921) 5–57.

JUAN DE JESÚS MARÍA, O.C.D., *El valor crítico del texto escrito por la primera mano en el códice de Sanlúcar de Barrameda:* Ephemerides Carmeliticae 1 (1947) 313–66.

LABOURDETTE, O.P., Michel M., *La foi théologale et la connaissance mystique d'après Saint Jean de la Croix:* Revue Thomiste (1936–1937) (Separate ed.: Saint-Maximin [1937] 116).

LEBRETON, Jules, *La nuit obscure d'après S. Jean de la Croix:* Revue d'Ascétique et de Mystique 9 (1928) 3–24.

LOUIS DE LA TRINITÉ, O.C.D., *La nuit de la foi:* Études Carmélitaines (1937) 189–224.

――――, *Le docteur mystique* (Paris 1929).

MARCELO DEL NIÑO JESÚS, O.C.D., *El tomismo de San Juan de la Cruz* (Burgos 1930).

MARITAIN, Jacques, *Distinguer pour unir ou les degrés du savoir* (Paris 1946).

――――, *Une question sur la vie mystique et la contemplation:* La Vie Spirituelle 7 (1923) 636–50.

MASSONET, O.P., A.-M., *Intuition mystique et foi théologale:* La Vie Spirituelle, Suppl. 51 (1937) 141–64.

――――, *Foi théologale et dons intellectuels:* ibid., Suppl. 54 (1938) 1–21.

PASTOUREL, O.S.B., L. *La doctrine mystique de Saint Jean de la Croix:* Annales de Philosophie Chrétienne (1912) 54–74.

WINKLHOFER, A., *Die Gnadenlehre in der Mystik des hl. Johannes vom Kreuz* (Freiburg i.B. 1936).

WILD, Karl, *Auf den Höhenwegen der christlichen Mystik* (München 1935).

――――, *Das Wesen der mystischen Beschauung nach dem hl. Johannes vom Kreuz:* Zeitschr. f. Aszese u. Mystique (1934) 107–34.

――――, *Die Begleterscheinungen des myst. Gnadelenlebens:* ibid. (1934) 306–23.

――――, *Das Höchstziel des mystischen Gnadenlebens:* ibid. (1937) 97 f.

――――, *Theresianische Mystik:* ibid. (1937).